The search for responsibility in complex organisat
ble undertaking. Adopting a multidisciplinary ap
science, ethics and organisational design, Mark Bovens analyses
this, and offers possible solutions. He begins by examining the problem of
'many hands' – because so many people contribute in so many different ways,
it is very difficult to determine who is accountable for organisational behaviour.
Four possible solutions – corporate, hierarchical, collective and individual
accountability – are analysed from normative, empirical and practical perspectives. Bovens argues that individual accountability is the most promising solution, but only if individuals have the chance to behave responsibly. The book
then explores the implications of this approach. What does it mean to be a
'responsible' employee or official? When is it legitimate to disobey the orders of
superiors? What institutional designs might be most appropriate?

THE QUEST FOR RESPONSIBILITY

THEORIES OF INSTITUTIONAL DESIGN

Series Editor
Robert E. Goodin
Research School of Social Sciences
Australian National University

Advisory Editors
Brian Barry, Russell Hardin, Carole Pateman, Barry Weingast,
Stephen Elkin, Claus Offe, Susan Rose-Ackerman

Social scientists have rediscovered institutions. They have been increasingly concerned with the myriad ways in which social and political institutions shape the patterns of individual interactions which produce social phenomena. They are equally concerned with the ways in which those institutions emerge from such interactions.

This series is devoted to the exploration of the more normative aspects of these issues. What makes one set of institutions better than another? How, if at all, might we move from a less desirable set of institutions to a more desirable set? Alongside the questions of what institutions we would design, if we were designing them afresh, are pragmatic questions of how we can best get from here to there: from our present institutions to new revitalized ones.

Theories of institutional design is insistently multidisciplinary and interdisciplinary, both in the institutions on which it focuses, and in the methodologies used to study them. There are interesting sociological questions to be asked about legal institutions, interesting legal question to be asked about economic institutions, and interesting social, economic and legal questions to be asked about political institutions. By juxtaposing these approaches in print, this series aims to enrich normative discourse surrounding important issues of designing and redesigning, shaping and reshaping the social, political and economic institutions of contemporary society.

The Quest
for Responsibility

Accountability and
Citizenship in Complex
Organisations

MARK BOVENS

Utrecht University

CAMBRIDGE
UNIVERSITY PRESS

PUBLISHED BY THE PRESS SYNDICATE OF THE UNIVERSITY OF CAMBRIDGE
The Pitt Building, Trumpington Street, Cambridge CB2 1RP, United Kingdom

CAMBRIDGE UNIVERSITY PRESS
The Edinburgh Building, Cambridge CB2 2RU, United Kingdom
40 West 20th Street, New York, NY 10011–4211, USA
10 Stamford Road, Oakleigh, Melbourne 3166, Australia

First published 1998

Typeset in 10.5/12pt Minion   [SE]

A catalogue record for this book is available from the British Library

Library of Congress cataloguing in publication data

Bovens, M. A. P.
    [Verantwoordelijkheid en organisatie. English]
    The quest for responsibility : accountability and citizenship in
complex organisations / Mark Bovens.
            p.   cm.
    Revised translation from Dutch of: Verantwoordelijkheid en
organisatie.
    Includes bibliographical references.
    ISBN 0 521 48163 5
    1. Organisational sociology.   2. Responsibility.
3. Organisational behavior.   4. Industries–Social aspects.
I. Title.
HM131.B66713   1997
302 3′5–dc21   97–10236   CIP

ISBN 0 521 48163 5 hardback
ISBN 0 521 62898 9 paperback

Transferred to digital printing 2004

Contents

Preface

> Most of the creations of the intellect or fancy pass away for good after a time
> that varies between an after-dinner hour and a generation.
>
> (Schumpeter 1950: 3)

The theme of this book first took shape at the Leidseplein in Amsterdam on
a fine April afternoon in the early 1980s. In an outdoor café, René Went and
I were having a couple of beers after a public demonstration for a better
system of legal aid. Inspired by *The Quest for Control* and other work by
Herman van Gunsteren, who later became my Ph.D. supervisor, I enter-
tained my companion with an impromptu lecture on the problematic character of responsibility within organisations. Often the burden of such
conversations is already forgotten by the time the bill is paid. This time,
however, such was not the case. The same evening, on the bus back home, I
wrote down my reflections on a sheet of paper. These ideas, I now see,
became a central element in my present argument.

Willem Witteveen stimulated me to turn those notes into a paper that I
read at a seminar in constitutional theory at the Faculty of Law in Leiden.
Subsequently, he enabled me to publish my paper. The LL.M. programme
of Columbia University Law School in New York later provided me with a
stimulating environment to develop and test my thoughts. When, after
graduating, I returned to Leiden as a junior lecturer in Political Science, I
decided to work up my notes and papers into a dissertation. The members
of the Leiden circle of postgraduate researchers, Marius de Geus, Paul den
Hoed, and Willem Witteveen, have through their stimulating comments
contributed greatly to the growth of a complete argument from that first
brief article. In intellectual respect, I am most indebted to my teacher,
Herman van Gunsteren. The title of this study is an attempt to give expression to that debt. The Leiden Centre for Law and Public Policy played a main
role both in the appearance of the Dutch-language edition of the book and
in this elaboration on it. It was, first in the late 1980s and after that in the

mid 1990s, the ideal place to pursue socio-legal studies. I was also able to bother many colleagues in the Department of Political Science and later as senior lecturer in the Department of Public Administration with my various versions and manuscripts. In these years I have particularly profited from conversations with Wim Derksen, Paul 't Hart, Hans Oversloot, Martin Rein, and the late Aaron Wildavsky.

When I finished my book in 1990, I said I hoped that my views, now that they had transcended the 'after-dinner hour', would at least address a generation. Within the Dutch-speaking world, that hope seems to have been fulfilled. In 1991 the Dutch version (*Verantwoordelijkheid en organisatie: beschouwingen over aansprakelijkheid, institutioneel burgerschap en ambtelijke ongehoorzaamheid*, Zwolle: W. E. J. Tjeenk Willink 1990) won the G. A. J. van Poelje prize for the best book on government studies. Meanwhile, it has been reprinted several times and at least one generation of Dutch students has toiled over it.

The Quest for Responsibility is a revised version of that earlier effort. The original manuscript has been abridged, updated, and adapted for an international audience. The first two parts more or less follow the original manuscript. The last part, about citizenship in organisations, has, however, been substantially modified, since my thoughts on active responsibility in organisations have progressed over the last five years. A grant from The Netherlands Institute of Government and a sabbatical leave from the Department of Public Administration of Leiden University provided me with the opportunity to further pursue my thoughts. The translation, by Gregor Benton, was made possible by a generous grant from the The Netherlands Organisation for Science Research (NWO). B. Guy Peters read the entire manuscript and I have benefited enormously from his comments. Hester van Beelen-Bergsma was of great help in the final editing. Figure 2.1 is from *Foundations of Social Theory* by James S. Coleman, copyright © 1990 by the President and Fellows of Harvard College. Reprinted by permission of Harvard University Press. Finally, I would like to thank Robert Goodin for the confidence that he gave me. If this book reaches even one English-speaking generation, it is mainly because of these various people and institutions.

PART I

THE QUEST FOR RESPONSIBILITY

1

Complex organisations and the quest for responsibility

> How can corporate actors be made appropriately responsible?
>
> (Coleman 1982: 90)

Organisational deviance and the quest for responsibility

Famous names have over the last few years become tarnished and venerable institutions have been brought into discredit. Large-scale embarrassments such as the collapse of the Bank of Credit and Commerce International (BCCI) have greatly dented international confidence in the solidity of the British banking world. For years BCCI had been able to conceal enormous financial losses through a complex system of fraudulent transactions. Eventually, the Bank of England was forced to close BCCI and all its branches in over sixty-eight countries, which amounted to the largest bank closure in history. In the United States, billions were lost as a result of the Savings and Loans scandal, which involved a series of banks who became insolvent as a result of excessive risktaking, mismanagement, and fraudulent practices. In the Netherlands, Slavenburg's Bank was engaged on a considerable scale in tax evasion and various other forms of illegal transactions. Not only the banking world but industry too was the arena of sensational scandals with a big social fall-out. Environmental disasters such as the explosion at the Union Carbide plant in Bhopal that killed thousands of people, the accident with the *Exxon Valdez* oil tanker that polluted a large part of the coast of Alaska, and the fire at the Sandox chemical plant in Basle which sent a toxic wave down the river Rhine, killing much of its wildlife, have given the petrochemical and chemical industry an extremely bad image. Such 'affairs' did not remain confined to industry, but also affected the public sector. With the downfall of the RSV shipbuilding conglomerate in the Netherlands, many hundreds of millions of guilders in government support were lost that could have been saved if the government officials had acted with greater prudence. In the United States, the accident with the

3

Space Shuttle *Challenger* led to a collective trauma and severely damaged the image and stature of NASA. If we examine these affairs more closely, they would appear, despite various differences and particularities, to have a few elements in common:

* They are not strictly personal affairs. In all cases the main role is reserved for organisations, often corporate bodies with a very complex structure and an intricate division of competencies.
* It is rarely a case of one-off and small-scale forms of corruption, bad management, or improper administration. In many cases, there is talk of activities that extend over long periods of time and large territories, and several organisations, institutions, and departments are involved.
* The damage, in the form of tax evasion, budget deficits, environmental pollution, or human suffering, not only runs into the millions but is in many cases irrevocable and irreparable and can, like some environmental disasters, lead to whole residential areas and ports becoming unusable or even to the dislocation of parts of society.
* Because of the complex structure of the organisations involved, it does not always appear possible for controlling organs, both within the organisations themselves and outside them, to become aware of potential problems sufficiently and in good time. As a consequence, after the event it is often particularly difficult to determine whether or to what extent certain individuals can be held responsible for the course of events. It means, moreover, that an adequate defence against a future repetition of such events is particularly difficult.

This study explores the issues of responsibility that such incidents call forth. Who can be held responsible for the behaviour of complex organisations? What constitutes responsible conduct inside complex organisations? To what extent can new conceptions of bureaucratic responsibility contribute to the prevention of such incidents?

My point of departure is what Dennis Thompson (1980) called *the problem of many hands*: because in complex organisations many different functionaries, at various levels and in various measure, often contribute to the policy and decisions of the organisation, it is often extraordinarily difficult to determine who is responsible for the organisation's conduct in the last instance. With respect to complex organisations, the problem of many hands often turns the quest for responsibility into a quest for the Holy Grail.

This study investigates to what extent current – as well as some new – models and conceptions of responsibility can help in resolving the problem of many hands. Later on (in chapter 4), we shall see that the problem of many hands has various dimensions and that these issues of responsibility can be grouped roughly into three sub-questions:

1. To what extent are the various constructions of accountability and concep-
    tions of responsible conduct within organisations *effective* in controlling
    complex organisations?
2. To what extent are these constructions and conceptions *acceptable* from a
    normative (moral, political, or legal-philosophical) point of view?
3. To what extent, in the light of the answers that we give to the first two ques-
    tions, are these constructions and conceptions *feasible* given the daily prac-
    tice of complex organisations?

The nature of such questions implies that the perspective changes constantly. To obtain an indication of an answer to the first question, I shall look
first and foremost to research in the fields of the sociology of law and organisation studies. For an answer to the second question, I shall engage in discussion with philosophers working in the field of business ethics, law, and
politics. For an answer to the third question, I shall look for clues in the fields
of law, government, and business administration.

Public and private organisations

The framework for this study is formed by contemporary, liberal democracies – those societies which Bernard Crick (1973: 56) in his classification of
forms of government calls 'modern republics'. Of this group of societies, I
shall look above all at the Netherlands, the United Kingdom, and the United
States, although the literature concerning other countries will also be
touched upon where necessary or relevant.

I shall discriminate only to a limited degree between private and government organisations. I shall frequently resort to the general idea of 'complex
organisations', and for a number of different reasons:

> With Bozeman (1987), one could say that 'all organizations are public'. Many
> of the activities of private companies have important public effects. The
> labour policy of Philips is more important for employment in large parts
> of the Netherlands than the activities of the Ministry of Economic Affairs.
> Therefore, many private organisations receive subsidies from the govern-
> ment and they are all to a greater or lesser extent subjected to public rules
> and political monitoring. To an increasing extent, companies behave as
> political actors and emerge into the public arena. On the other hand, as a
> result of privatisation and mixed arrangements, even the conduct of many
> government organisations is to a certain degree influenced by market
> factors and economic considerations
> Risks are tied to activities, not to legal regimes. The 'corporate risks' that
> Coleman (1982) distinguishes (see chapter 2) are 'corporate' only in the
> sense that they are the outcome of the activities of *incorporated* actors,
> namely, of private or public corporate bodies. Pollution, waste, and social

dislocation can be brought about both by corporate and governmental deviance alike.

Many of the phenomena and social mechanisms relevant for answering the questions about responsibility that this book addresses exhibit a similar pattern inside both private and public organisations. That is true, for example, of the problem of many hands, but it is also true for many internal and extraneous questions of control and for many mechanisms of social coercion. The complex structure of modern organisations is often, at that level, more dominant than the legal character of the organisation.

On the basis of these considerations, I have taken the liberty in analysing the *controlling* aspects of the passive and active forms of responsibility of making relatively few distinctions between private companies and public organisations. In the case of the third perspective, the *practical* design of the various models and conceptions, more account is already taken of the legal status of organisations, as in most western countries, different legal regimes apply to public and private organisations. Finally, when we are engaged in *normative* considerations, the particular character and the explicit public aims of an organisation will play the largest role. From a political-philosophical perspective, the legal status of an organisation is crucially important. Though the social mechanisms and effects are in many cases similar, our moral and political judgements are not always so. Questions of responsibility are more complicated in the case of public organisations because the tasks, competencies, and duties of officials and political administrators are more complex than are those of their counterparts in business. In the latter case, there are fewer questions of equality, political responsibility, and fairness and there are no issues that involve the monopoly of violence.

The Plan

It would seem obvious to treat the different questions and disciplines addressed in this book in separate chapters. First, a separate, empirically oriented section about the controlling aspects, then a section dealing with normative discussions, and finally a practical section that focuses on a number of concrete legal adaptations, policy recommendations, and proposals for organisational design. The models of accountability and the conceptions of responsible conduct that are discussed here, however, are not easily fitted into a disciplinary bodices. It would appear that, precisely in questions of responsibility, the orthodox separation of facts and norms, of empirical investigation and the forming of judgements, and of analysis and recommendation is scarcely fruitful. If against the background of the problem of many hands one wishes to deliver a considered judgement of a given model of accountability, or of a notion of appropriate conduct, the controlling issues and the moral considerations must be viewed in one and the same context.

I have therefore decided to give precedence to the systematic set of issues that flowed from my analysis of the concept of 'responsibility' over an explanation on the basis of disciplines. Mapping out a number of important issues of responsibility that crop up in the case of complex organisations has assumed priority. Lest I lose my way in the course of my reconnaissance of this complicated topic, I have, like Theseus in the labyrinth, unrolled a few threads along which to find my way back to the entrance.

A first thread begins with the observation that the rise of complex organisations, their great social importance, and the type of risk that as a result of their conduct is called into being, requires a certain control of their behaviour (chapter 2). Processes of calling to account, being taken to task before a forum, have constituted as of old one of the most important means of controlling the conduct of natural individuals. The question now is to what extent current notions of responsibility drawn from law, ethical discourse, and politics are also applicable to the control of complex organisations. Is it really the case that these important social actors can be compared with rationally acting citizens? To get more insight into this question, the idea of 'responsibility' must first be analysed more closely (chapter 3). Such an analysis yields a number of meanings and two more or less independent forms of responsibility. Together with the introduction, these two chapters form the first, general part of this study.

In part II (chapters 4 to 8) and part III (chapters 9 to 12), these two forms of responsibility are consequently elaborated in greater detail in regard to complex organisations. In part II, the main focus is on passive responsibility – responsibility in the sense of accountability (chapter 4). Who is in the event accountable for the misbehaviour of complex organisations? Four ways of analyzing accountability – corporate, hierarchical, collective, and individual – are described and examined (chapters 5 to 8).

At this point a second thread of Ariadne is unrolled, namely, an emphasis on individual responsibility. In part III of this study, I investigate to what extent active forms of individual responsibility can play a role in overcoming the problem of many hands. To that end, I focus on a second meaning: responsibility as virtue. How should a responsible functionary behave? Several conceptions of active individual responsibility within organisations shall be judged each on its merits (chapter 9). One particular conception, the idea of citizenship within organisations, is then further developed. Particular attention will be paid to employee civil disobedience, such as resignation and refusal to work, whistle-blowing and leaking, and to forms of critical loyalty (chapters 10 to 12).

In treating these questions, I shall not, however, lose sight of the first thread. Even in these last chapters, my interest is not only in questions of managerial and business ethics. I shall also consider whether, and to what extent, these conceptions could contribute to the control of complex organisations. In the concluding chapter 12, I shall briefly reel in the two threads and suggest a number of practical organisational designs and management tools that might help to combine individual responsibility and organisational accountability.

However, this is not a how-to-do-book on managing complex organisations. Also, it is not a book on the economic control of enterprises. It is an attempt to apply fundamental notions of responsibility to a new and powerful actor in society. Therefore, the emphasis is on a combination of empirical and normative analysis. There is no systematic treatment of the modern management literature, nor of the literature on the economics of the firm. These literatures will be dealt with whenever relevant for the argument. Matters of management usually are addressed within the third, practical perspective. The economic control of firms is addressed to some extent in chapter 5, when the corporate model of accountability is discussed.

The combination of disciplines and perspectives treated in this study means that the readership, as is often the case in this sort of tour through a conceptual labyrinth, consists of a number of varied groups that do not all share the same background or language. The control perspective will be particularly interesting for people working in the field of government, organisation studies, or the sociology of law. The normative perspective will be more familiar to legal and political philosophers, and to those with a background in business ethics. Managers, consultants, and policymakers will probably be more interested in the practical issues of organisational design. I have tried to reckon with this disciplinary diversity by aiming in my presentations at a general, non specialist audience. However, in a number of places, digressions that are mainly of interest to specialists can be found. These digressions are not necessary for understanding the chief line of argument and can, if one wishes, be skipped. The book as a whole, however, is intended for each and every philosopher, lawyer, social scientist, or academically trained manager who has an interest in organisations. An important part of this study consists, therefore, of 'mapping'. On the basis of secondary material, derived from various disciplines, the labyrinth is charted and a guided tour of it is organized. At the end, we shall find no compelling conclusions or summary of findings, but – as I hope – a greater degree of insight and understanding. Many paths can be taken in the quest for responsibility, and I would consider that my plan had succeeded if, after finishing my book, readers were in a position to discover a path of their own.

2

Complex organisations as corporate actors

... the law has facilitated, and technological developments have motivated, an enormous growth of a new kind of person in society, a person not like you and me, but one which can and does act, and one whose actions have extensive consequences for natural persons like you and me.

(Coleman 1982: 19)

The age of complex organisations

Individual autonomy is a central value in contemporary western societies. An extensive system of legal protection greatly limits the extent to which government can intervene in the personal life of individual citizens. Basic rights guarantee everyone, within broad limits, the freedom to go and stay wherever one wants to go or stay, to join together with others, to speak out freely, or otherwise to employ one's time. In recognizing political rights, we no longer think in terms of households, as we still did well into the nineteenth century, but in terms of individual men and women. The criminal law is characterized by the concept of individual culpability; in fiscal and social security law, too, claims and duties have to a great extent been individualized. The same goes for many theories and rules in the sphere of ethics and morality. Authenticity, development, and individual responsibility are to the fore.

There is, however, another phenomenon that can be seen as typical of contemporary western societies and that is apparently at odds with this notion of individual autonomy: the fact that organisations play a big role in social and political life. Every one of those autonomous individuals has daily contact as citizen, employee, customer, or resident with organisations. As citizens for example, individuals are confronted with a large and opaque agency, the tax office, or a number of other barely penetrable government institutions. As people eligible for state benefits, they are confronted with a social security office, a welfare department, or the NHS. As employees, they work for a limited or private company, a foundation, or a government service. As customers, they are confronted with a fast-food chain, a hospital, or an insurance conglomerate. As residents, they have to put up with a chemical concern, a military-training ground, or a waste-disposal company. We thus live in what Sheldon Wolin has called an 'age of organization' (Wolin 1960: 352). Organisations have penetrated into almost all facets of daily life and their importance as social actors on a number of terrains is much greater than that of any single individual.

This discrepancy between the enlightenment ideal of the autonomous individual and the social reality of dominant bureaucratic organisations has in increasing measure attracted the attention of political theorists, sociologists, and philosophers. In this study, too, these two elements, individual autonomy and organisational dominance, are taken as points of departure for a number of theoretical, philosophical and empirical reflections. The emphasis, however, shall lie not so much on the threat to the autonomy of the individual as a result of these ever advancing processes of bureaucratization and rationalization – a concern that characterizes much of the work on this terrain.[1] Instead, I shall pay most attention to the question to what extent and in what way notions of individual autonomy, and in particular of individual responsibility, can contribute to increasing our ability to control the conduct of organisations.

In what ways do we live in an 'age of organization'? One can already speak of an 'organisation' as soon as two or more people consciously and deliberately cooperate in order to achieve a certain end (Barnard 1938: 4; Etzioni 1975: xi). Not only big companies, public utilities, hospitals, armies, prisons, state services, municipalities, independent administrative agencies and other government institutions, political parties, professional associations, universities, and schools fall within this broad definition, but so, too, do small businesses with only a handful of employees, football teams, fraternities, residential groups, action groups, families, toddlers' creches, and youth gangs. However, the extent and social importance of this second group is presumably not an essential characteristic of contemporary society. Even in earlier times, individuals had to do with such small-scale, relatively informal types of organisation. Think, for example, of tribes, militias, feudal courts, households, church institutions, and charitable associations.

It is above all the first group of large-scale, formal organisations whose presence can be seen as typical of the twentieth century and that form the point of departure for this study. Following (among others) Etzioni (1969, 1975) and Perrow (1979), such organisations are here denoted by the term *complex organisations*. The complexity of these organisations is often the result of a combination of two or three elements: large scale, bureaucratic structure, and formal status.

None of these elements can in itself be employed as denominator. True,

---

[1] See, for example, Arendt (1958); Adorno (1971: 67); and Habermas (1981).

the organisations to which I refer are mostly characterized by *largeness of scale* in terms of personnel, package of tasks, or activities; but not all complex organisations are large and not all big organisations are complex. (Think, for example, of a network of empty limited companies or of a club of football supporters.)

Nor is the element of *bureaucratic structure* wholly suitable as a central term. The concept of 'bureaucracy' has in the course of time acquired too many meanings and connotations to be useful as an independent, unequivocal denominator (Albrow 1970: 84–105). It is true that the most complex organisations in greater or lesser extent have a structure that is currently called 'bureaucratic'. There is a division of labour, a hierarchical structure of authority, and tenure of office based on expertise (Heady 1984: 67). Other elements that some include under the idea of bureaucracy in the sense of 'organisational structure' are often found in complex organisations: an oligarchical distribution of power, formally determined spheres of competency, an impersonal character, and a rational and impartial management on the basis and with the help of regulations (Weber 1980 (1920): 551–6; Albrow 1970: 102). On the other hand, many public and private organisations nowadays are trying to move away from the classical bureaucratic structure towards more flexible, decentralised structures, such as matrix organisations, 'adhocracies', semi-independent agencies, and workunits.

A final element that contributes to the 'complexity' of complex organisations is their formal status. It was above all the development by jurists of various forms of *charter of incorporation* that made possible the enormous growth in the number and importance of complex organisations (Pollock and Maitland 1968: II, 486–511; Stone 1975: 8–25; Coleman 1974: 13–31; Williamson 1985). Moreover, it is precisely this element of incorporation that puts complex organisations in many respects on a similar footing with natural individuals. Yet even this element is not the essential characteristic that distinguishes complex organisations from other forms of organisation. It is too large as it includes all those one-person businesses that for fiscal reasons or in order to protect the private fortune of the owner are transformed into private companies. On the other hand, it is too restricted, for some complex organisations formally lack an independent charter of incorporation, like the Dutch departments that are under the jurisdiction of the state.

Complex organisations as corporate actors

Over the last century, complex organisations have achieved prominent positions in society, often at the expense of the position of independently operating natural individuals. They have become 'corporate actors' (cf. Galbraith 1967: 72; Dahl 1970: 115–21; Coleman 1974, 1990). This shift of power and

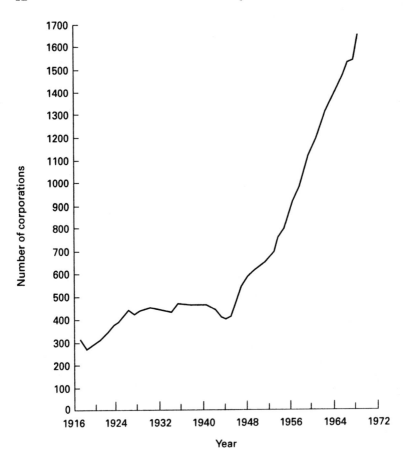

Figure 2.1   Number of profit-making corporations filing an income tax return in the United States, 1917–1969. From Coleman (1990:551).

influence can be exemplified easily in terms of a comparison of the daily transactions and worries of a modern family with those of a family at the beginning of the twentieth century. Our grandparents and great-grandparents often received their incomes directly and in cash from a 'boss' or from their customers; we, on the other hand, mostly receive our income through a salary administration, the social services, or some other sort of administrative office, and mostly by way of a bank or giro. For goods and services, our immediate forebears depended on independent shopkeepers and artisans; we, on the other hand, depend above all on supermarkets or big stores, private companies, and public service corporations. They had a landlord, we have a mortgage with a building society, or we rent from a housing association, a municipality, or a real estate developer.

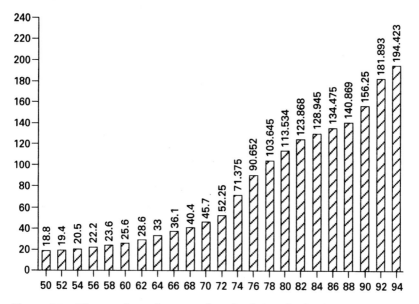

Figure 2.2   The number of corporations in the Netherlands (×1000). From Dutch Central Bureau of Statistics.

It is less easy to substantiate with empirical data the thesis that complex organisations in this century have increased enormously in number and social importance – if only because of the methodological problems that such an investigation entails. There are, however, several indicators:

An increase in the number of corporate bodies in the course of the century. Though not all corporate bodies are complex organisations, in so far as not all complex organisations have charters of incorporation, by far the great majority of them do, and many corporate bodies are at the same time complex organisations. A strong growth in the number of corporate bodies can therefore be taken as an indication of a growth in the number of complex organisations. James Coleman (1982: 10; 1990: 551) has pointed out that the number of profit-seeking corporate bodies in the United States increased more than fivefold between 1917 and 1969, many times more quickly than the population (figure 2.1). A similar development is evident in the Netherlands. In 1950, more than 18,000 businesses existed in the form of limited companies, a number that gradually rose to more than 45,000 in 1970. After a new form of corporation, the private limited company, was created in 1971, the number of companies and concerns with a charter of incorporation rose spectacularly to more than 194,000 in 1994 (see figure 2.2), a tenfold increase in just forty years.

An increase in the number of bureaucratic organisations. Bendix concluded on the basis of research in the United States, England, France, Germany, and Sweden that in the first half of the twentieth century a 'rather dramatic change in the organisational structure of economic enterprises' took place (1963: 221). In all the countries where he carried out research, he discerned a strong bureaucratization of life in industry. This bureaucratization was evident for example in a relatively strong growth in the number of employees occupied with administration as compared with the number working in the production of goods. Also, small family businesses gave way to large-scale, strongly bureaucratized concerns at whose pinnacle the place of the 'self-made man', the independent 'entrepreneur', and the manufacturer's son was taken by anonymous, salaried, and highly educated career-managers (Burnham 1947; Bendix 1963: 221–36; see also Galbraith 1967: 14). By now, at the end of the twentieth century, in most OECD-countries between 80 or 90 per cent of the civilian employment consists of wage earners and salaried employees. Only a limited part of the labour force consists of unpaid family workers, employers, or self-employed persons (OECD 1995).[2]

The increase in the number of law suits to which a complex organisation is party. According to Coleman (1982: 11–12), in 1853 in the New York State Court of Appeals, 15 per cent of parties to trials were corporate bodies; in 1973, more than half were. Dutch research in the sociology of law points in the same direction. Of all the legal problems analyzed by Schuyt, Groenendijk, and Sloot (1976: 161), 63 per cent involved conflicts between individuals and complex organisations. Vos (1985) even arrives at a figure of 75 per cent. In that connection, one can point, too, to the strong growth

---

[2] For example, the OECD labour force statistics 1973–1993 give the following figures for some of the major OECD countries:

	1973	1993
United States		
wage earners & salaried employees	90.3	91.1
others (unpaid family workers, employers, self-employed persons)	9.7	8.9
Germany		
wage earners & salaried employees	85.2	89.9
others	14.8	10.1
France		
wage earners & salaried employees	80.9	87.7
others	19.1	12.3
United Kingdom		
wage earners & salaried employees	91.8	86.1
others	8.2	13.9
Japan		
wage earners & salaried employees	58.7	77.0
others	41.2	22.8

in the number of administrative appeals – cases that by definition involve complex organisations.

The increase in attention to complex organisations in the media. Finally, a good indication of the social importance of the activities of complex organisations is provided by the front page of the *New York Times.* The space devoted to reports about natural individuals fell from approximately 45 per cent of the front page in 1876 to just 20 per cent in 1972; in general, this fall was matched by a rise in the amount of attention paid to complex organisations (Coleman 1982: 10–13). A sample investigation of the front page of the *Algemeen (NRC) Handelsblad* in the Netherlands yields similar findings (Baelemans and Van Zuilekom 1987: 17).

A new asymmetry in society

The legal system considers natural individuals and complex organisations as largely equivalent parties. They can contract with one another, fulfil obligations, acquire property, administer estates, and establish and acquire business rights. Organisations, just like natural individuals, can commit illegal acts, commit default, and consequently appear as party to a trial. Only in family law concerning, for example, marriages or parenthood, and some parts of criminal law, do organisations not have the same rights as natural individuals. If one considers the relations between both groups of actors from a less formal point of view, then the symmetry suggested by law often appears in practice to be wholly illusory. Many of the social relations between natural individuals and complex organisations are highly asymmetrical.

In the first place, most complex organisations have at their disposal a host of financial, technical, and administrative *means* that natural individuals do not have (see also Galbraith 1967: 85–8; Coleman 1982: 21). Complex organisations mostly have big laboratories and teams of researchers or a number of other experts in house. This gives them a large information advantage over individual clients, residents, or citizens. They can afford to wage advertising campaigns, run extensive lobbies, and, if such measures do not produce results, resort to law with the help of legal specialists and attorneys, in more or less unrestricted measure. Moreover, many organisations are, in the words of Marc Galanter (1974: 97–125), 'repeat players'; they are frequently involved in the same sort of legal procedures and become adept in the field. As a result they can better structure their future relations with others, develop specific expertise, maintain informal relations with people in the legal apparatus, and more easily negotiate and spread their risks and costs over a series of different endeavours. All those skills and abilities give them a considerable advantage over individuals. Most natural individuals are, after all, 'single-shooters'; they seldom resort to the courts, and, as a result of inexperience, often come up against big barriers.[3]

Both actors differ in terms not only of staying power and social skills but also of *life-span*. There are in principle no limits to the life-span of a complex organisation. Its continuing existence bears no relation to the life-span of the individuals that give form to it (see also Galbraith 1967: 14). This fact means that in the case of complex organisations, both social expansion (the increase in the organisation's share of the market and movable and immovable capital) and the consolidation of its own position are not weighed down by the burdens of death and ageing, as they are in the case of natural individuals. For example, almost half of the fifty biggest American companies (defined according to the extent of their 'assets') in 1909 came up on the list of the seventy companies that were at the top both in 1948 as 1959 (Chandler 1962: 3–6; Chandler and Salisbury 1971). If one then compares these two lists with the American top seventy (defined according to the extent of their sales) in 1983, at least nine of the biggest companies from 1909 are still at the top, and four of them are in the top ten (see also Sobel 1984: xi/xii). No less than twenty-nine companies that were among the biggest in 1948 were still among the top seventy in 1983, and no less than eight were among the top ten.[4] A considerable number of those companies had already been set up in the nineteenth century; one even came into being in the eighteenth century (Philips 1972: 431). Developments in the Netherlands confirm Chandler's findings. Table 2.1 shows the history of the top ten concerns of Dutch industry in 1990, defined according to the volume of their transactions. The date of their establishment is indicated in parentheses. Some of these concerns resulted from fusions of already existing companies whose history stretches even further into the past. (Fusions are indicated in the table with an F.)

The average age of these companies, or of their constituent parts, is more than 100 years. Other than in the case of people, this great age has not affected their vitality. The top ten show a large measure of stability over the years. The top six, for example, have remained the same ever since 1930.

---

[3] Research by Bruinsma (1988: 20) on the Dutch right of appeal points in the same direction. Organisations that proceed against private individuals win their cases significantly more often than do the private individuals.

[4] In reality these figures will presumably be even higher, since a number of the companies, both in the list of 1909 and in that of 1948/1959, now operate under another name or have merged. This phenomenon proved impossible to investigate. Moreover, at this point one quickly comes up against technical and philosophical questions. What does one mean by one and the same organisation? What is decisive: continuity in name, in legal form, of stock-exchange quotation, of ownership of shares, of a listing in the register of trade, of organisational structure, of personnel, of capital goods, or of a combination of two or more of all these elements?

Table 2.1 *History of the top ten Dutch industries*

	1990	1973	1950	1930	1913
Koninklijke Petroleum	1	1	1	1	1 (1890)
Phillips	2	2	3	3	17 (1891)
Unilever	3	4	2	2 (F1927)	
Van den Bergh					2 (1872)
Jurgens					4 (1871)
AKZO	4	3 (F1969)			
AKU			5	4	102 (1911)
Kon. Zout			33	85 (1918)	
Zwanenberg-Organon			22	67	(1887)
Ketjen			73	84	104 (1888)
DSM/Staatsmijnen	5	5	4	5	(1907)
Hoogovens	6	7	6	7 (1918)	
Heineken	7	9	20	23	38 (1873)
Fokker	8	8	15	68 (1919)	
Albert Heijn	9	18	28	?	? (1887)
Bührmann-Tetterode	10	17 (F1963)			
Bührmann			43	122	? (1887)
Tetterode			83	52	92 (1901)

Source: Bloemen, Kok, Van Zanden (1993).

Similar observations can be made with regard to government institutions (Kaufman 1973b).

In the third place, complex organisations, and especially the bigger concerns, are as a result of these developments often *oligopolist* or even, as, for example, in the case of many government institutions, monopolist. Natural individuals, on the other hand, 'come in crowds'. As individual clients, employees, residents, or citizens, they are mutually exchangeable, while they themselves, however, have only a few choices, or none at all. Individuals are therefore dependent on complex organisations, while complex organisations themselves are dependent only on big groups of individuals that act in unison (as action groups, political parties, consumer organisations, and trade unions; organisations that are often themselves also complex in nature). The result is that natural individuals, other than in the case of many of their mutual relations, often have little influence on the conditions within which their relations with complex organisations are enacted. Work and working conditions, products and services, and the conditions under which one and the other is offered are often decided unilaterally by the organisa-tions.[5]

Finally, the activities of complex organisations can also bring *risks* along, for individual citizens or for the society as a whole, risks that are somewhat different in quality from those that affect the activities of natural individu-als.[6] The nature of the risks is in some cases unknown or differs strongly from previously known risks. Complex organisations bring new products into the world based on production processes whose effect, or controllabil-ity, is not always known or predictable (certainly not in the long term). Examples of this are the risks, unknown at the time to the users, of medi-cines like Softenon or DES and the type of deformities that these products create. One might even mention the lack of clarity and security regarding environmental disasters – often, no one knows in what measure and for how long the expelled materials remain poisonous – or the uncertainties regard-ing the long-term effects of some forms of genetic manipulation (Beck 1992). Activities of complex organisations can produce risks for very many individuals at the same time as well. Some activities can disrupt society, or parts of society, for a brief while or even bring about far-reaching changes in society's structure in the long term. An example of the first situation is the leak in Union Carbide's chemical factory in Bhopal in India, which cost the lives of more than 2,500 people. The introduction of nuclear energy generally, and the fire in the Soviet nuclear reactor at Chernobyl in particu-lar, are examples of the second type of risks.

Environmental disasters, radioactive contamination, and other forms of environmental pollution are examples of risk-causing conduct that speak strongly to the imagination. The same goes for disasters involving ferries, oil tankers, or trains. Even in the socio-economic sphere, however, the increase in scale, which became possible as a result of the use and emergence of cor-porate actors, has resulted in increased damage to society. A case can be

[5] The flip-side of this unilateral and impersonal character of the relationship between individual and complex organizations is, however, that it gives the individual the opportunity, and perhaps even the occasion, for malversation. Protected by anonymity and relatively unhampered by the moral considerations that play a role in relations between individuals, one is more inclined to commit acts of shop-lifting, fraud, and vandalism when the damage is at the cost of a complex organization than when it is at the cost of a recognisably natural person (cf. Coleman 1974; 1982: 22).

[6] Coleman even goes so far as to talk of 'new risks', in distinction to the 'old' risks that flow from natural disasters or from the conduct of natural persons (1982: 88–90). Whether we are really dealing here in all respects with 'new' risks remains to be seen (there are, for example, substantial similarities with natural disasters), but the question is in any event less pertinent in this connection. One can in any case defend the proposition that these 'corporate risks' can be clearly distinguished on a number of points from the risks that flow from the conduct of natural individuals.

made that the damage to the economy and to state finances as a result of wilful fraud on the part of private or public organisations far exceeds the effects of malversation by natural individuals (Clinard and Yeager 1980: 7–12; Finney and Lesieur 1982: 257; Snider 1991: 209–10).

Similar considerations caused Coleman to describe modern, western society as asymmetrical: 'The first and perhaps most compelling attribute of the modern social structure which we inhabit is the *asymmetry* of a large portion of its relations' (1982: 19). What is new in the social structure as sketched is not, however, its asymmetrical character. Feudal societies had a structure in which the relationship between individuals from the various estates was both in formal and material regard one between unequal parties. And the analyses of Marx laid bare the discrepancy in capitalistic societies between the formal individual equality of the civil rights, and the actual asymmetry of class relationships (Marx 1844). New in the structure of modern western societies is above all the fact that the asymmetry is no longer between individuals, but between two fundamentally different types of actors: people and complex organisations.

Complex organisations as Chinese boxes

Asymmetrical or not, modern western societies stand or fall with complex organisations. Without complex organisations, we would still be at the level of prosperity and civilization of the late middle ages. It would be non-sensical to think of doing without them; as long as more efficient organisational forms have not emerged, complex organisations are here with us to stay. How can we, however, prevent this asymmetry from degenerating into a tyranny? How can we prevent the risks getting out of hand? In most 'modern republics', people have tried in various ways to maintain a balance between natural individuals and complex organisations. One can distinguish at least three such ways.

Indirect and passive intervention. In the first place, governments have tried to strengthen the social and legal position of natural individuals, the weaker party, in relation to complex organisations. In that connection, one can think of regulations concerning food and drugs, the extension of credit, colportage, working conditions, minimum wages, dismissal procedures, or employee participation in corporate decision-making. These and a number of other measures offer individual consumers and employees a certain basis upon which to negotiate on a slightly more equal footing. Similar developments can be found in the courtrooms. The difference in social position can play an important role when judges have to decide whether to award compensation for damages. Sometimes the government assists citizens financially or in terms of expertise. The extension of the legal-aid system is one example of such an intervention. Through legal aid for the indigent, natural individuals are provided with a measure of compensation for their lack of knowledge and means.

Support by interest organisations. In a number of areas interest groups – often themselves complex organisations – have been allowed to act as 'countervailing powers'. For example, unions and intermediary associations play a major supporting role in wage negotiations, in decision-making about consumer affairs, and in forming welfare or environmental policy. The appointment of a national ombudsman in many countries also fits within this general frame.

Active and direct state intervention. In a number of areas, however, the government also tries to influence the conduct of complex organisations directly. This happens by way of an extensive system of regulations and often with the help of special inspections and institutions that have the authority to check and, where necessary, enforce rule observation. For example, the government not only establishes rules regarding working conditions, goods and prices, or the creation of cartels, but also checks by means of its own inspection services whether these rules are actually observed. Environmental legislation is a good example of active government intervention to protect the interests of individual residents against encroachment by powerful complex organisations not only by establishing rules but also by means of inspection.

Each category is distinguished by a number of instruments that are applied in various ways and with varying degrees of success to bring the asymmetrical society into balance.[7] In the case of the first form, the emphasis lies on control by the individual natural persons themselves. The two last, which from the point of view of society are by far the most important categories, are a form of control by or with the help of (other) complex organisations. In fact, it is a case of 'setting thieves to catch thieves'. In most cases, such supporting organisations and inspection bodies are themselves also complex organisations (Coleman 1974: 73).

When complex organisations are used to control other complex organisations, we are in fact dealing with Chinese boxes: the government, for example, a conglomerate of complex organisations itself, tries to control complex organisations that themselves often consist in their turn of complex organisations or parts of organisations. At every level, the same questions arise again and again: an organisation oversees an organisation

---

[7] This is not the place to look into the effectiveness of these instruments. A number of them have already been the subject of empirical research and evaluation. See, for example, Nagel (1975), Stone (1975), Ermann and Lundman (1982a), Vaughan (1983), Fisse and French (1985), and McCahery, Picciotto, and Scott (1993). In the following chapters, I shall discuss these studies.

that oversees an organisation and so on. A minister of environmental affairs who wants to do something about the discharge of waste materials by industry is thus often confronted with a myriad of complex organisations. In order to achieve adequate control over industry, it will be necessary to set up an environmental inspection-service that will almost inevitably have a certain complex structure itself. The minister lacks the time to oversee and control this service; in practice, the department will do that, but the department is, of course, a complex organisation itself. We thus already have two layers of complex organisation. The well-intentioned CEO, or the board of directors of a company, questioned by the inspection service about its discharges, has, however, precisely the same problem. Many complex organisations are characterized by divisions, departments, and sections that themselves have a complex structure. That fact creates a third and sometimes even a fourth layer of control problems.[8]

In the first instance, this study will therefore address an issue of control. How can we prevent individuals or parts of society falling victim to the risks created by complex organisations? However, this study is no general investigation into the possibilities of controlling complex organisations. Attention will be paid to only one of the mechanisms that play a role in this issue: the imputation of responsibility. Most notions of control cannot do without a concept of responsibility. A central place in the practice of controlling complex organisations is occupied by processes of calling to account. Many of the instruments touched on above work, for example, by calling to account complex organisation or the individual functionaries that give shape to them. The central question of this study concerns, therefore, to what degree current notions of 'responsibility' are suitable for controlling the behaviour of complex organisations and controlling the emergence of those new 'corporate risks'. For that purpose, we must first ascertain what the current notions actually entail.

---

[8] With the rise of even more complex business organisations, such as corporate groups, another Chinese box seems to have been added (Williamson 1985: ch. 11; Antunes 1994).

3

Two concepts of responsibility

Responsibility is so integral a part of human relationships that in its various meanings and shadings it serves as a synonym for almost every important political word.

(Wildavsky 1986a: 1)

The problem of many responsibilities

Anyone who reflects on the concept of 'responsibility' will quickly discover that, just like 'freedom', 'equality', or 'solidarity', it is one of those big political words that is easily said but whose precise meaning is only too often obscure. If a word were ever to be described as a 'container concept', then that word is 'responsibility'. It is a vessel from which speakers can apparently draw at will; a tub in which almost all important moral, legal, and political ideas are to be found if only one rummages about in it long enough. It is also, and precisely for that very reason, an example of what the philosopher Gallie has called an 'essentially contested concept' (1962: 121). 'Responsibility' is a complex idea that has many equally plausible definitions, though these definitions are rarely compatible. 'Responsibility' or 'responsible' are terms that express values, but the values they embody are not generally accepted, and differ from time to time, place to place, and speaker to speaker. In the third place, 'responsibility' is a real 'right-on word', an idea that everybody supports. Who could possibly object to responsible conduct or a responsible organisation? Finally, 'responsibility' is in some respects what Bart Tromp has called a 'Sunday concept'. A 'Sunday concept' is an idea of which no one dares to say that he finds it particularly useful as a point of departure for his actions, or as an indication of a given state of affairs, but which 'in Sunday rhetoric sounds all the better when everyone knows that it can do no harm because everyday life throughout the week is not burdened by it' (Tromp 1985: 73). It is above all this last feature that is regularly present, and can sometimes cause considerable irritation, when responsibility is the issue. 'Responsibility' is only too often used as an intellectual stop-gap in party programmes, pamphlets, and sermons. It is, however, by no means useless, either in normative or in descriptive respect. It is simply that there are many 'responsibilities', which, moreover, can differ according to the context, the discourse, and the views of the speaker. To be able to work with it, the idea must therefore first be brought back to weekday proportions.[1]

What do we do when we say that someone is responsible for a given state of affairs? What do we mean when we say that someone 'has acted irresponsibly' and 'can be held responsible'? What do I mean when I ask who is responsible for the conduct of complex organisations? An obvious point at which to begin to seek an answer to these and other questions is the etymology of the word. The term 'to be responsible' suggests, both in its Germanic as in its Romance origin, the notion of giving an answer, *respondere*.[2] It is, however, not the answer to a request for information, such as 'who is Mary?' or 'what is the capital of Bourkina Fasso?', but an answer in the sense of giving account, justifying oneself, or defending oneself against an accusation. 'The root-notion is that of answering, in the sense of rebutting charges; or [. . .] giving an account' (Haydon 1978: 55). The core of responsibility is that 'I can be asked the question "why did you do it?" and be obliged to give an answer' (Lucas 1993: 5).

Accounting for oneself, taking responsibility, and justifying oneself never, however, happen in a vacuum; there is always something or someone who asks the questions or makes the accusations. Such asking and accusing happens mostly at the instigation and in the presence of some *forum* or other, varying in constitution from the *forum internum* of the conscience to

---

[1] In 1950 Chester Barnard could still say: 'Unlike "authority", "responsibility" has not been the subject of extensive literature [. . .] [C]onsidering the common use of "responsibility" and "responsible" in connection with politics, government, and organization, this is a matter of astonishment' (Barnard 1950: 1,001, note 2). Since then there has been a good deal more literature on this subject, literature that is above all philosophical in nature – about organisations, there is less. For this paragraph, I have among others used Pennock (1952), Arendt (1964), Hart (1968), Spiro (1969), Glover (1970), Feinberg (1970), Van Gunsteren (1974), Haydon (1978), Kenny (1978), Thompson (1980), Hart and Honoré (1985), and Lucas (1993). For general treatments of the concept of responsibility in the context of organisations see also Burke (1986), Day and Klein (1987), Romzek and Dubnick (1987), and Harmon (1995).

[2] 'Responsibility' is rendered as *Verantwortlichkeit* in German (*verantwoordelijkheid* in Dutch), formed on the basis of the noun *Antwort* (*antwoord*), 'answer'. Both the English *responsibility* and the French *responsabilité* can presumably be traced back to *responsabilis*. The word does not occur in the classic Latin vocabularies and probably dates from the legal jargon of the late Middle Ages. The *Lexicon Manual ad Scriptorem Mediae et Infimae Latinitatis* (1890: 1926) gives the following lemma: 'Responsabilis: "Responsabilis petitio"; Actio juridica, cui *respondere* debit (Anno 1351)'.

the informal forum of family members, friends, and colleagues, the much more formal disciplinary committee, tribunal, or parliamentary committee of inquiry, or even the television, the forum of the nation. According to Van Gunsteren, the basic significance of being responsible lies in the fact of being liable to be held to account before a forum. In the absence of a forum, our thinking about responsibility runs into trouble (Van Gunsteren 1974: 16). The idea of having to answer to a forum is of great importance for a good insight into issues of responsibility; later, I shall return many times to this notion. It is tempting to seek the essence of the idea in this very notion, without further ado. However, when we look at a few other ways in which we employ the idea, we see that the presence of a forum sometimes plays little or no role at all. When we say that someone is pursuing an irresponsible policy, is behaving irresponsibly, or is an irresponsible driver, we are making a value judgment whereby whether or not one is (or wishes) to be taken before a forum is only of incidental importance. We could at most say that those who realize that they might at some point be called to account will behave 'more responsibly' than others. It is even more difficult to demonstrate a connection with the idea of a forum when we employ the word 'responsible' in a causal sense, for example, in the pronouncement 'the guilder's high exchange rate was responsible for the downturn in exports' or, even more remote from the realm of human behaviour, 'the prolonged drought was responsible for the failure of the harvest'. Responsibility exists in such cases without a forum, not even in the shape of the board of the Dutch Bank or the meteorological office.

'Responsibility' is therefore a concept that can presumably best be clarified by making a sketch of what Wittgenstein called a family resemblance. Just as the members of a family are recognizable because they have various features in common, with (say) two of them sharing the same sort of nose and two others the same eye colour or shape of mouth, though there is no facial feature common to them all, so, too, the various forms of 'responsibility' are related to one another, though they cannot be reduced to one essential meaning. Let us therefore list the different ways the word 'responsibility', in its various forms, can be used. The well-known classification of Hart is a good point at which to start (1968: 211–30). Hart distinguishes four different forms that I have here rendered in my own words and in a somewhat adapted form:

1. Responsibility as *cause*. 'Responsible for' can in a number of contexts be replaced by 'caused' or 'to have as a consequence' or some such expression that indicates a causal connection. Above, I have given a few examples of such causal responsibility. As we also saw, not only people or their behaviour but also things, situations, and circumstances can be responsible for

something in this sense. Therefore, we not only say that 'the director's consumption of alcohol was responsible for his poor functioning', but also that 'the collapse of the market was responsible for bankrupting the coffee broker' or 'a virus was responsible for the flu epidemic'.

2. Responsibility as *accountability*.[3] Very often 'being responsible' is used in the sense of political, moral, or legal liability (or in all or some of these senses) for the results, mostly harmful, of a given form of behaviour or event. This is the meaning in which going before a forum most obviously applies. We can in such cases ask ourselves 'who must be held responsible for the sinking of the "Herald of Free Enterprise"', 'who is responsible for the greenhouse effect', or – food for lawyers, policy analists, and engineers – 'who was responsible for the fault hole in the o-ring of the propulsion rockets of the Space Shuttle *Challenger*'.

3. Responsibility as *capacity*. To be responsible in the sense of 'accountable', one must in most cases also have been in a position to exercise a certain amount of responsibility. Some people, however, lack the intellectual capacity that is necessary for this exercise of responsibility. Mentally ill people are often not in a position to reflect, to grasp connections, or to control and justify their actions and impulses. Of such people we say that they 'are not fully responsible for their deeds'. 'Responsibility' in this sense is often synonymous with *compos mentis* ('soundness of mind').

4. Responsibility as *task*.[4] When someone fulfils a given social role, holds an office, or is allotted a task or function in an organisation from which competencies flow and that entail certain duties in regard to others or in regard to the organisation, then we mostly speak of his or her competencies and duties as 'responsibilities'. For example, we say sometimes that 'parenthood brings with it responsibilities'; and where complex organisations are concerned, we say that 'the Under-secretary to the Ministry of Justice is responsible for our policy toward aliens' and 'the head of the internal accounting service has responsibility for controlling accounts'; in family circles, we might pronounce with some awe that 'he has a job with many

---

[3] Hart (1968: 215) speaks of 'liability-responsibility'. However, I prefer the word 'accountability', since it has fewer strictly legal connotations and also entails an element of moral or political responsibility.

[4] Hart (1968: 212) speaks of 'role-responsibility'. This includes for him, however, both the concrete tasks and duties that flow from a given role and concepts such as 'sense of responsibility' or 'responsible behaviour'. In order to get a better understanding of the term 'responsibility' it is more useful to consider the latter category separately. Below, I shall call this category responsibility as 'virtue'.

responsibilities'. In so far as 'responsibility' in this sense refers to the extent to which one makes decisions about and acts on important issues, it is synonymous with 'authority'; in so far as it refers to the burdens and tasks that flow from authority, 'responsibility' is often synonymous with 'duty'.[5]

These four categories more or less cover the basic features of the concept of 'responsibility'. However, one extremely important family member is lacking, namely:

5. Responsibility as *virtue*. We can also employ the concept to voice a positive value judgment or to sketch the outlines of a character trait. We can therefore say of someone that he is a 'responsible lecturer', that he pursues a 'responsible policy', or that he behaves 'responsibly', in short, that he is a person with a 'sense of responsibility'. In this sense, the concept refers to a virtue, it suggests that someone takes his tasks and duties seriously, acts only after due deliberation, and considers himself answerable to others for the consequences of his actions. It is a sense that is often neglected in discussions about responsibility, but that deserves a place of its own alongside those that Hart lists.[6]

Two concepts of responsibility

In this study only two forms are discussed in any depth. The first is responsibility in the sense of accountability, since this notion is central to the (semi-)legal context of complex organisations and 'corporate risks'. I call this *passive responsibility*. I shall also pay considerable attention to responsibility as virtue, which I call *active responsibility*. I do so not only because this latter meaning is very important within an organisational context, but also because it is a form that is, unfortunately, rarely dealt with.

---

[5] 'Responsible work' can thus refer to at least two situations that in no way overlap: (1) One has great powers of decision, but also, and as a result, a great burden in regard to decision-making. (2) One has only small powers of decision and action, but one still has a great burden in regard to decision-making, since the consequences of wrong decisions can be particularly serious. The role of a director or of the head of an operations team are examples of the first situation; a maintenance mechanic in a nuclear power station or a nurse in an operating theatre are examples of the second situation.

[6] This latter meaning of responsibility is classified by Hart under the rubric of responsibility as task ('role-responsibility') and not separately distinguished. That classification is understandable in the light of Hart's concentration on criminal-law aspects of the issue of responsibility. In his study, it is not so much a case of rewarding 'virtuous' acts as of determining the responsibility for damage done to persons and things. A more detailed discussion of responsibility-as-virtue and a clearer definition of the various meanings that Hart distinguishes can be found in Haydon (1978).

Some of the linguistic confusions and misunderstandings that often attend the use of 'responsibility' can perhaps be cleared up if we make a clear distinction between accountability and virtue. Moreover, it is possible with the help of these two forms to divide into two main categories the various possibilities of controlling the conduct of complex organisations by resort to notions of responsibility.[7]

In the case of passive forms of responsibility, one is called to account after the event and either held responsible or not. It is a question of who *bears* the responsibility for a given state of affairs. The central question is: 'Why *did* you do it?' In the case of active forms, the emphasis lies much more on action in the present, on the prevention of unwanted situations and events. Above all, it is a question of responsible acting, of taking responsibility, of *behaving* responsibly. The central question here is: 'what *is* to be done?'

A third meaning, responsibility as task, forms the connective element between the two. Both in the determining of responsibilities after the event and in determining a responsible line of conduct in a concrete situation, the notion of responsibility as task or competency is of very great importance. Tasks and competencies often entail responsibilities, too. And in order to be able to take responsibility, in order to be able to 'rise above oneself', one must in most cases also have at one's disposal certain responsibilities, in the sense of tasks and competencies. Both forms therefore are closely connected. The moral acceptability of the passive form will mostly be dependent on the availability of the active form. We will not easily accept the idea of bearing responsibility unless we have at our disposal the possibilities of behaving responsibly. We would be asking a lot of someone if we held him responsible in a situation in which he had no choice other than to behave in the way he did.

There is also a reverse connection between active and passive responsibility. Individual opinions about a responsible line of behaviour are not formed in a vacuum. 'The power of judgement rests on a potential agreement with others, and the thinking process which is active in judging something [. . .] finds itself always and primarily, even if I am quite alone in making up my mind, in an anticipated communication with others with whom I know I must finally come to some agreement' (Arendt 1968: 220).

---

[7] The only authors who to my knowledge have at least begun to make such a classification of the various forms of responsibility are Finer (1941: 336) and Pennock (1952: 797). The latter distinguishes between 'accountability, in the sense of answerability' and on the other hand 'explicability'. He describes the latter meaning as follows: 'A person's conduct is responsible if it is susceptible to rational explanation and, furthermore, if it is conditioned upon an attempt to obtain the pertinent facts, upon deliberation, and upon consideration of, and with due regard for, the consequences'.

To feel responsible for something and to take action on it happens mostly in the realization that you will at some point have to answer for your action or inaction; whether to a formal institution, such as a tribunal or commission of inquiry; to an informal, but no less concrete, forum such as your circle of friends, your parents, or your children (even if they are not yet born); or to a more metaphysical type of forum such as God or humankind. In the case of responsibility as virtue, the forums are thus often internalised in the form of what George Herbert Mead has called the 'generalized other'.

These connections do not imply that it is meaningless to make this distinction, for it allows us to divide the question of how to control the behaviour of complex organisations with the help of models of responsibility into more viable sub-questions. In the first part of this study, the emphasis will lie on questions of accountability, while in the second part, bureaucratic virtues will be the focus of discussion.

Passive responsibility

When do we hold someone responsible and when do we say that someone behaves responsibly? What are, in short, the *criteria* for these two important forms of responsibility? I will first examine accountability, the most classical form.

It is impossible to produce an unambiguous and universally acceptable list of criteria for responsibility in the sense of accountability. Classic forms are after all the subject of classic debates. Also, the content and application of some criteria differ according to discourse and according to the type of accountability. Political, legal, and moral responsibility, for example, do not always coincide. Moreover, when one tries to apply the discrete criteria in hard cases, it appears that they often exist in such narrow mutual coherence that one can scarcely speak of independent testing. The following survey is, therefore, no more than a global map; it could certainly not be used as an ordnance map. If for the moment we abstract from the scholarly issues, there are (broadly speaking) four categories according to which the diverse criteria for responsibility-as-accountability can be classified.

1. *Transgression of a norm.* This category falls into two sub-parts. In the first place, there must be some question of human *conduct*, of action or inaction, that appears to have contributed to a situation or event. (The high guilder cannot be blamed for the downturn in exports, though the directors of the Dutch Bank, who persisted too long with their monetary policy perhaps can.) Processes of calling to account begin mostly when an event or situation is perceived as harmful or shameful. We have already seen that answering for something means answering accusations. However, there can

be no accusation without norms and values. If someone is to be held responsible for the conduct of a complex organisation, it must at some point be established that that person has by his conduct contravened some *norm*. That norm need not explicitly exist; in many cases, it is explicitly formulated only in the course of the process of calling to account by the forum.

Both of these elements have been the topic of extensive debates in the philosophy of law. In the case of the first criterion, for example, one may enquire under what circumstances one can speak of an action (what about, for example, twitches, reflex movements, or motor disturbances?), or of one single action (think of the legal problem of concurrence), and what factors must play a role in the qualification of an action (think, for example, of the nuances between murder, manslaughter, and death by default). Also, there are numerous nuances in regard to the nature and formulation of the norm. In criminal law, this norm must be explicitly formulated (*nullum crimen, nulla poena sine praevia lege poenali*), whereas in civil law norms often are much vaguer, and in politics, the great majority of rules are unwritten and fluctuating.

2. *Causal connection*. In the second place, there has to be a certain causal connection between the conduct of the person held to account and the damage done. Usually, we only hold someone responsible when it can be shown that there is a relation between that person's action or negligence and the event or situation that is under challenge. Many theories have been developed about the nature of this causal connection, above all in the field of (criminal) law.[8] The theories of equivalence are quite comprehensive. In them, each form of behaviour that can be considered as a *conditio sine qua non*, as a precondition for the given state of affairs, is viewed as cause. Alongside such theories are the theories of adequacy in which a relevant causal connection is considered present only if it could reasonably have been foreseen that a given form of behaviour would result in a negative state of affairs. In the Netherlands, the Supreme Court also has been applying an assumption of reasonableness. It looks not only for a scientific connection but also looks into the question of whether or not the consequences, in the light of all the circumstances, can in all reasonableness be attributed to the person who has been called to account. With that statement, we have arrived in the vicinity of the third category.

3. *Blameworthiness*. It is important not only whether someone as a result of his conduct has contributed to the situation that has given rise to the grievance; it must also be possible to attribute the conduct to him. In order

[8] For Anglo-Saxon law, see Hart and Honoré (1985).

to be responsible, in the sense of liable, one must have had a real possibility of acting otherwise than one actually did. Someone who could not help getting involved in the causal chain is rarely blamed. This category, too, can be divided into a number of separate parts. To be held fully accountable, at least two things must be shown to be true.

a) The person held to account must at the moment of engaging in the form of behaviour under consideration have been in adequate possession of his mental faculties. This criterion is concerned above all with the internal aspect of blame. It points in the first place to the notion of responsibility as capacity, which we dealt with earlier. Young children and people who are mentally disturbed (either temporarily or permanently) are not at all, or only in slight measure, held accountable for their behaviour. They are often insufficiently able to determine their wishes and to do otherwise than they actually did. For those who were so able, it must be possible to show that they knew or could reasonably – as the lawyers say – have foreseen at the moment that they performed, or neglected to perform, a given action that damage to people or things might ensue. In order to be in a position to be responsible, one must act (or have been able to act) deliberately and knowingly.

b) Alternative forms of conduct were available. This criterion considers extraneous inhibitions. It is not only necessary that someone was in a position to determine his own will, but he must also have had the opportunity of putting his will into effect. No one will readily be held responsible when extraneous factors prevented him from doing other than he did. In criminal law, one speaks in such a case of *force majeure* or, if one's own life or safety was at stake, of self-defence. In the case of functionaries in an organisation, these inhibitions often consist of legislative prescriptions, official commands, and (other) role obligations.[9]

4. *The relationship with the agent.* This criterion only plays a role in particular cases. In most cases, the person made to answer and held responsible is also the one who performed the action that gave rise to the offence. Sometimes, however, someone is held to account for deeds committed by somebody else. In civil law, we hold parents accountable for their children and – of great importance for the control of complex organisations – employers accountable for their employees. A good example in the Netherlands is also ministerial accountability for the conduct of the Royal House. When questions arise concerning the conduct of the Queen, the

[9] The category of blameworthiness has up to now produced the fiercest debates and the most nuanced distinctions. Here, too, criminal law is an important source. In Anglo-Saxon law, this category is in general treated under the heading 'mens rea'. See for a general discussion of this subject Hart (1968), Feinberg (1970), and Kenny (1978).

prime minister rather than she herself is called to account in parliament. In all these cases, however, there is a particular and close relationship with the agent; without this relationship, the person held to account could not be held responsible.[10]

Speaking very generally, these are, then, the criteria at play when we are dealing with responsibility in the sense of accountability. These criteria are in most cases necessary conditions. To be responsible means that every one of these elements must be present; if even one is lacking, then accountability, too, frequently does not apply. Responsibility in this passive form is, moreover, to employ a distinction made by Schuyt (1983: 278–87), *digital* in nature. You are either accountable or you are not. There is no middle way, you cannot be 'somewhat' or 'fairly' accountable, and you cannot call someone a little bit to account.[11]

---

[10] I have with some hesitation taken over this fourth criterion from Hart (1968: 220). To what extent are we dealing with a discrete category? Does that particular relation not in most cases consist of a sort of obligation of care? If that is the case, then we can make do with the first three categories, and have no need of a fourth. As soon as there is the need to construct an – extremely far-reaching – obligation of care, this can as a *norm* be done in terms of the first category. The employer is responsible for the illegal acts of his employees because he deliberately and knowingly (blameworthiness) took insufficient care in instituting the structures of his company (transgression of the norm), as a result of which the employee could act as he did (causal connection). But ministerial responsibility for the Royal House remains a problem. There, it is difficult to construct any more than a restricted obligation of care. The responsibility of the prime minister can rather be traced back to old values of a ritual character. This form probably goes back to the idea of 'the King can do no wrong'; his mistakes are attributed to his servants, who appear in parliament on his behalf. This part of ministerial responsibility is therefore no more than a ritual that maintains the fiction of royal inviolability. Another explanation could be that in such cases we operate on the edge of the idea of responsibility. This category belongs in the discussion only because we coincidentally speak of responsibility-as-accountability. In a legal context, the two concepts coincide, but not in moral respect. We do not hold parents, employers, and the prime minister who have behaved with normal care in relation to their children, employees, and the Royal House *morally* responsible for wrongdoing by their children, their employees, or the royal family. Those persons are themselves morally responsible for their own conduct. For social reasons (redistributive justice, prevention of serious risks, preservation of the monarchy), an additional type of accountability has been created that can be understood only in a strictly legal or political sense as 'responsibility'.

[11] True, we speak of 'shared' responsibility or of 'a certain moral responsibility'. In my view, however, that has to do not so much with whether or not one can be held to account but with the fact that others, too, can be held to account on the same grounds, or with the measure of blameworthiness, or, in legal discourse, with the extent of the sanction or reparation that results from the accountability. See for a very subtle distinction of the various dimensions of passive responsibility Baier (1972: 55–6).

Active responsibility

Most theories about the passive side of responsibility have strong roots in legal science. It has nearly always been jurists and philosophers interested in law, for example Aristotle, Bradley, Mill, Von Savigny, Traeger, Von Buri, Rümelin, Hart, and Feinberg, who have reflected on issues of accountability. For views on the active side of responsibility, for responsibility as virtue, one must consult another tradition. In law, virtues only occasionally play a role, for example, in the case of the *diligens pater familias*, or they do so only very indirectly, in the form of 'negligence'. Rather than virtues it is human vices that underlie most legal questions. For modern treatises on virtues one must turn to moral philosophers and theologians.

Alasdair Macintyre (1981) has shown that the content and also the ranking order of the principal virtues can differ strongly from century to century, from (sub)culture to (sub)culture, and from thinker to thinker. The properties that brought someone respect in the Homeric society of warriors and farmers were in later societies only moderately prized or not prized at all. Even the established/solid Athenian citizen from the last era of the polis would, if he tried to behave according to the Nicomachean Ethics of Aristotle, have looked little like the heroes of the Trojan war. In the Ilias and the Odyssey, bravery, physical force, cunning, and loyalty to one's own group were the prime virtues. As Greek society became more complex and social life became concentrated in the city, the catalogue of virtues changed greatly. Contributions to public affairs and an aristocratic attitude to life became much more important (Adkins 1960). The chief virtues that Aristotle discusses in his *Nicomachean Ethics* are courage, temperance, liberality, magnificence, pride, equability, friendliness, truthfulness, ready wit, justice, and practical wisdom. With the reception of Aristotle in the Middle Ages, this classical concept of 'virtue', *aretè* (which originally signified little more than power, ability, or excellence), was elaborated and adapted in a Christian direction by thinkers like St Thomas Aquinas. Under the influence of the New Testament, virtues such as faith, hope, and the love of one's neighbour became more prominent.[12] In Machiavelli's *virtù*, however, one still finds many of the classical virtues, such as bravery, energy, cunning, eloquence, and ambition. The reformation, in combination with the rise of capitalism, led to a further transformation. In the Protestant ethic – one of the main sources of many of contemporary western moral conceptions – virtues were emphasised that are in many respects the antitheses of the virtues that made the Aristotelian Athenian a gentleman. In the wake of

---

[12] A neo-Thomist like Peter Geach (1977) names faith, hope, charity, prudence, justice, temperance, and courage as the most important virtues.

Luther, Calvin, Kant, Benjamin Franklin and other puritan moralists, virtues such as love of the truth, obedience, zeal, frugality, sobriety, chastity, temperance, industry, and cleanliness – *innerweltliche Askese* (Weber 1981 (1920): 179) – were emphasised.[13]

Responsibility or, better still, a sense of responsibility does not occur in most traditional ethics. Its appearance in the higher regions of the top ten of virtues is presumably of a more recent date. In any case, there is a close connection with Christian ethics. Many of the virtues that are implied in the expression 'a sense of responsibility' are closely related to Christian virtues, such as love of one's neighbour, frugality, and zeal. The idea of the human being as steward over God's creation is also an important element. Among the authors who have given consideration to this active side of responsibility, theologians and thinkers inspired by Christianity have been predominant.[14]

Responsibility as virtue is *analogous* in character. You can act responsibly to a greater or lesser extent; in this sense, the concept allows a fluid transition. The qualification of someone, some form of conduct, or a policy can vary from 'very irresponsible' through 'rather (ir)responsible' to 'very responsible', according to the (degree of) presence of the various contributory elements. Because of the analogous character of responsibility as virtue the debates have been far less vehement than with responsibility as accountability. Unlike in the case of the passive form, this analogous character means that none of the criteria constitutes a necessary precondition. Even if only some of the preconditions are fulfilled, this can suffice to establish whether or not someone is behaving responsibly, is endowed with the necessary sense of responsibility, in short, is a responsible person. Therefore, the criteria for determining whether conduct is responsible are less clearly delineated and more dependent on context and speaker than in the case of responsibility as accountability. I shall therefore confine myself more or less to conceptual elements – although it is not always possible to separate conceptual and substantive aspects. The following summary is, moreover, not

[13] It would be interesting to put together a top ten of the virtues prized by modern western societies. An important complication is formed by the fact that those societies are characterized by a social, cultural, and ethical pluralism of values. The top ten of a Christian entrepreneur would presumably not deviate all that much from that of Benjamin Franklin; the top ten of a liberal, urban 'professional', on the other hand, would hardly show signs of 'innerweltliche Askese', and would presumably have more in common with the Aristotelian aristocrat; while the top ten of an Arsenal supporter would look most like those of the Homeric heroes.

[14] See, for example, Niebuhr (1963) and Bonhoeffer (1971). The notion of stewardship and of a worldly asceticism also underlies one of the most important contemporary books on responsibility as virtue, *Das Prinzip Verantwortung*, by Jonas (1979).

meant to be restrictive; I do not exclude that more independent elements can be found and invite the reader to consider which elements he or she would employ. My own cogitations lead to the following five categories.[15]

1. *An adequate perception of threatened violations of the norm.* A policy or a form of conduct often acquires the epithet 'responsible' or 'justified' when it is based on, or shows signs of, an adequate perception of possible dangers. In the fable of the grasshopper and the ant, the ants are presented to us as an example of responsible folk because they realize that, when winter comes, food will no longer be abundant. The grasshopper, according to the moral of the story, behaved irresponsibly because it wrongly thought that everything would be allright. Responsibility in the sense of virtue is thus closely related to ideas such as 'reasonable', 'rational', or 'prudent'.[16]

The adequate weighing up of mutually conflicting norms and interests is a part of this category as well. Responsible conduct can sometimes consist of the wilful contravening of certain norms in order to avert the threatened violation of other norms. In that situation, too, adequate perception is indispensable. When, for example, I am driving my car and one of my passengers seems to be suffering a heart attack, the fact that I rush to a hospital without worrying too much about speed limits, can be a sign of a sense of responsibility. Saving a life then, takes precedence over obeying traffic regulations. If, once we have arrived at the hospital, it turns out that my passenger had simply fallen asleep, judgment will be quite different. In order to act responsibly, one must be aware of all relevant aspects of the situation.

This requirement of adequate perception bears on at least four questions: (a) Which norms are in danger of being contravened? (b) What is the importance of those norms? (c) How great is the chance they will be contravened? (d) How serious would the results of transgression be in the concrete situation at hand? A serious and plausible, albeit in many cases implicit, answer to this sort of question precedes 'responsible conduct'. We see that on this point the two forms of responsibility are connected. These questions will also play an important role when someone is held to account by, or in

---

[15] In the course of my deliberations, I have used the somewhat comparable views of Stone (1975: 113–15) and Haydon (1978: 48–53). See also Lucas (1993: chapter 9.4).

[16] One might ask oneself whether the ants also demonstrated their wisdom by subordinating the fulfilment of their present desires to the prevention of possible accidents in the future. In his version of this fable, Martin Hollis has nicely shown how responsibility and wisdom can be two different things: 'The Grasshopper expired, and the Ant lived on into grey old age without ever once doing anything which caused him a moment's overall regret. '"It is hard never to be able to do what one wants most to do", he mused arthritically, "but then the life of a rational being is a hard life." Moral: *It is hard to be wise, but there are many ways to be foolish*' (Hollis 1987: 98).

the presence of, a forum. The aspect of adequate perception will be important above all in determining blameworthiness.[17]

2. *Consideration for consequences.* This element was already vaguely
present in the previous four questions. 'Consequences' have a place of
honour in the vocabulary of responsibility as virtue. A responsible person
allows the possible consequences of his conduct to play a role in his decisions. In so doing, he must pay special attention to the consequences of his
conduct for others. A responsible driver not only takes care that he himself
and his car arrive home without a scratch, but drives in such a way that his
passengers and other road users arrive home in the same condition. This
element has a strongly utilitarian undertone. Responsible conduct implies
seeking and weighing alternatives on the basis of a calculation of the consequences for the interests of all those involved. Attention to consequences can
also sometimes cause people to feel obliged to contravene certain norms or
forsake certain duties.

However, we already have one foot on substantive terrain. For not everybody will accept this element in the same way. Strict deontologists, such as
the Kantian puritans who strictly interpret the commandment to speak the
truth, or principled pacifists who are under no circumstances prepared to
apply violence, will not let the consequences of their principled attitude play
a decisive role in their decisions. For them, responsibility as virtue is in the
first place an issue of purity of conscience. Max Weber calls such a point of
departure *gesinnungsethisch*. He himself is a proponent of an opposite, con-
sequentialistic attitude, at least where politics are concerned: 'der *verant-
wortungsethischen*: dass man für die (voraussehbaren) Folgen seines
Handelns aufzukommen hat' (1977 (1919): 57–8; my italics). For Weber, the
politician who takes account for the results of his policy is the truly responsible politician.

3. *Autonomy.* In order to be in a position to act responsibly, one often
needs to be independent in the sense of autonomous. This is the mirror
image of the criterion of blameworthiness that is posed by the concept of
responsibility as accountability. It has both an internal and an external side.
A responsible person listens to the advice and commands of others, but acts
and eventually decides on his own account and on the basis of his own per-

---

[17] The adequate weighing up of mutually conflicting norms will, for example, be very
important in appraising a legal defence based on civil disobedience, or in the
opposite case of an appeal to official orders or role obligations. (I shall return in
greater detail to this question in later chapters, when I consider certain forms of
administrative disobedience.)

ceptions and norms. Someone who only reacts to what others say, who leaves his own judgments out of consideration, and who obediently does what others require him to do is not often considered 'responsible' – even though there may be material notions of responsibility according to which such conduct on the part of functionaries actually would be called 'responsible', as we shall see later. In the second place, there is the external aspect; there must also be sufficient space in which to act independently. Someone whose hand is forced, and who cannot be blamed for having put himself in that situation, will not readily be accused of irresponsible conduct.

At this point, responsibility as virtue touches on responsibility in the sense of task. The more responsibilities one has, the more important a sense of responsibility becomes. More room for decision within the framework of the task at hand, as, for example, in the case of the director in regard to the proverbial man or woman on the production line, means an even greater chance of irresponsible conduct. And the more serious the results of mistakes and neglect of duty, as, for example, in the case of a nurse in an operating theatre, the more important is responsibility in the sense of virtue.

4. *Conduct based on a verifiable and consistent code.* This general description includes three elements that lie very narrowly together. A responsible person acts in the first place on the basis of (moral) norms and values and not on the basis of emotional impulses, sudden feelings, or violent instincts: 'Responsibility [. . .] is the power of a particular private code of morals to control the conduct of the individual in the presence of strong contrary desires or impulses' (Barnard 1938: 263). A personnel chief who nominates someone as head of a department because he is passionately in love with that particular candidate, although he knows very well that almost all the other candidates are better suited to the post in question, will not readily be called 'responsible' from a bureaucratic point of view. In such a context, we mostly find that the person best qualified for the job is the one who should be appointed.

Good intentions and elevated moral values do not in themselves, however, amount to a sense of responsibility. In the second place, it is a question, as has already become obvious, of concrete conduct. A sense of responsibility is demonstrated not through fine words but through actual conduct in concrete situations: 'The point is that responsibility is the property of an individual by which whatever morality exists in him becomes effective in conduct' (Barnard 1938: 267). Only by our actions do we show who and what we are.

The third element is that this conduct must be comprehensible to and verifiable by outsiders. A manager who cannot explain why he has taken a certain decision, on which rules he bases his behaviour, or who in ostensibly equivalent situations arrives at wholly different decisions will not readily be called a 'responsible manager'. In many situations, 'responsibility' also implies that you keep a hold on your caprices. Others must not only be able to understand why you acted as you did, they must also be able to build on your conduct and attune their own conduct to it. Responsibility and caprice are not easily reconciled.

5. *Taking role obligations seriously.* When we wish to answer the question whether or not someone has acted responsibly in a given situation, the office that that person holds, the function that he or she fulfils, or the social role that he or she occupies and the obligations that flow from it are very important. Within western liberal democracies, the responsibility of a judge is quite other than that of the Minister of Justice or of a member of parliament. The question whether or not a functionary is acting responsibly will therefore depend in large part on the function that he or she fulfils within the organisation. The supervisor in the Union Carbide plant in the Indian city of Bhopal who first went to have a cup of tea before examining the leakage that eventually led to the death of some 2,500 people acted irresponsibly. But we would not readily reach the same conclusion about a postman who suspected something yet continued delivering his letters. (If, however, he had come across casualties and yet simply continued on his round without reporting the incident, our judgment would be quite different.)

For Hart, this is the sole criterion; with responsibility as virtue he means role responsibility: 'A "responsible person", "behaving responsibly" (not "irresponsibly"), require for their elucidation a reference to role-responsibility. A responsible person is one who is disposed to take his duties seriously; to think about them, and to make serious efforts to fulfil them. To behave seriously is to behave as a man who took his duties in this serious way' (1968: 213). Taking role obligations seriously, then, is a sufficient, though not necessary, and certainly not the sole condition for responsible conduct. Even if a functionary punctually fulfils all his role obligations, his conduct, measured according to the other criteria, can still be experienced as very irresponsible. Think, for example, of the case of Eichmann and many other dutiful officials in the territories of the Third Reich. Furthermore, responsibility as virtue is a concept that can also be meaningfully applied without there being talk of a specific role, function, or task and of the obligations that flow from them.[18] A police officer who in the course of surveillance comes across the beginnings of a conflagration but neglects to warn the fire-brigade is not taking his obligations seriously and is therefore acting

---

[18] See also Haydon (1978: 47–52).

irresponsibly. The same judgment would also apply, however, to the passer-by who has promised his wife to take the dog for a walk and first finishes that task before calling the fire-brigade. He, too, acts irresponsibly, though he takes his task seriously.[19]

It is obvious that various meanings are possible within each criterion. Little has been said about the nature of the norms that may not be contravened, about how to choose between conflicting norms, about the criteria on the basis of which one determines whether or not a perception is adequate, about what should and should not be reckoned among the consequences, and about which obligations flow from a given role. Many conceptions about responsible conduct are therefore possible. By a *conception* of the concept of responsibility as virtue, I mean a concrete interpretation of the criteria I have just discussed. Such an interpretation can be in the form of a professional code or code of behaviour: a set of duties, the fulfilment of which earns someone public or social esteem, and the transgression of which evokes disapproval. There are many such codes of behaviour and responsibilities; the content depends on the role that one has or the situation in which one finds oneself. A responsible father behaves differently from a responsible police officer, a civil servant with a sense of responsibility is not the same as a responsible politician. Moreover, different views of the correct performance of a role are often possible. I have already mentioned the Weberian distinction between *Gesinnungsethik* and *Verantwortungsethik*, two conceptions of politically responsible conduct that differ greatly in how they weigh up possible consequences. A principled pacifist would presumably follow a different view of responsible defense policy from that of a pragmatic conservative; and the expression 'a responsible soldier' would, even in the age of peace-keeping operations, probably strike the pacifist as a contradiction in terms.

Responsibility and the control of complex organisations

By holding each other to account, people maintain a certain order and regularity in society. Norms are (re)produced, internalised, and, where necessary, adjusted through accountability. The person held to account is told about the standards he must hold to and about the fact that in the future he may again (and, in that case, more strictly) be called to account in connection with his conduct. In such cases, outsiders are often addressed as well, particularly those outsiders likely to find themselves in a similar position to

---

[19] Hart's thesis on this point can perhaps be saved if the concept of role is understood in its broadest sense and the passer-by is held to account in his role as citizen or as 'fellow human being'.

that of the person or persons being called to account. After the Nuremberg trial, for example, functionaries can put forward superior orders as a defence of their misconduct only in particular circumstances.

Active notions of responsibility are thus created, made explicit, or discarded in the process of calling someone to account. These notions, however, also cast their shadows ahead, they set the norms for future conduct and can thus play an independent role in the control of conduct. The knowledge (or the probability) that we shall be held to account for things that go wrong often forces us to seek new ways of preventing such a situation from arising.

> As a result of constructions of responsibility, our quest to enlarge our control of given points is concentrated [...] We will reconstruct what happened until we are able to relate it to the actions of an individual capable of being held to account. Until we can say: you were responsible and you had control, you could have acted otherwise. But we know somehow or other that the original situation was not like that. Speaking in terms of responsibility, it is a learning process. An appeal to do more, to surpass yourself. We ask too much. And this asking too much, this hypocrisy, is necessary in order to steal from reality all the potential that it contains.
>
> (Van Gunsteren 1974: 23)

The realisation that one will or might be held to account, the passive side of responsibility, stimulates people to behave responsibly, the active side. Giving account of oneself is therefore one of the most important means by which we can try to maintain the fragile public sphere and to make sure that the way in which society is arranged does not at crucial points slip through our collective fingers. In the course of this process, control and prevention, accountabilities and virtues, go hand in hand.

Sanctions will often play an important part. At the end of a process of holding to account, a decision is often taken as to whether and in what measure the violation of the norm should be punished. In such cases, it is not always solely a question of how to compensate the victims. Even when victims are not evident, one still imposes sanctions (think, for example, of administrative fines) in order to underline the importance of the norms that were contravened. The connection between responsibility and sanction is, however, ambiguous. Even without (formal) sanctions, processes of calling to account can be meaningful and produce learning effects. In the first place, one must realize that 'sanction' is an elastic concept. In a number of cases, and for many people, the fact that one must appear before a forum in order to explain one's conduct is already experienced as a *démarche*. It signifies that one is not trusted. Also, giving account of oneself, certainly when that happens in public and when the discrepancy between the norms and the actual behaviour is there for everyone to see, can in itself be particularly painful. The sanction is therefore present in the very process of being held responsible.[20] Moreover, a process of holding to account can in the nature of things also lead precisely to 'positive' sanctions, to a restoration to honour, and the repolishing of the tarnished escutcheon. The forum can free those called to account before it of all blame and declare groundless the imputations levelled at them.

But even when giving account of oneself is not experienced as painful, when no sanctions are imposed, and when no one is restored to honour, the procedure can still be meaningful and effective. Giving account of oneself is not only about determining ignominy, guilt, and damage, about conviction and compensation; it is also about telling a story, reconstructing events and drawing lessons from the past. Such processes of calling to account often have a ritual purifying function. They bring a period to an end, they allow people to get things off their chests, to voice their grievances, or even to give account of themselves. The fact that, in the end, a balance is drawn up makes a new beginning possible. Processes of calling to account create the opportunity for penitence, reparation, and forgiveness and can thus prevent the past remaining a burden on the shoulders of all those involved and on their mutual relations. Processes of calling to account clear the air, they can round off a business that is tending to drag on and offer the chance of a new start. One can start up one's life again, 'sadder and wiser' perhaps, but not full of resentment and bitterness, of a sort that could seriously frustrate every form of cooperation.

When, and on the basis of which elements, can we say that a process of calling someone to account before a forum, has been meaningful? The analysis of the connections between responsibility and control can be summarized in four series of questions that should be able to play a role in appraising processes of calling to account.

First, has holding someone to account ended social unrest? Does the process of being held to account act as a purification ritual, does it help to close off a painful period? Secondly, did the holding to account and the subsequent arrival at a judgment happen in a satisfactory way? Was the process of holding to account fair? Were both sides given the chance to air their views, did the person held to account have enough time to prepare and to defend himself, was the judgment sufficiently motivated? – and similar procedural rules. But also: were the material criteria for responsibility taken

---

[20] That sanction can be extremely grave and can sometimes assume terrible forms. Think, for example, of the practice in some socialist countries of forcing dissidents and other 'enemies of the people' to practice self-criticism in public, at popular tribunals.

into account in reaching the judgment? Choosing a scapegoat or holding a lynch party for example, will not readily be counted as successfully executed processes of calling to account. The answer to these first two questions can in turn be important for the third question that one can ask oneself. Does the process of holding to account make a new beginning possible? Will the process, and above all the way in which it was conducted, not perhaps lead to a further disturbance in relationships? If the discussion remains open, will people get back onto 'speaking terms'? As Arendt (1958: 236–47) puts it is there sufficient opportunity for forgiveness and for promises to do better?

Another step futher along in time, the fourth question arises. Does the process of accounting produce learning effects? Will it lead to a situation in which those involved, and possibly outsiders who are in a position similar to that of the persons held to account, learn from the mistakes made? Does the process of accounting lead to particular and to general prevention and to other conceptions of responsibility as virtue? But also, what in the long term are the negative effects of a strict accountability and an only too strict judgment? Accounting for oneself does not always have healing effects. Too much emphasis on responsibility can lead to apathy, pushing the buck, and a general cramping of relationships and behaviour.

In a word: responsibility does not have to be a mere clever-sounding term of self-congratulation or a 'Sunday concept', and its pluriformity does not have to be a source of cynicism and scepticism, provided that one takes account of the variety of meanings, criteria, and conceptions. As we have seen, that pluriformity finds expression at various levels. In the first place, the word is used in different but mutually connected senses. Whether a given sense is applicable to (the concrete behaviour of) a person is consequently dependent on various criteria. In most cases, there is no unanimity concerning the meaning of those criteria. It is dependent both on the role of the person concerned and the situation in which he finds himself, and on the political and moral views of the person who makes the judgment. The way in which an idea such as 'responsibility' is interpreted shows what kind of person the speaker is.

Two forms, passive and active responsibility, will here be applied to those new social actors, complex organisations. Is their effect the same in the case of corporate actors as in that of natural persons? When we consider the control of complex organisations, it is in the first place a matter of passive responsibility. After the event, natural persons or corporate bodies are held to account before various forums for the conduct of the organisation. These issues are the topic of part II. In order to be able after the event to determine whether someone or some organisation can be held liable, however, one must have some idea of what in the given situation would have constituted responsible behaviour. In this way, active notions of responsibility can play an independent role in the control of individual behaviour within organisations. Moreover, passive responsibility can only be established after the event and its preventive effect relates only to future cases. In the case of active responsibility, the most important moment of control comes before the potential deviance. Prevention is better than cure when misbehaviour can have very serious social consequences, as is sometimes the case with complex organisations. In the third part of this study, the emphasis will therefore lie on the important role played by various bureaucratic virtues (and vices) in the control of complex organisations.

PART II

PASSIVE RESPONSIBILITY

4

Accountability: the problem of many hands

The practical difficulties in the operation of organization seldom lie in the excessive desire of individuals to assume responsibility for the organization action of themselves or others, but rather lie in the reluctance to take responsibility for their own actions in organization.

(Barnard 1938:170–171)

The paradox of shared responsibility

The conduct of complex organisations has major consequences both for society and for individual citizens, for good as well as for bad. Although in the last analysis they are the product of human action, many of those consequences, such as environmental disasters, sometimes appear to us as natural disasters. This raises the question whether the Enlightenment ideal of a rationally organised society is feasible in this respect. Must we accept 'corporate risks' as inevitable by-products – as the price to pay for the great prosperity made possible by the existence of complex organisations? Or can the notions of responsibility currently to be found in the fields of ethics, politics, and the law that were addressed in the previous chapter also play a role in the control of complex organisations? In considering that question, we must first direct our attention to responsibility in the sense of accountability.

In the prevention of unwanted or risky behaviour on the part of natural persons, processes of calling to account play a very important role. From childhood onward, our conduct is influenced by the fact that we can be called to account for our actions. Whenever we contravene social, moral, or legal rules, we can expect parents, schoolteachers, friends, customers, colleagues, bosses, journalists, inspectors, or judges to demand an explanation and an accounting for what we have done. Accounting for oneself is one of the ways in which we ensure that the brittle public sphere remains in being.

But who shall be held responsible for the conduct of complex organisations? The way to this important form of responsibility leads irrevocably along the avenue of *the problem of many hands*. Dennis Thompson, who first

45

put a name to this problem, described it as follows: 'Because many different officials contribute in many ways to decisions and policies of government, it is difficult even in principle to identify who is morally responsible for political outcomes' (1980: 905). For outsiders who want to hold functionaries to account regarding the policy or conduct of a complex organisation, it is particularly difficult, and often impossible, to find any one person who can be said independently and by his or her own hands to have formed and carried out the policy: 'They often cannot even discover anyone whose contribution to the collective outcome seems significant enough to warrant credit or blame for it' (Thompson 1987: 40). Thompson restricted his analysis to public organisations and moral accountability, but it is equally applicable to complex organisations of a private character and to political and legal accountability. A similar fragmentation of accountability can be found in companies and other complex organisations in the private sphere (Ladd 1970: 514; Stone 1975: 45; Antunes 1994).

It would therefore seem that in complex organisations we are confronted with a paradox of shared responsibility. As the responsibility for any given instance of conduct is scattered across more people, the discrete responsibility of every individual diminishes proportionately: 'The bigger the organization, the fewer the individuals that can be held responsible, it would seem' (van Gunsteren 1974: 3).

When we look more closely at this problem of many hands, it appears to have several dimensions. It is above all a *practical problem*. For outsiders, it is often particularly difficult to unravel who, and in what way, has contributed to the conduct of a complex organisation and who, and to what degree, can be made to account for its actions. In the first instance, it is therefore above all a question of identification and proof. This element of the problem of many hands was evident, for example, in the course of the parliamentary inquiry in the Netherlands into the downfall of the Rijn-Schelde-Verolme ship-building concern. This débâcle, which led to the loss of many hundreds of millions of pounds for the government, was the result of a number of decisions by a number of actors, not just natural individuals but also complex organisations – the Chinese boxes of chapter 2 – over a large number of years. It turned out to be virtually impossible after the event to identify one or more organisations, let alone individuals within them, as specifically responsible. Everyone – the participating concerns and the management of the various divisions, the board of directors and the trade unions, the General Directorate for Industry and a succession of Ministers of Economic Affairs, the cabinet and parliament – bore a certain degree of responsibility for the débâcle, but it eventually transpired that no one could be held entirely responsible.

At least three closely related reasons make it very difficult to identify the 'responsible' functionaries or actors and to prove their involvement.

Complex organisations are surrounded by paper walls. From the outside, it is rarely possible at a glance to determine and to prove who was formally and actually in a position to take or withhold a dubious decision. Unlike in the case of the conduct of an individual, the conduct of an organisation rarely bears a personal stamp.

Policies pass through many hands before they are actually put into effect. Decrees and decisions are often made in committees and cross a number of desks before they (often at different stages and at different levels) are implemented. This means that in most cases there are more individuals or groups who satisfy all criteria; or – and this makes things even more difficult – that the various criteria for accountability are spread across various individuals or groups.

Individual continuity is often lacking. That fact sometimes makes it very difficult to reduce the conduct of the organisation to the discrete actions of individuals. New members of committees, of administrative bodies, and of departments conform to the traditions, rules, and existing practices (or what they think are the traditions, rules, and existing practices) and sometimes contribute ideas and rules of their own; however, they often leave before those ideas and rules can be put into practice, or before it becomes obvious that they did not work very well. Thus, the conduct of an organisation often is the result of the interplay between fatherless traditions and orphaned decisions.

In the second place, the problem of many hands also has a *normative dimension*. It raises the question whether the responsibility of the collectivity, the organisation, can be reduced to the individual responsibilities of discrete functionaries not just in practical but also in moral regard. Could it not be that only the collectivity, and not the individual members, has contravened a norm by virtue of its blameworthy conduct? It is possible to conceive of situations in which the sum, at least at first glance, seems more liable to be held to account than each of the parts:

Each partial action is in itself morally correct or neutral, but the sum total of the actions is not. At the individual level there is no violation of the norm, but at the collective level there is such a violation. An example of this is provided by the the implementation of the Dutch Social Security Act. This law has a provision that allows social workers in certain individual cases, as a result of particular circumstances, to give people additional benefits.[1] This clause was specifically intended to give extra support to large, 'needy'

---

[1] I owe this example to Romke van der Veen.

families. Research shows, however, that in practice the provision is applied
above all to assertive single people and not to the 'genuine' cases for which
the provision was originally intended. Although most individual cases can
be defended within the widely constructed framework of the provision, the
overall outcome can hardly be so defended.

Each partial action is morally neutral or at most doubtful and is not in itself
enough to bring about the offending outcome, but the sum of all the
partial actions does lead to a very undesirable result. In this way, small or
even negligible individual immoralities can lead to large collective
immoralities. Parfit provides an extreme, but nevertheless illuminating,
example of this situation in his hypothetical case of the 'Harmless
Torturers' (1984: 80–81). In it, a prisoner is attached to an ingenious
instrument of torture. Each time that the button on the apparatus is
pressed, the victim's pain increases to such a small extent that the increase
is imperceptible to him. There are, however, more than 1,000 officials who
all press the button once; their joint action results in severe torture. At the
individual level, there is hardly any causal link, but at the collective level,
there is such a link.

Each partial action was dubious and obviously contributed to the offending
outcome, but it could nevertheless be extenuated. The collectivity is in the
wrong, but every member has an excuse. One often comes across such
cases in war situations, as for example in the case of the mass murder committed by US soldiers in My Lai during the Vietnam War (French 1972;
Kelman and Hamilton 1989). Lieutenant Calley, the commander of the
platoon of soldiers that in 1968 killed at least 107 civilians in the village of
My Lai, defended himself by referring to the extreme tension under which
he and his men had to operate and to the fact that during the preceding
'briefing' he had been told that the village was a Vietcong base. That the
information was incorrect could only be established after the event.
Furthermore, he had been expressly instructed to destroy the village; it was
a so-called 'search-and-destroy mission' which, as such, fitted within the
anti-guerrilla campaign mapped out by the military staff. Refusal to obey
such a command, in those circumstances, would moreover have been
interpreted by Calley's superiors as insubordination. The superiors, for
their part, denied that such an explicit order had been issued; Calley had
wrongly interpreted their words. Moreover they could hardly know about
and prevent an incident that took place at such a great distance from their
headquarters. Eventually, of all those involved, only Calley was convicted.
His sentencing – initially to imprisonment for life – met with enormous
resistance in the United States among broad layers of the population; many
found it unjust that Calley should be found guilty for doing what was
expected of him.[2] In 1975, Calley, after four years' detention (served partly

---

[2] See the findings of the extensive research by Kelman and Hamilton (1989: 167–235).

under house arrest), received an official pardon. Blame at the collective level thus often appears in such cases to be difficult to translate into blame at the individual level.

In each of these problematic cases, the collectivity – the Municipal Social Service, the prison, the US army – meets the criteria for moral accountability, but it is doubtful whether the same can be said of individual members of those bodies. Everyone seems to be either not at all or to only a very limited extent at fault, while it is obvious that the organisation as a whole is indubitably at fault. At this point, I will not yet start to examine the question of whether and in which cases the problem of many hands is a 'genuine' moral problem. It is doubtful whether in each such case individual justifications really are tenable. In chapter 8, where the individual model of accountability is treated, I shall analyse at greater length the tenability of a number of current individual justifications and excuses.

In the third place, the problem of many hands is also a *problem of control*. Who is called upon to prevent the recurrence in the future of such undesired conduct on the part of the complex organisation? Who is expected to draw the necessary lessons from the process of calling to account? This subproblem can also be specified in greater detail.

> A meaningful calling to account is rendered extremely difficult and sometimes even impossible by the above variations on the problem of many hands. This frustrates the need for compensation and retribution on the part of the victims ('the guilty still run around freely'). More important still, such outcomes signify that what began as a conscious and rational human act can be transformed by the structure and the dynamics of complex organisations into a sort of 'act of God' with its own dynamic, which seems to be independent of any specific individual human action ('there are no guilty ones').
>
> The fact that no one can be meaningfully called to account after the event also means, however, that no one need feel responsible beforehand. Just as processes of calling to account can throw their shadows ahead, so the problem of many hands frustrates attempts at preventing undesired conduct on the part of complex organisations.

The problem of many hands is therefore also, and above all, a problem of control. It can form an important obstacle in the way of attempts on the part of society, or of general managers, to prevent misconduct by complex organisations.

In the following chapters, I shall therefore look at issues of responsibility from three different angles. In the first place, I will consider the *controlling perspective*. To what extent do the various models of accountability and the various conceptions of responsible conduct offer solace in the external control of complex organisations? Of great importance is also the question whether they can help to prevent the corporate risks. But I shall also pay attention to the *normative perspective*. To what extent are these models and conceptions satisfactory from a moral, political, or legal-philosophical point of view? Perhaps there are constructions of accountability that are efficient from the point of view of control but which for moral reasons we would probably not accept – some forms of collective accountability, for example. In the light of the practical sides of the problem of many hands I shall, finally, give some attention to the *practical consequences* of these empirical and normative considerations. How can one, in the light of the answers to the previous two questions, give shape in practice to the constructions of accountability and the conceptions of responsible conduct? Each chapter will close with a brief discussion of the possible adjustments and applications of the form of responsibility that has been discussed in it.

Passive responsibility: four models

Whom can one hold responsible after the event for the conduct of complex organisations? Two possibilities suggest themselves in the first instance. One could begin by holding the organisation itself to account. Complex organisations, whether companies, departments, or institutions, are treated in modern society as autonomous actors. They are in almost all cases corporate bodies that can be independently addressed in law. The parallel with natural individuals is therefore obvious: 'corporate risks' can be curbed by considering complex organisations as a type of natural individual and addressing them accordingly. This 'corporate' model of accountability is discussed first, in chapter 5.

Alongside the corporate body one could address the natural individuals that give the organisation shape. Individuals are not just the hands and feet but the head and heart of organisations. Without the decisions and activities of natural individuals, the complex organisation would be no more than an entry in the registers of the Chamber of Commerce or a paragraph in the State Directory. Alongside 'corporative' accountability, there is therefore also the possibility of *personal* responsibilities for the conduct of complex organisations.

This personal accountability, in its turn, knows various forms. One could, in conformity with the hierarchical structure of complex organisations, turn to the individuals at the top of the organisation, the CEO, the members of the board of directors, the minister, or the undersecretary, and hold them exclusively and wholly liable for its conduct. That is the *hierarchical* model, which is discussed in chapter 6. One could, alternatively, draw an even more

Figure 4.1

radical conclusion from the problem of many hands: 'many hands' means equally many responsibilities. Complex organisations act by virtue of the collective conduct of natural individuals; so every member of the organisation, simply by virtue of his or her membership of that collectivity, is in equal measure liable to be held responsible for the conduct of the organisation. That, in crude outline, is the *collective* model, which is discussed in chapter 7. Finally, one could make distinctions and hold to account individual members of the organisation only if, and in so far as, they have contributed by their actions to the conduct of the organisation. That is the *individual* model of accountability, which is discussed in chapter 8. The resulting scheme is shown in figure 4.1.

Dennis Thompson (1980; 1987) selected the individual, personal model of accountability as his solution to the problem of many hands: 'I [...] argue that the two most common ways of ascribing responsibility to officials – the hierarchical and the collective models – do not adequately respond to this problem, and that personal responsibility suitably interpreted, can be imputed to these officials more often than these models suggest' (1980: 905; cf. 915). It cannot be denied that the hierarchical and collective models, both from the normative point of view and from the perspective of control, have important shortcomings. In the relevant chapters I shall go into this question in greater detail. That does not mean to say, however, that a one-sided emphasis on the individual model is not without its shortcomings either. The solution to the problem of many hands, it would appear, lies not in a unilateral choice for one or the other of these various models. On the contrary: 'Cultural pluralism is the solution to the problem of responsibility' (Wildavsky 1986: 23). It depends on the structure, the environment, and the culture of an organisation, along which lines responsibility inside the organisation is regulated. In practice, responsibility after the event flows from the type of organisation and not the other way round. Often a combined approach, whereby various models are held in readiness alongside one another, will therefore produce the best result. In many cases it is better to employ corporate and personal forms of accountability alongside one another. This possibility (represented by 'both' in figure 4.1) shall, for the sake of furthering the argument, be discussed not separately but together with the corporate model.

From chapter 8 onward, the emphasis will nevertheless lie on the individual model. Quite apart from the points of departure of this study, there is another reason for so doing. Of the four models that I have distinguished, the individual model is recommended by many authors (Arendt 1964; Levinson 1973; Van Gunsteren 1974; Thompson 1980; 1987; Fisse and Braithwaite 1993), and above all for normative reasons. With the exception of Fisse and Braithwaite, these authors do not go beyond the stage of recommendation. Most analyses fail to answer the question as to how that individual responsibility can take shape in the practice of complex organisations, with their large size and hierarchical structure. In which cases, under which conditions, and in which forms can such an individual model actually help prevent 'corporate risks'? Much of part III is given over to answering such questions.

First, however, I will consider the possibilities of the other forms of passive responsibility.

5

Corporate accountability: the organisation as a person

... no soul to be damned, and no body to be kicked.[1]

Passive responsibility of complex organisations

A dominant metaphor in the literature about complex organisations is the notion of 'personality'. The complex organisation is often presented as a person, albeit a person of a somewhat special character. This metaphor has its origin largely in law, which has solved the problems that arose as a result of the appearance of organisations in social intercourse by treating them as 'corporate bodies'. One can, however, also find the metaphor in other disciplines. In the organisation studies, it is not unusual to portray complex organisations as model-individuals, as practically perfect rational beings that in their actions are led exclusively by utilistic calculations. We also speak of 'agents', a term that is used above all in the more philosophical literature (Donaldson 1982: 19). And as we have already seen, James Coleman (1974, 1982) added a similar image to the social-science language-game. Complex organisations are not just rational, robot-like servants that quietly hover in the corners of society until their assistance is required. They also act on their own account. Complex organisations are 'corporate actors', a new type of social actor alongside the traditional, human actors.

This personification of complex organisations would seem to be the solution to the problem of many hands. Outsiders, whether public agencies or

---

[1] The full quotation, which can be found in almost any book on the subject, is as follows: 'Did you ever expect a corporation to have a conscience, when it has no soul to be damned, and no body to be kicked?' This passage is ascribed by most authors to Edward, First Baron Thurlow (1731–1806), Lord Chancellor of England, who, according to one story, added in a whisper: 'and, by God, it ought to have both' (Coffee 1981: 386, n1).

individual citizens, can in this way circumnavigate the troublesome issues of identification and verification. In the event of organisational deviance they can turn directly to the organisation and hold it to account for the collective outcome, without having to worry too much about which official has met what criteria for accountability. From a *practical* point of view, this 'corporate' model, in which the organisation itself, as actor, is addressed, is therefore a promising device for curbing 'corporate risks'. And what of the other two angles of approach?

To start with, this manner of tackling the problem raises questions of a dogmatic nature in the areas of legal and moral philosophy. To what extent can non-natural actors be bearers of legal or moral responsibilities? Originally, law and morality recognised only individual responsibility for actions undertaken in an organised context (*societas delinquere non potest*). The question whether artificial entities can be bearers of *legal* rights and duties was decided long ago by the development of the idea of a charter of incorporation. In many countries, it is now generally accepted that a corporation can act illegally and, as such, be called to account for such actions both in civil and in criminal law. This goes not only for private but often also for public corporate bodies.[2]

Among philosophers, on the other hand, there is still no consensus as to whether organisations, with or without charters of incorporation, can also be seen as *moral* persons. Roughly, one can distinguish three positions in those debates. At one end of the spectrum are people such as John Ladd, who maintain that moral categories are not applicable to complex organisations:

> Thus, for logical reasons it is improper to expect organizational conduct to conform to the ordinary principles of morality. We cannot, and must not expect formal organizations, or their representatives acting in official capacities, to be honest, courageous, considerate, sympathetic, or to have any kind of moral integrity. Such concepts are not in the vocabulary, so to speak, of the organizational language-game. (We do not find them in the vocabulary of chess either!) Actions that are wrong by ordinary moral standards are not so for organizations; indeed they may often be required. [. . .] Therefore, if one expects social decisions to conform to the principles of morality, he is simply committing a logical mistake, perhaps even what Ryle calls a category mistake. In a sense as we shall see, organizations are like machines, and it would be a category mistake to expect a machine to comply with the principles of morality.
>
> (1970: 500)

---

[2] For Anglo-American law, see Wells (1993: 94–122), and for the Netherlands, see Torringa (1984: 153–8).

But Ladd's argument is not in all respects convincing.[3] One important objection is that he bases it on a model of complex organisations that is a combination of the Weberian ideal-type of the rational bureaucracy and Simon's description of formal organisations. Those models are not, however, value-free and universal. The observations that Ladd presented as logical facts are largely an echo of the political values that underlie the organisational model with which he works.[4] Other forms and models of complex organisations do not necessarily lead to identical conclusions. Ladd seems to fall victim to a variant (not in itself uninteresting) of the naturalistic fallacy. From the empirical observation that inside many organisations 'secrecy, espionage and deception do not make organizational action wrong; rather they are right, proper and, indeed, *rational*, if they serve the objectives of the organization' (1970: 500), he concludes that such characteristics must always hold in the case of organisations, and that it is therefore impossible to condemn such a state of affairs on moral grounds. That is a strange, normative jump. Why is practice elevated to the level of an infrangible norm? This general conclusion is, moreover, hard to reconcile with the likewise empirical observation that in everyday language a number of moral categories are without too much difficulty also applied to organisations. Are all the people who do so apply them wrong? In this connection, it is above all important to note that 'responsibility' seems at least to have acquired a place for itself in the 'organisational language-game'. For example, it is, not in itself nonsense to say that Union Carbide is not only legally liable but also morally responsible for the outcome of the poison disaster in Bhopal in India. And the 'corporate social responsibility' debate, which has waged with great fervour for a number of years both inside and outside organisations, has in the meantime led even to the formation of discrete subdisciplines in business and public administration, such as business ethics and the philosophy

[3] See also Donaldson (1982: 23–32) and DeGeorge (1983: 57–62).
[4] A good example of this is Ladd's denial of the possibility of active moral responsibility on the part of individual functionaries. 'By the same token, an official or agent of a formal organization is simply violating the basic rules of organizational activity if he allows his moral scruples rather than the objectives of the organization to determine his decision. In particular, he is violating the rule of administrative impartiality, that is, the rule that administrative officials "faithfully execute policies of which they personally disapprove"' (1970: 500). What Ladd here presents as a 'logical mistake' is at most a conflict of values. This 'basic rule of organizational activity' comes, by way of an article by Reinhard Bendix (1952), almost word for word from *Politik als Beruf* ('Politics as a vocation'), one of the most normative components of Weber's work (1919/1977: 28). Unless one accepts Weber's political theory, Ladd's logic more or less collapses (see further chapter 9).

of public administration.[5] Ladd's argument is therefore not sufficient to allow us to dismiss the moral responsibility of complex organisations on dogmatic grounds – although his arguments are, on the other hand, important if the effectiveness of such an approach is under discussion.

Diametrically opposed to Ladd is Peter French (1979; 1984), according to whom complex organisations can be viewed as 'full-fledged members of the moral community' (1984: 32). French's point of departure is to a certain extent comparable with mine in this chapter: how can the idea of 'responsibility' be applied to collectivities and organisations? However, he goes beyond the problem of 'corporate responsibility' and argues the case for 'moral personhood', a complete equation of complex organisations and natural persons in the moral arena. That approach not only goes much further than is necessary (here) but is also difficult to sustain. The crucial criterion for 'moral personhood', according to French, is the presence of intentions. However, that criterion is both too narrow and too wide. It is too wide because it remains relatively unqualified and includes even animals among moral persons (we could, for example, argue that a dog that barks and jumps up onto its owner in an attempt to persuade him to go for a walk is acting intentionally). On the other hand, it is also too essentialistic; other elements such as guilt feelings, a conscience, or self-reflection, will often also play a role in determining whether we view a person as moral. (Even with responsibility, intention is the essential element in restricted cases only, as we saw in the previous chapter). Finally, one can ask whether it is possible

[5] The term 'corporate social responsibility', or 'social responsibility of corporate actors', refers to the debates that have been going on ever since the 1950s, especially in the USA, about the social responsibilities of firms. Their particular focus is on the social responsibilities of firms. The main question is whether firms should, alongside making profits, also aim at social and ethical goals (see for an overview Stone 1976: 71–118; Donaldson 1982: 36–108; Beauchamp and Bowie 1983: 68–106). Although these debates are conducted very sharply and with a great deal of philosophical ingenuity, I shall look at them only in passing. This is in the first place because they are concerned not with questions of accountability, the passive form of responsibility, but with views about the virtuous conduct of commercial concerns, the active responsibilities of concerns. In the second place, people have on the whole contented themselves with justifying starting points and expressing intentions, without elaborating on the concepts and proposals and investigating whether or not they are feasible. Often the proponents of a broad view of the social responsibilities of concerns restrict themselves to calling for a change in mentality; that way out, however noble, is doomed to failure unless one at the same time takes account of the continuing threat of 'free-rider' behaviour, which can only be exorcised by collective measures, and unless one takes account of the fundamental importance of economic motives for concerns and of the comparatively feeble power of moral restrictions for complex organisations and individual managers (cf. Jackall 1988).

to attribute independent intentions, i.e., intentions other than those of the relevant functionaries, to an organisation, and where those intentions should be localised or whence they should be derived.[6] Even aside from French's specific argumentation, it is not easy to accept that complex organisations can in all respects be considered as moral entities. As we shall see, they scarcely (for example) have a conscience in the usual – i.e., human – sense of the word. The idea of a 'moral person' is used in a wholly aberrant and restricted sense if one declares it applicable to complex organisations.[7]

Luckily, we do not have to go the way of 'moral personhood'. For our question, it is enough that the idea of 'moral responsibility' can be meaningfully applied to complex organisations. To be able to talk of the moral responsibility of an organisation, it is not necessary to establish first that at least one individual member of that organisation meets all the criteria for responsibility, while on the other hand it is also unnecessary to furnish complete proof – a proof that would in any case be impossible to assemble – of the moral agency of organisations. One can make do with a personification that is merely temporary or of restricted extent, and that comes into being only for the purposes of the argument and not under the pretension of discovering a new moral entity. Or, as Dworkin (1986: 171) puts it: 'The personification is deep: it consists in taking the corporation seriously as a moral agent. But it is still a personification not a discovery, because we recognize that the community has no independent metaphysical existence, that it is itself a creature of the practices of thought and language in which it figures.'

In the rest of this chapter, I shall therefore seek a third position: some moral categories are not easily applicable to complex organisations, but other moral categories, including 'responsibility', are indeed applicable.[8] This summary argument implies, at least on the basis of our current legal and moral practices, that there is insufficient reason to dismiss in advance the most obvious, 'corporate' responsibility. Alongside its pragmatic evidential advantages, which I have already mentioned, this model also has practical advantages of a (legal-) philosophical sort. For the time being, we need not worry about the question of whether, and, to what extent, individual functionaries can be held to account for the conduct of the collectivity, the organisation. The organisation is itself addressed on account of its conduct. What remains is the control question.

[6] Cf. Donaldson (1982: 21–3).   [7] Cf. Van Haersolte (1971: 121, 179–81).
[8] Others who share a similar standpoint include Donaldson (1982), DeGeorge (1983), Flores and Johnson (1983: 539), Thompson (1987: 76), Fisse and Braithwaite (1993: 22–31), and Wells (1993: 90).

The complex organisation as a rational person

The metaphor of the organisation as a person is not confined to law and business ethics. Particularly since the work of Max Weber and Chester Barnard, it is common in social science literature to sketch a contrast between complex organisations with their essentially rational and utilitarian character and natural persons who, in greater or lesser measure, are led by emotions and irrational motives (Barnard 1938: 186; Perrow 1979: 87; Braithwaite and Geiss 1982: 300). Thus complex organisations are often presented as greater-than-life persons, model-individuals who finally behave according to the rules of 'rational choice' and try to maximise their gains on the basis of cost-benefit analyses. This approach provides excellent perspectives to solve the third element of the problem of many hands, namely, the control issue.

From the point of view of neo-classical law and economics, the direct addressing of the organisation is strongly recommended.[9] The organisation itself is best able to regulate its own conduct and to discipline its functionaries. If the sanction, together with the risk of being caught,[10] is big enough, complex organisations will of themselves seek to maximise their profits along other paths. Rational actors will refrain from socially undesired conduct when the expected costs are greater than the profit.

> '[D]eterrence is doubtful with traditional crime, but may well be strong with corporate crime', among other reasons because 'corporate crimes are almost never crimes of passion; they are not spontaneous or emotional, but calculated risks taken by rational actors. As such, they should be more amenable to control by policies based on the utilitarian assumptions of the deterrence doctrine.'
>
> (Braithwaite and Geiss 1982: 301–2, cited in Braithwaite and Makkai 1991: 10)

Prevention is therefore above all a question of careful econometric calculation. Moreover, if '"corporate actors" have become examples of rationally acting citizens, for whom the advantages and disadvantages of legislative measures can be calculated on a profit and loss basis' (Schuyt 1985: 120), we can apply most of the instruments and mechanisms that are used to control the conduct of natural persons to complex organisations. What is more: the

---

[9] For an overview of the literature, see Fisse and Braithwaite (1993: ch. 3).
[10] A sanction that simply confiscates the profits of irregular conduct is insufficient; the chance of being caught must also be taken into consideration. If an infringement of the cartel law yields a concern a sum of one million, and the chance of being caught is 25 per cent, the fine should be 4 million (Posner 1972: 360).

rational, bureaucratic structure of complex organisations, with its division of labour and specialisation, a more or less strict hierarchy, clearly delineated competencies and procedures, and a form of business management based on documents and archives would appear to be much easier to control than simpler organisational forms or than emotional and fickle natural persons.

To what extent are these utilitarian assumptions of law and economics viable in the practice of control? Relatively little research has been done on the effectiveness of control specifically directed at complex organisations. In so far as we do have relevant data, they often relate to sub-areas, such as environmental policy and economic criminal law; it is difficult to generalise on the basis of such findings. Moreover, there are big differences between organisations, not just in legal form and character (private, public, or semi-public), but also in structure and extent. What we do have, however, is a stream of disconnected cases, disasters, and fiascoes in which it did appear to be less easy to prevent undesired conduct on the part of complex organisations, with all the resulting risks and consequences. In the Netherlands, the names of infamous affairs such as those connected with RSV, Uniser, Slavenburg's Bank, Walrus and ABP, come to mind. In the United Kingdom we have, for example, the Westland affair, the sinking of the *Herald of Free Enterprise*, the BCCI scandal, and the collapse of Barings Bank. In the United States, the list is a lot longer: Love Canal, Watergate, Three Mile Island, the New York City Police Department, Ford Pinto, the Santa Barbara oil-spill, the Bendectine cover-up, Challenger, and the Savings and Loans scandal are just a few of the best known of a whole series of cases of 'corporate and governmental deviance' (Ermann and Lundman 1982a; Ermann and Lundman 1982b). On the basis of these cases and with the help of other scholars[11] who by examining a number of cases have tried to create a body of theory on this point, it is possible to distinguish a few general problems that are specific to the control of complex organisations. In every one of these cases, it seems that instruments and mechanisms that are reasonably effective in the control of natural persons become problematic when applied to complex organisations. The rosy and comfortable image that underlies the 'corporate' model is in need of a certain measure of adjustment. Complex organisations sometimes appear not to behave at all as if they were almost perfectly rational, natural persons.

---

[11] In particular, Stone (1974), Coleman (1974; 1982), Thompson (1980; 1987), Coffee (1981), Ermann and Lundman (1982a), Vaughan (1983), French (1984), Fisse and French (1985), Vogel (1986), and Braithwaite and Makkai (1991).

The problem of prevention

The nature of 'corporate risks' makes prevention of organisational deviance of the utmost importance. The consequences of environmental disasters, airplane accidents, birth defects, or financial misconduct are often difficult or even impossible to remedy. However, prevention is very problematic in the case of complex organisations. Control through passive responsibility is, by its very nature, a procedure that nearly always takes place after the event. Most of the mechanisms and instruments, in particular actions claiming damages, fines, judicial orders, shutdown, or forced reorganisation, can be used by outsiders only when things have already gone wrong, and, what is much more important, when the damage is of a sufficient extent to come to people's notice. These instruments are above all indirect; the most important thing that they can do is to put an end to existing practices and prevent their future continuation.

This *ex post* character would not be too much of a problem in the case of natural persons; a series of *ex post* sanctions applied to transgressions that cause a relatively small amount of damage can have a strongly preventive effect in the long term and on a large scale. In the case of complex organisations, however, one can not always afford to gamble on long-term prevention; the 'economies of scale' also make themselves felt in the amount of damage. Moreover, after the event, unlike in the case of natural persons, sanctions sometimes no longer make sense from the point of view of compensation and repayment. The company is bankrupt and the corporation has disbanded, or the sanction means unemployment for the mainly innocent employees.

What happened in the case of the Dutch waste-disposal company Krimpen BV (EMK) is a good illustration of the failing of government control for those very reasons. This company was established in 1970 at Krimpen and was formally engaged in the storage and processing of waste oils. Almost immediately afterward, complaints about the smell began to reach the municipality, and it soon transpired that in a number of respects EMK was failing to abide by the terms of its licence under the Nuisance Act. Years of jousting between the municipality and EMK followed; the municipality wrote numerous letters, once even closed the business down for a while, and eventually strengthened the terms of the licence. EMK frequently appealed, above all to win time, and made many promises that it rarely kept, but effectively won even more delays. Eventually, on 13 June 1980, the municipality won an appeal by EMK against its final shutdown. Meanwhile, EMK announced that it would transfer its activities to the mother company, Uniser Holding BV, in Moerdijk; in the summer of 1980, it began to dismantle its equipment. This did not last long, however, for

Uniser rapidly went bankrupt. What happened next is described as follows in the report of the committee that undertook an official investigation:

> The government was confronted with a collection of often dilapidated and worn-out tanks that contained large quantities of unknown chemical materials and mixtures of chemicals, while in a number of cellars on the site a large amount of chemical waste was to be found. At the dock there was a ship (Delta XIII) carrying some 170 tons of chemical waste. The soil on the site is polluted to a depth of some dozens of meters by chemical waste, tar products, and waste oil. While during the period in which the company was actually working the main preoccupation of the authorities was to prevent or restrict transgressions of the Nuisance Law, after 1980 the emphasis was on ascertaining the true extent of the environmental scandal with which the government, and thus the community, was confronted. A start was made in 1983 with cleaning up the contents of the tanks, the cellars, and the ship. Right up to this very time, various public bodies have been attempting by way of lawsuits to present the bill for this activity (and for the measures that remain to be taken to deal with the consequences of the pollution of the soil) to those whom they deem responsible for the mess.
>
> (Report of the Hellinga Commission 1983: 42)

But has the threat of sanctions no *ex ante* effect? Will not the risk of a fine, of a shutdown, or of a reparations order be calculated into the decision-making of the organisation? That is much less self-evident than the legal and economic arguments would seem to suppose. Research by Braithwaite and Makkai (1991) on corporate deterrence in the case of relatively simple corporate actors such as nursing homes shows, for example, that the certainty or severity of sanctions does not influence the degree to which one is prepared is follow the rules. Only the perceived certainty of detection played a partial role in the decision-making. Financial and economic sanctions seem for example to be much more sensitive and unstable than one might at first sight think.

> An often heard complaint is that in practice the size of the fines or of the damages is much too small in proportion to the total budget of a company or to the profits that flow from the wrongful conduct.[12] Financial sanctions are often no more than one small item of expenditure among many. A fine of just £10,000 on account of illegal discharges of chemical waste is completely out of proportion to the extra costs of the legal processing of the waste.
>
> A big increase in fines and damages is, however, just one part of the solution. If fines and damages are to be meaningful, they must not exceed the capac-

---

[12] See, for example, Stone (1975: 36–40, 50); Coffee (1981: 388); Vaughan (1983: 84); Gosewehr and Maas (1984: 75); Fisse (1985: 138–9).

ity of an organisation, but they must on the other hand take into account the risk of being caught. The smaller the risk of being caught becomes, the greater must be the fine, if it is to have a deterrent effect from the point of view of a rational actor – one that, unlike natural persons, would not be constrained by moral considerations. If the fine is too big, however, it will scarcely deter, since after a given threshold, the organisation can no longer pay it anyway.[13] This is known as the 'deterrence trap'.

The risk of being caught is, however, notoriously low in the case of complex organisations, as we shall soon see, since illegitimate conduct in that context is often easy to camouflage, particularly difficult to prove, and, both for insiders and for outsiders, hard to recognize as such.

In practice, the finetuning of monetary sanctions turns out to be extremely difficult. One must not simply make a realistic estimate of the potential costs and benefits for the organisations involved but also include in the calculation the various probabilities (risk of being caught, risk of conviction, the advantages of deviant conduct, the disadvantages of conviction, and so on). All this makes a strictly legal-economic approach a difficult and rarely fruitful exercise (cf. Fisse and Braithwaite 1993: 88–93).

The limited rationality of complex organisations

Beside fines and damages, several other sanctions are also possible. However, here too there is no certainty that the threat of sanctions will, after a utilistic, rational consideration of costs and benefits, automatically lead to conduct in conformity with the norm. The rationality of complex organisations has its own imperfections. In a number of cases there is no guarantee that extraneous norms, laid down in regulations and maintained by sanctions or rewards, will actually penetrate through to a complex organisation. There are several more or less structural reasons for this:

Complex organisations are often split up into divisions, sections, and subsections. The goals of each of these 'sub-units' are often only tangentially connected to the goals – profit maximalisation, an increase in sales volume, provision of services – of the organisation as a whole. Satisfying legal obligations (or preventing sanctions that would eat into profits) is sometimes an objective only of the top levels of an organisation or of the staff departments involved with legal affairs. At the level of the lower depart-

---

[13] Cf. the example provided by Coffee (1981: 390):

for example, if a corporation having $10 million of wealth were faced with an opportunity to gain $1 million through some criminal act or omission, such conduct could not logically be deterred by monetary penalties directed at the corporation if the risk of apprehension were below 10%. That is, if the likelihood of apprehension were 8%, the necessary penalty would have to be $12,5 million (i.e., $1 million times 12.5, the reciprocal of 8%). Yet such a fine exceeds the corporation's ability to pay.

ments, people are often not spontaneously inclined to take measures, since each extra obligation costs time and money and makes it more difficult to strive toward one's own goals (Stone 1975: 43; Braithwaite 1985: 48–49).

The top levels of the organisation or the department for legal affairs that is charged with ensuring that legal obligations are complied with is sometimes either not sufficiently informed, or informed too late, to be able to take necessary measures. The extent and complexity of many organisations often make it very difficult for internal controllers to keep an eye on the course of affairs (cf. Finney and Lesieur 1982: 278).[14] Legal experts must moreover often contend with other departments that have no need of troublesome snoopers: 'the lawyer is regarded by his co-workers as the "no" man' (Stone 1975: 43; see also Finney and Lesieur 1982: 280–1).

For individual functionaries, there is often no reason to pay special attention to observing legal obligations. Transgressions that lead to sanctions on the organisation usually have no consequences for the (financial) position of managers and officials. The corporation is accountable; in extreme cases, any debts that might have ensued are liquidated in the course of a bankruptcy action. Only in exceptional cases are individual persons held directly to account. The transgression of legal regulations need have no consequences even for their internal careers, as long as they achieve successes in the short term (Jackall 1988: 90–100). According to Ermann and Lundman,

> Evaluation of performance [...] generally is limited to short-term goals, as with production or profit figures [...] Rarely are executives sanctioned for long-term failures. It generally is recognized that calculation of the long-term costs of a particular decision is extremely difficult [...] [T]here frequently is such a gap between decision and consequence that corporations find it difficult, if not impossible, to sanction executives responsible for long-term blunders. Executives who make these decisions are promoted, retired, or dead, which makes them invulnerable to corporate penalties.
>
> (Ermann and Lundman 1982a: 70–2)

Legal sanctions are rather seen as business risks that cast no particular blot on the reputation of those who incur them (Stone 1975: 40).

Complex organisations are moreover 'less inclined than an individual person to display consistency over the long run. Members of committees, for example, change and often the changing ideas of even existing members combine in surprising ways' (Donaldson 1982: 115). This discontinuity diminishes the rational character of decisions and undermines the learning capacity of the organisation.

---

[14] A more extensive analysis of the possible complications in the internal provision of information in complex organisations follows in chapter 6.

In the case of most natural persons, there is a large measure of continuity and uniformity across the years. Extreme cases apart, we are dealing with people who are hewn from a single piece, with a memory and a capacity to learn from earlier mistakes. Extraneous stimuli therefore often lead to changes in behaviour. That is the anthropomorphic viewpoint that partly underlies the utilitarian model of law and economics. In the case of complex organisations, this notion of the 'self', of a central, rational core that not only functions as the memory of the entity but even gives it identity and direction, is, however, even more problematic than in the case of natural persons.[15] To the outside world, organisations may exhibit considerable continuity and uniformity, but internally, this is often far from the case. A large turnover of the experienced members of an organisation can lead to the loss of many habits, rational routines, and valuable rules-of-thumb learned by trial and error. Office politics and individual interests can acquire precedence over averting extraneous sanctions that affect the organisation as a whole. The theoretically interesting image of the complex organisation as a rational actor should therefore be strongly relativised in practice.

The lack of external insight

In a modern, liberal society the conduct of citizens is controlled by means and sanctions that work on them from the outside and leave the physical constitution of those citizens intact (with the exception of certain serious mental disturbances, which are subject to certain forms of intrusive treatment). We no longer hack off the hands of thieves. Complex organisations are also preponderantly controlled by extraneous means; think, for example, of subsidies and tax concessions, systems of regulation and licensing, and fines and other punishments levied on property. Control from the outside, however, can be effective only when one knows or suspects that undesirable behaviour is taking place or is likely to take place. External control therefore stands or falls with access to good information. But such information is often lacking.

In the first place, a lack of information and expertise often plays a role in the very process of drawing up the rules. Especially when production processes are complex and technological developments rapid, it can be extraordinarily difficult for a relative outsider such as the government to acquire proper insight into the possible harmful consequences of production processes, into the causes of any eventual damage, and into the effects of its own regulations (Stone 1975: 96; Ackerman and Hassler 1981: 2; Crandall and Lave 1981: 14–17).

[15] For the problematic character of personal identity, see Parfit (1984).

In the second place, outsiders, for example nearby residents, fraud officers, council officials, and controlling bodies, often lack insight into the factual course of affairs. When controlling by means of extraneous mechanisms, one must be in a position to know from the outside what happens in and around a complex organisation. However, most organisations will not go out of their way to provide outsiders with information about what is going on within their own bodies. Moreover, the complicated and technical character of the transactions that take place inside and between organisations often makes it particularly difficult to detect irregularities. That goes, by the way, not only for outsiders but often also for many members of the organisation itself:

> When insiders do witness illegal behaviour, they may see only a portion of a very involved transaction, not recognizing it as illegal because they did not see the entire transaction. The complexity of corporate law and regulations, in many cases interpretable only by experts, further complicates identification, for potential witnesses may see misconduct, but lack the expertise to interpret it as a violation.
>
> (Vaughan 1983: 90)

The supervision of the observance of regulations becomes even more difficult, and in many cases impossible, in the case of wilful fraud (Ermann and Lundman 1982a: 87–92; Finney and Lesieur 1982: 280).

Finally, the lack of insight, information, and expertise can continue to have an effect even after irregular business management, harmful side-effects, or fraud has been successfully tracked down. It can sometimes be extraordinarily difficult and costly to gather together the evidence on the basis of which a complex organisation can be held to account or criminally prosecuted for any damage that it has caused. '[E]conomic crimes are far more complex than most other federal offenses. The events in issue usually have occurred at a far more remote time and over a far more extensive period. The "proof" consists not merely of relatively few items of real evidence but a large roomful of obscure documents' (Wilson and Matz 1977: 651, cited in Fisse and Braithwaite 1993: 37).

The administrative and technical complexity of many organisations and of their deviant conduct therefore requires extremely specialised research facilities and techniques. Diane Vaughan concluded on the basis of her investigation of the Ohio Revco affair, a case of large-scale fraud with medicines paid for by health insurance, in which various private and public organisations were involved, that the specialist character of many complex organisations, and of their transgressions, makes necessary the development of new and innovative methods of detection in each new case. Controlling bodies can therefore only to a very limited extent learn from their mistakes and develop a certain degree of routine. Techniques and products follow each other at high speed; much of the research experience that one acquires in a given case is of restricted use in future cases. Moreover, the organisation that is to be controlled is sometimes itself the only body that has the necessary expertise. Often controlling bodies exist as a result of this specialisation in a sort of symbiosis with the organisations that they are supposed to regulate. They speak the same language, and knowledge and personnel are mutually exchanged. This can endanger the independence of the supervisory organs (Vaughan 1983: 92–104; Finney and Lesieur 1982: 281).

Outsiders who wish to control the conduct of complex organisations therefore have to do with actors whose structure is hard to penetrate, whose conduct is difficult to monitor, let alone to interpret, and whose means, knowledge, and skills are often much greater than their own. Controlling on the basis of a 'corporate' model of accountability is often controlling from the outside, and therefore places most of the helmsmen not on the ship but on the quay.[16]

The impotence of morality

Many citizens will refrain from deviant behaviour even when there is no specific sanction on transgression of the norm or when the risk of being caught is small (Spicer and Lundstedt 1976). The behaviour of natural persons is not regulated only by the threat of sanctions. In the course of our upbringing and other socialisation processes, we internalise many of the norms that are maintained by means of sanctions. The government takes advantage of this and tries, for example by way of information and publicity campaigns or propaganda, to control the conduct of citizens. An important part of the prevention of undesirable conduct on the part of natural persons happens in this way; obviously resort to the same tactic is advisable in controlling complex organisations, where prevention is of such major importance.

Controlling organisations by way of moral conventions or calls for a change in mentality is, however, highly problematic. Organisations have no conscience in the usual (Christian, Kantian, or Freudian) sense of the word. Among the first things that one comes across in the literature on this point is the utterance, which has since degenerated to the status of a platitude, attributed to Baron Thurlow, Lord Chancellor of England: 'Did you ever

---

[16] See further Galbraith (1968: 91). In chapter 6, it will be argued that many of the helmsmen on the ship, those who control the organisation itself, are in many cases themselves to a great extent outsiders.

expect a corporation to have a conscience, when it has no soul to be damned, and no body to be kicked?' Natural persons are in general in a position, in conformity with the Kantian categorical imperative or the Christian golden rule, to put themselves in the position of those who will bear the consequences of their actions. Complex organisations, on the other hand, as should by now be obvious, have hardly anything in common with natural persons; they are actors with an entirely different structure. 'Do not unto others as you would not have them do unto you' is for them a sensible injunction at most in the course of their dealings with other organisations. In their dealings with natural persons, they are not quickly led by feelings of sympathy; for them, individuals are mutually interchangeable (Coleman 1974: 94–8; S. Nagel 1975: 349). The motives that drive their own objectives (maximisation of turnover, profit, market share, competencies, or tasks) will be their primary consideration.[17]

That does not, however, mean to say that corporate bodies have absolutely no 'conscience' and therefore know only one source of inhibition, namely external incentives. In some respects a company's board of directors can fulfil such a function of conscience – even though they too will presumably judge the conduct of the organisation above all in the light of its statutes and aims. Many companies and institutions furthermore have a specific corporate culture or some sort of unwritten ethos in which norms concerning permitted ways of acting ('we don't do that sort of thing here') are passed on. Research in the United States into industrial accidents in the mining industry shows that in mines that were exploited by traditional mining companies, on average many more accidents occurred than in others exploited by the steel industry. Differences in business culture were advanced as the principal cause of this disparity: 'traditionally the steel companies' top corporate executives, being used to a relatively good safety record in their steel mills, have never been willing to tolerate poor safety performance in their mines' (Stone 1975: 238).

Whether norms of the sort associated with a business or administrative culture could play a role within organisations comparable to the role of internalised moral norms in the case of individuals, is a question that, even

---

[17] Coleman (1976: 97; 1982: 22) points out that the inability to put oneself in the position of another is also true of a natural person in relation to a complex organisation. Fraud and destruction committed against corporate bodies lead to fewer feelings of guilt, a fact that is apparently confirmed by the correlation between the rise of complex organisations since the Second World War and the rise of above all petty criminality during the last few decades. A rather extensive empirical proof of this thesis, as well a description of the way in which similar processes of rationalisation happen, can be found in the volume edited by Smigel and Ross (1970) and especially those parts of it by Smigel, Horning, and Cressey.

in the light of much more detailed research, is difficult to answer. The chances that they might be able to play such a role must, however, be assessed as low. John Ladd is presumably right – on empirical, not dogmatic, grounds – when he claims that 'morality as such must be excluded as irrelevant in organisational decision making – by the rules of the language-game' (1970: 498–9). Norms associated with organisational cultures cannot be likened to the moral considerations, feelings of pity and of guilt, and the ability to put oneself in the place of another that inhibit most natural persons from harming others. That is also the reason why the 'social responsibility debate' has yielded relatively little fruit despite all the years that it has been going on. Complex organisations are 'by nature' disinclined to take the interests of individuals into account on their own initiative in the course of their deliberations: 'In a sense [. . .] organizations are like machines, and it would be a category mistake to expect a machine to comply with the principles of morality' (Ladd 1970: 500).

But, one might object, without the help of natural persons, organisations are not much more than lifeless abbreviations; and those natural persons are certainly not insensitive to moral inhibitions. However, even that is apparently far from always being the case. There are strong indications that the moral barriers that in private life help prevent injury to others, function much less stringently when natural persons are operating within the framework of a complex organisation. Natural persons seem to be much less sensitive to those internalised moral norms when, and in so far as, they function within an institutional and hierarchical framework (Milgram 1974; Robbins 1980: 237–9; Finney and Lesieur 1982: 275–6; Meeus and Raaijmakers 1984; Jackall 1988; Kelman and Hamilton 1989; Vaughan 1996). In chapter 8, when I look at the question of individual accountability, I shall look more extensively at the possible explanations for this phenomenon.

The limits of the law

Needless to say, it is not just complex organisations and their functionaries that find it difficult to behave in accordance with the categorical imperative. Even natural persons, as common citizens, fail all too often in the observance of their Kantian duties. An extensive legal system, with commandments and prohibitions, is called into being to make provision for such moments of weakness. Legal instruments that are reasonably effective in the case of natural persons cannot, however, be applied without further ado to complex organisations. The structural differences between complex organisations and natural persons also make themselves felt in the applicability and effectiveness of legal means.

Sometimes there is no longer any complex organisation to be held to account before a forum; in the case of a liquidation or bankruptcy, one ends up – sometimes literally as well as figuratively – talking to a brick-wall. In cases where companies are split up, taken over by another company, or sold to the management, it is an open question as to how far the accountability is transferred along with the assets.

If the organisation continues to exist in its original shape, the question arises, whom should the forum address? An organisation cannot appear as such before a forum; for that purpose, individuals are always necessary to function as spokespeople, or fall-guys. Even a model of strict corporate accountability demands a specification of individual representatives.

The consequences that flow from punishing corporate bodies are far from always borne by those who have profited most from the transgressions, and often affect individuals – for example, small shareholders, creditors, employees, and consumers – who were not at all in a position to prevent the misconduct. 'Punishing the organization spreads the blame beyond the responsibility and is to that extent without moral justification' (Thompson 1987: 76). Hefty fines can, for example, mean unemployment for the employees, most of whom are innocent. This is the problem of the 'external costs' of penalties: 'the costs of deterrence tend to spill over onto parties who cannot be characterized as culpable' (Coffee 1981: 401).

Some important sanctions, like detention during Her Majesty's pleasure, prison sentences, or programmes of compulsory education, are not applicable to complex organisations as such. Other sanctions have little effect, work the wrong way, or come into conflict with other important goals of government policy. The imposition of a fine on a public institution is not excluded in Dutch criminal law (Torringa 1984: 153–8), but will in many cases be meaningless because it will lead to a budgetary deficit that can be cleared only by public means or, if one is not prepared to do so, by a decrease in the provision of services. Even the closing of a department, service, or company will in most cases amount to throwing the baby out with the bathwater; and this *ultimum remedium* is seldom applied in practice (Vogel 1986: 16).

Decisions about the actual application of sanctions are quite often influenced, or, if one wishes, biased, by extraneous considerations. Governments may hold back from acting against bad working conditions or environmental pollution because of a high level of unemployment or because they have an interest in the processing of waste. A related issue, which I addressed earlier, is the complaint that those fines that are imposed are often out of proportion when compared with the big financial advantages that sometimes accrue to a complex organisation when it contravenes regulations (Stone 1975: 36–40, 50; Coffee 1981: 388; Finney and Lesieur 1982: 282; Vaughan 1983: 84; Gosewehr and Maas 1984: 75; Fisse 1985: 138–9).

Legal means cannot be applied at will. The law recognises important intrinsic values that resist a strictly instrumental application (Schuyt 1985: 118–119). Extensive procedural prescriptions and material principles protect the objects of control against an arbitrary or improper use of administrative competencies. Corporate actors can appeal to this protection too. Complex organisations are moreover, as we have already seen, mostly 'repeat-players'; they have extensive legal expertise at their disposal and make optimal use of all the means of protection and of the opportunities for winning time that the formal procedures offer – as, for example, in the case of the EMK/Uniser affair.

The organisation as a semi-autonomous social field

The difference between the rational and calculating complex organisation and the fickle and emotional natural person is only one of degree and certainly not a sharp contrast. Complex organisations can, just like natural persons, be bothered by rather serious 'subversions of rationality' (Elster 1983a). Perfectly rational behaviour on the part of benefit-maximising managers or departments can, in dynamic combination, lead to irrational conduct on the part of the organisation as a whole.[18]

This does not, however, imply that complex organisations have much in common with natural persons in other respects. The conceptualisation in terms of 'personality' and 'actorship' should not make us forget that both types of actors have an absolutely different structure and react quite differently to the same instrument of control. Van Haersolte warns quite rightly against the mistake of 'makranthropie', the temptation to consider a corporation as a more than life-size natural person (Van Haersolte 1971: 121). The image of the organisation as a person should be used with circumspection. Like any metaphor, it is, in the words of De Jouvenel, 'une servante dangereuse: ne paraissant d'abord que pour modestement illustrer le raisonnement, elle s'en rend bientôt maîtresse et le governe' (De Jouvenel 1945: 86).[19]

The problem with the 'corporate', legal-economic model of accountability is that the complex organisation is too often treated as a 'black box', as an entity hewn from a single piece. The personification of the complex organisation disguises the fact that, unlike most natural persons, a complex organisation does not have a central core that reacts to incentives, draws

---

[18] For a similar argument already, see Arrow (1974).

[19] Jurists, who have been working with the complex organisation as a social actor for a much longer time than have management scientists and philosophers, have long known the temptations and restrictions of fiction in general and of that of corporate personality in particular. See for example Fuller (1967).

lessons from the past, and regulates its conduct. We have seen that external norms by no means always penetrate through into the organisation; and even if they do so, they tend to lose out to other objectives. Sanctions that are directed against the organisation often come too late, hit the innocent as well as the guilty, or cannot be made effective because of the actual or threatened liquidation of the organisation.

Legal anthropology offers us another image of complex organisations that is more adequate to our purposes than the metaphor dominant in the field of legal economics and in the organisation sciences. The complex organisation is more readily to be understood as a semi-autonomous social field, than as a rational person. That is a field that 'can generate rules and customs and symbols internally, but [. . .] is also vulnerable to rules and decisions and other forces emanating from the larger world by which it is surrounded' (Falk Moore 1978: 55). The complex organisation is not a person, but a social field that in its turn consists of a number of mutually connected individuals and groups of individuals, who themselves can again have a semi-autonomous character. Within complex organisations, the external norms, laid down in regulations, must take a stand against (and sometimes loose out to) already existing norms, obligations, and arrangements that are sturdily rooted in the daily practice of the organisation (cf. Falk Moore 1978: 29, 58, 80).

This raises the following question: to what extent are organisations in a position to learn from processes of calling to account? 'Learning' is after all an anthropomorphic idea that, to a certain extent, assumes a memory and a unity of personality. Who ensures that a lesson is stored in the working memory of the organisation? Who or what is the bearer of the lessons from the past?[20] How are these lessons made available in decision-making? The semi-autonomous character of organisations will often severely weaken the learning effects of corporate models of accountability. Due to the lack of independently responsible individuals a source of change often is also lacking. Who is responsible for the structure of the complex organisation? Who is expected to, and can, give the initial impetus to a modification of that structure, of changing the internal norms and practices in the sense desired by the outside forum? Because of their semi-autonomous character, many complex organisations have great difficulty with learning processes that are concerned with the conduct of the whole organisation or that are expected to result in uniform, centrally controlled behaviour. This means, once more, that we should not expect complete salvation from the legal-economic, corporate model of accountability.

---

[20] For an answer to these questions for small, not too complex organisations, see Cook and Yanow (1993).

Corporate accountability and personal accountability

To what extent is the 'corporate' model capable of repair? On the basis of what I have said so far, it should be obvious that prevention, control *ex ante*, is of major importance in the light of the scale and the irrevocable character of the damage that can flow from 'corporate risks'. Various proposals have been made to strengthen the preventive power of strictly 'corporate' accountability. Coffee has come up with the ingenious proposal that fines and damages should no longer be paid in money but in company shares, to be administered by a damages fund (1981: 413–24). This procedure would, according to Coffee, achieve a greater degree of deterrence, since it makes a much higher actual sanction possible than would a fine, which is expressed in the form of liquid means. Such a procedure would also make the results of the sanction felt more strongly in circles that can exercise an influence on decision-making: big shareholders who see their ownership drop in value; and the management (in so far as it is not already itself a shareholder), which sees its chance of acquiring capital by way of the issue of extra shares diminish and the chance of a hostile take-over increase.

There is still the problem, however, that an external instrument of this sort can have relatively little preventive power, because of a lack of adequate and timely information and because of the possibility of counter-strategies on the part of the organisation. It can therefore also be necessary to penetrate the organisation and enforce change in its internal structure. Particularly in those sectors with large corporate risks, one might contemplate the possibility of allowing outsiders, by way of a judge's order or in the shape of regulatory bodies and inspections, to intervene in the decision-making structure of such organisations. There are other ways, too, of achieving the same aim:

> By nominating general or special public directors to companies in sectors at high risk; these directors would function as a sort of public 'conscience' inside the organisation and serve as points of application (Stone 1975: 152–183).
> By making it obligatory to follow special procedures in the case of high-risk production processes and by requiring special qualifications on the part of controlling personnel (Stone 1985: 18).
> By making it possible for judicial bodies to oblige organisations to undertake internal reforms, for example as part of a conditional penalty (Fisse 1985: 144–7).

Each of these proposals deserves to be considered separately, on its merits. However, in the light of our previous observation, that the image of the organisation as a semi-autonomous field is more adequate than that of the organisation as a rational person, no miracles can be expected of these direct, interventions in the internal functioning of organisations. The rise and fall of the RSV-Concern teaches us, moreover, that the government has only restricted possibilities to control internal decision-making in organisations and that the dangers of such an intervention are particularly great. When outsiders, for example judges or public directors become involved with administration and management, they enter a mine-field from which few emerge unscathed. Direct interventions can cause more harm than good and should therefore be reserved for particularly risky sectors and easily monitored processes.

Regardless of the possibilities of these proposals, the conclusion must be that this first solution of the problem of many hands, namely an *exclusive* reliance on 'corporate' accountability, must be rejected if only on pragmatic grounds. It would simply increase the problem. This means, moreover, that this model falls short in moral respect, as well. It is hardly acceptable that serious human suffering, which has its ultimate cause in conscious (collective) human acts, is permitted and allowed to repeat itself. In so far as the corporate model results in a situation in which no one can be held to account for the conduct of complex organisations, it must be said to fail in moral respect. For that reason, most western democracies, at least in legal and political regard, and for the most part in moral regard too, recognise one or the other form of responsibility of natural persons *alongside* the responsibility of complex organisations.

Most of the remedies that one comes across in the recent literature[21] and in practice aims (partly) at controlling the natural persons, i.e., the managers, employees, and officials who give form to the complex organisation. The organisation as such, as well as certain individuals within it, can simultaneously be held responsible for the actions of the organisation. The responsibility of the one need not exclude or cancel the responsibility of the other (or others), for the actions of complex organisations are always bound up with the actions of individuals.

But far more difficult than determining this duality, is the question which individuals can be held responsible for the actions of the organisation, and to what extent they can be held responsible. In that sense, the problem of many hands lies in all its complexity ahead of us again.

[21] See, for example, Coffee (1981: 455–9), Stone (1975; 1985: 19–34), Coleman (1982: 102–11); Braithwaite (1985); Fisse and Braithwaite (1993: chapter 5).

6

Hierarchical accountability: one for all

There is no danger in power, if only it be not irresponsible. If it be divided, dealt out in shares to many, it is obscured; and if obscured it is made irresponsible. But if it be centred in the heads of the service and in heads of branches of the service, it is easily watched and brought to book.

(W. Wilson 1925 [1887]: 148–9)

The pyramid of accountability

Underlying hierarchical schemes of accountability is a pyramidical image of complex organisations. Processes of calling to account start at the top. The external responsibility for the conduct of the complex organisation lies, in the first instance, wholly with that person who *de jure* or *de facto* leads the organisation. The process of accounting can in principle address the conduct of each part of the organisation and all of its policy, implemented or intended. Only one person or a small group of persons can be held accountable: the minister, director, chief executive officer or commander in chief. Usually, the rank and file do not appear before that external forum but hide behind the broad shoulders of the leaders, who, at least in dealings with the outside world, assume complete responsibility. The lower echelons can in their turn, however, be addressed by the leaders of the organisation regarding questions of internal accountability. In the case of hierarchical schemes, processes of calling to account thus happen along the strict lines of the 'chain of command' and the middle managers are in turn both the persons addressed and the internal forum.

I have deliberately spoken of hierarchical schemes of responsibility. The scheme as here described is after all no more than an ideal type – in the Weberian sense of the word – that has many variants. The roots of this model lie, certainly in so far as the public sector is concerned, largely in the nineteenth-century state administration of a number of German principalities. After the Prussian defeat by Napoleon, in a number of German states the previous system of collegial administration (*Kollegialsystem*) was in whole or in part replaced by a more hierarchical model, the unitary or office system (*Einheits- oder Bureausystem*), in which at every level in the organ-

74

ism of administration only one official was charged with making arrangements and implementing them (von Malchus 1823: 7). The classical formulation of this German hierarchical model of responsibility is naturally to be found in the work of Max Weber.[1] As a result of the work of writers such as Bluntschli, this German model has also had an important influence on American administrative practices. Woodrow Wilson (1887) and Frank Goodnow (1900) in particular propagated – partly by appealing to the example of continental administrative practice – a strict separation between a responsible political leadership and an executive administrative staff as a remedy for the partisan, venal, and inefficient spoils system.

Not only Wilson and Goodnow but also Weber and many modern thinkers in the field of public administration thus frequently combine a hierarchical scheme of accountability with a strict separation of 'politics' and 'administration'. For most authors, this has important consequences for their conception of administrative responsibility-as-virtue. In the third part of this study I shall therefore look more extensively at the tradition regarding this point and at the link with hierarchical schemes. Here I shall make do with the comment that the separation of politics and administration and a hierarchical conception of responsibility as *virtue* do not necessarily and automatically follow from a hierarchical scheme of *accountability*. For example, it is quite possible to apply hierarchical schemes of accountability even within a strongly politicised organisation.

Managers are outsiders

Hierarchical schemes are by virtue of their simplicity and clarity highly attractive for the control of complex organisations. Whenever one wants to hold someone to account for the conduct of a complex organisation, one knows immediately what steps to take. There is an easily identifiable small group of responsible persons. It is not necessary to penetrate the organisation and to unravel the intricate complex of powers and contributory actions.

The preventive power of the attribution of accountability along hierarchical lines stands or falls with the possibilities open to the leadership of controlling its own organisation. However, one of the fixed themes of the literature on modern organisation is precisely the restricted capability of the higher levels to control the organisation.[2] Various structural factors contrib-

---

[1] Although for that purpose a reconstruction is necessary using various elements that are scattered across a whole range of writings (especially Weber, 1980: 551; 1977: 27–8; 1958: 322–3).

[2] See, for example, Ames (1965), Tullock (1965), Downs (1967), Wilensky (1967), Kaufman (1973a), and Van Gunsteren (1976).

ute to a restricted capacity to control on the part of the leading bodies of complex organisations. Christopher Hood makes a distinction between 'detecting', the procuring of the relevant information, and 'effecting', the influencing of behaviour, which is of great help in analysing these factors (Hood 1983).

Detecting. The chances that leading levels will be in a position to control the conduct of the organisation depend on a healthy level of information about cooperation at the lower levels and about the effects of the activities of those lower levels on the outside world.[3] That provision of information is often highly defective:

> In complex or turbulent situations, the information is often inadequate or already out-of-date by the time that it percolates up to highest levels (cf. van Gunsteren 1976: 14–15).
>
> Lines of communication in complex organisations are often defective if only because of their very length. At each intermediary link, some information is lost or, in some way or another, distorted. Calculations show that as the number of links grows, so this 'mechanical noise' becomes ever stronger and a large part of the message may as a result become deformed (Ames 1965: 238; Tullock 1965: 137).
>
> Sometimes the problem is not so much a shortage as an abundance of information; this information remains unstructured, as a result of which the 'detecting' of problems is hardly possible (Ermann and Lundman 1982a: 50). Often only the technical experts, and not the generalists at leading levels, are in a position to interpret the information and to discover or predict failings.
>
> Finally, sometimes there can be deliberate noise or even the deliberate withholding of incriminating information. This can be prompted by the need of functionaries and departments to defend their own territory and interests. Few people gladly act as harbingers of bad news, certainly when it concerns their own performance, and the tendency is often to trivialise the problems in the interests of one's own budget or career (Wilensky 1967: 43; Jackall 1988: 20–1). In the case of fraud or conscious transgressions, those involved can have every reason, and often also the chance, to withhold the pertinent information from the leading bodies in the organisa-

---

[3] Some of the authors mentioned in note 2, Kaufman in particular, are principally interested in the question of whether or not the leading levels have at their disposal sufficient information about the behaviour and the level of obedience of the lower levels. However, extremely important for the control of complex organisations from the top is the question of whether or not the leading bodies can acquire sufficient insight into the effects of their policy and of the obedience (or disobedience) of their subordinates on the outside world. Can the leading levels discover timely that assignments, even when they are correctly implemented, do not have the effect that they are meant to have?

tion (Stone 1975: 45, 58–62; Ermann and Lundman 1982a: 89; Vaughan 1983: 73–6).

Effecting. Let us assume that the higher levels have managed to find out that transgression of important norms has taken place deliberately or through a concurrence of circumstances. That does not, however, necessarily mean that they will succeed in taking timely and adequate countermeasures.

> In the first place, one is often thwarted by a lack of time. The information is, for example, so fragmentary and unstructured that for that very reason there is insufficient time to think about the effectiveness of the countermeasures. But even when enough good structured information is available, there might not be an opportunity to react adequately, because there are (for example) no available rules that make it possible within a brief period of time to select the correct solution.
>
> Consequently, the problem of imperfect lines of communication makes itself felt here as well. Hierarchical noise also occurs in communication from the top to the bottom, although it is probably somewhat weaker than in the reverse direction (Andeweg 1985: 215).
>
> Moreover, the message must not only be clear to the subordinate but must also be adequate – something that is far from always easy to establish from the top (and from a distance) in complex and turbulent situations. One must also bear in mind that an assignment in a concrete situation can be wrongly understood, always requires interpretation and adaptation, and can often be put into effect in various plausible ways (Tullock 1965: 183, 184).
>
> Finally, even when the message has come through clearly, has been properly understood, and meets our criteria of adequacy, that does not yet mean that it will lead to actual changes in behaviour. Attempts to control the conduct of the lower echelons often elicit counter-strategies and evasive tactics on the part of those whom one is trying to control.

Anthony Downs once formulated a number of 'laws' that briefly and concisely reflect the sort of problems of control that can crop up in bureaucratic organisations:

> The first is the Law of Imperfect Control: No one can fully control the behaviour of a large organization. The second is the Law of Diminishing Control: The larger any organization becomes, the weaker is the control over its actions exercised by those at the top. The third is the Law of Decreasing Coordination. The larger any organization becomes, the poorer is the coordination among its actions. These rather obvious laws are inescapable results of the fact that each person's mental capacity is limited.
>
> (Downs 1967: 143)

Finally, he also came up with: 'The Law of Counter Control [...]: The greater the effort made by a sovereign or top-level official to control the behaviour of subordinate officials, the greater the efforts made by those subordinates to evade or counteract such control' (1967: 147). These and other mechanisms mean that 'effecting' does not naturally and automatically result from 'detecting'.[4] The idea of Chinese boxes that we spoke of in chapter 2 is definitely applicable here. Many complex organisations consist of collections of semi-autonomous fields within which central guidelines and rules must make a stand against the informal norms and practices of the lower levels.

This means that policy formulation and decision-making in many complex organisations is far from always conducted along official, hierarchical lines. Formal powers and actual decisions often diverge. In complex circumstances and turbulent situations, quick decisions are often necessary on the part of those directly involved. Lower levels therefore often have at their disposal the necessary discretionary powers. The actual use of these powers can only to a very restricted degree be managed and controlled from the top. Alongside, between, and behind the official lines of authority and jurisdictions exist informal networks and power relations in which knowledge, social contacts, and negotiating techniques are more important than formal powers.[5] Strictly hierarchical models of decision-making are in reality therefore only sporadically encountered. Many managers are outsiders in their own organisation.

Blameworthiness: the Achilles' heel of the hierarchical model

This relative inability of the leading bodies to control their own complex organisation has consequences for the normative evaluation of hierarchical schemes of accountability. In practice an apportioning of accountability along hierarchical lines often comes up against moral resistance. Stone (1975: 58–69) has shown, on the basis of research conducted in the United States, that the effectiveness of hierarchical responsibilities in (criminal) law is, as a result, often relatively small. This has various reasons, but the most important reason is the issue of blameworthiness. We saw in chapter 3 that

---

[4] These 'laws' are confirmed by various case-studies. See, for example, Punch on police organisations: 'To put my evidence in a nutshell, I would say that the police organization has a major schism between the work cultures of the upper and lower ranks – and this can be documented for London, New York and Amsterdam – and that attempts at imposing accountability and control from above have largely failed to penetrate the informal practices of street-level police work' (1981: 26).

[5] See also Allison and his 'Model III' (1971: 144–84), Perrow (1979: 42–4), and Kastelein (1985).

in the case of responsibility as accountability, the first three criteria – violation of the norm, causal link, blameworthiness – are necessary preconditions for accountability. It is above all the element of blameworthiness, and in some respects also the causal link, that in many cases cannot be sufficiently established to hold the leading bodies of complex organisations completely responsible in a moral, and also often in a legal, sense.

In the case of organisational deviance, many top functionaries seem to be able successfully to put forward the excuse that they did not know what was going on or that, in so far they knew, they had done everything in their power to prevent the misconduct; in short, they could hardly have done otherwise than they actually did.

This excuse is reinforced by the fact that in many organisations an almost natural screening of bad news takes place. The leading bodies are often automatically screened from incriminating or damaging information in order to protect them from legal or political problems. Sometimes, a boomerang effect even results from strict hierarchical accountability. On a number of terrains, the law imposes a penalty on knowledge of the course of events and puts a premium on ignorance. Precisely those people who might have been in a position to do something about the misconduct of the organisation can have an interest in knowing the least possible about what has actually happened.

Especially the top civil-servants and chief executive officers are often in a position to push the responsibility for the disfunctioning of their organisation onto others lower down in the hierarchy. These scapegoats are sacrificed – for example, by dismissal – while the leaders can remain at their posts and the organisation can pay penance without having to make any substantive changes (Jackall 1988: 85–91; Boeke 1992).

Hard-working entrepreneurs and respectable officials can reckon in lawsuits on a large measure of benevolence on the part of juries and judges (Nagel 1975: 349). In the United States it seems that 'in cases of "white-collar" crime, the prosecution finds itself trying to convict church-going, well-dressed, well-spoken, community leaders – men not apt to be judged harshly, except in the most extreme cases where responsibility and bad faith are unmistakable' (Stone 1975: 63). As a result, the penalties for white-collar crime are systematically far lower than for common crime. Within the category of white-collar crime even greater leniency is shown in the case of corporate offenders: 'Few members of corporate management ever go to prison, even if convicted, generally they are put on probation. . . . If executives do go to prison, it is almost always for a short period of time, usually only a few days' (Clinard and Yeager 1980: 286). In many cases, convictions have no further consequences for the position of the corporate executives within the company (Clinard and Yaeger 1980: 294–7).

The effects of penalties other than prison sentences are often doubtful.

'Probation, for the corporate offender, is generally viewed as a slap on the wrist, and monetary penalties, unless unusually severe, are usually meaningless to corporate executives' (Clinard and Yeager 1980: 286). The fines are often extraordinarily low in proportion to the salaries that top managers command. In some American states, moreover, companies can insure their top officials against any financial losses that might flow from their legal responsibilities; other companies pay for lawyers' fees and fines, or write them off as running costs.

Processes of calling to account that proceed only along hierarchical lines are for these reasons often experienced as highly unsatisfactory. That goes in the first place for the victims, to whom few possibilities of retribution, compensation, and remission are open. But even more importantly, the failures of hierarchical schemes also undermine the learning effects of such processes of calling to account – where no one can be called to heel, no one need in the future feel responsible.

That this problematic character of strictly hierarchical schemes of accountability is not restricted to the United States is evident from one of the most sensational business scandals of the last decades in the Netherlands: the large-scale fraud involving Slavenburg's Bank.

The hierarchical scheme in criminal law: the Slavenburg affair

In Dutch criminal law, the untenable nature of strictly formal schemes of hierarchical responsibility was apparent in an early stage and the necessary consequences were subsequently drawn. Instead of looking at the formal structure, one looks at the actual hierarchy within the corporation. Art. 51, of the Penal Code, for example, says: 'In the case of a culpable fact committed by a corporation, a criminal prosecution can be brought against that corporation and the penalties and measures available in law [. . .] can be applied [. . .] against those who gave the actual assignment that led to the offense, as well as against *those under whose actual direction the prohibited act was committed*' (emphasis added). Yet even this subtle modification of hierarchical accountability still leads in practice to big problems of an evidential nature in the case of culpable acts committed by big, complex organisations. This is illustrated by the Slavenburg affair, a *cause célèbre* in the sphere of company fraud.[6]

---

[6] The description of this case is based principally on the extensive overview-article by Brants (1988), on a case-study regarding the affair by Heleen den Haan, a student in the department of Political Sciences at the University of Leiden (1987), on the closing speech of the public prosecutor, De Doelder (1986), on the judgments mentioned in the text, and on numerous articles in *NRC Handelsblad* and *de Volkskrant*. I have also consulted Torringa (1984), 't Hart and De Vries-Leemans (1986), and Torringa (1988).

Slavenburg's Bank, founded by Thijs Slavenburg in 1925 as a small family firm, went through a period of spectacular growth in the 1960s and 1970s. Mindful of the founder's motto – 'the prettiest flowers grow along the edge of the abyss' – the bank was prepared to take huge risks in the management of its affairs. The name of the bank regularly cropped up in connection with various dubious transactions. At the time of the winding up of a bankrupt property company, in the course of 1982, a number of constructions came to light whereby an Amsterdam branch of the bank had 'laundered' various sums of money. The head of Slavenburg's Internal Accountants' Service was interrogated in that connection by the Public Prosecutor. It appeared that for years he had had big objections to these laundering operations and had several times complained in vain to his superior. He now took the opportunity to make a clean breast of the whole business and informed the Public Prosecutor of the existence of a system (started by him) of shadow-accounting and he handed over a number of incriminating dossiers.

On 18 February 1983, a judicial investigation team carried out a spectacular raid, attended by a great deal of publicity, on the bank's main office and three of its branch-offices. The preliminary legal investigation brought a number of culpable acts to light, principally in the sphere of tax fraud and forgery. Over a period of many years, offices of the bank had offered customers the chance to launder large amounts of black money by means of false name accounts, numbered accounts, safe-deposit credits, and the so-called 'envelope trick'.[7]

From the point of view of the system described in art. 51 of the Penal Code, it should have gone without saying that the corporation, Slavenburg's Bank Inc., would have been the first target of the criminal justice system – the corporate accountability considered in the previous chapter. After all, corporate bodies can commit culpable acts and thus be condemned on the basis of art. 51; moreover, in this affair no one doubted that the bank committed the offending act. But considerations of a political and monetary nature won out over considerations of criminal law – and that, too, is in conformity with the findings of the previous chapter. Slavenburg's Bank had just been taken over by Credit Lyonnais, in close cooperation with the Nederlandse Bank. To have prosecuted the bank and caused a possible bankruptcy would have had big financial consequences for the Nederlandse Bank and could have seriously shaken confidence in the Dutch banking system.

---

[7] The envelope-trick worked via Switzerland. If a customer wanted to launder some black money, an envelope that was either empty or filled with newspaper cuttings was sent out by the daughter-company Slavo-Schweiz A.G. in Zurich bearing the sum concerned and an account number of Slavo-Schweiz. The money received by the customer was subsequently booked as 'received by Slavo-Schweiz'; the envelope served to suggest that the money actually had been transferred from Switzerland. For the other methods, see Brants (1988: 35, note 11).

The Minister of Finance feared furthermore that it would wreak great damage in the monetary field, for example by causing a flight of capital and a possible drop in the value of the guilder, and therefore put heavy pressure on the Department of Justice to drop any idea of prosecution.[8]

A decision was taken to ignore the corporation as such and to prosecute only natural persons, the so-called 'central figures'. At first, more than twenty suspects were identified, including the whole of the board of directors. A number of cases against regional directors were eventually dismissed; according to the public prosecutor, the decision to do so was taken because the people concerned were lower-level personnel: 'In our view, they could not in the long run be blamed for the entire course of events. The lower one stood in the organization, the truer the adage that "he who pays the piper calls the tune". The actions of the employees were carried out not for personal gain but in the interests of and within the sphere of the corporation' (De Doelder 1986: 11). Also the case against the head of the Internal Accounting Service, the man who had given the initial impetus to the whole affair, was dismissed; the same happened with the cases against two members of the board of directors who had no direct tie to departments within which the culpable acts had been committed. A number of other regional office managers and managers in the main office were given the chance to pay their way out of a prosecution. They paid a settlement that varied from 5–10,000 guilders.

In the end, four people remained on the accused list, among them three members of the board of directors: Gonggrijp who was in charge of the bank's foreign offices; Piet Slavenburg., the former chairman and senior figure in the bank; Ruud Slavenburg, who was in charge of the domestic offices; and Veltena, the director of the finance company, one of Ruud Slavenburg's subordinates. They were each prosecuted because they had actually directed the committing of the forgeries at Slavenburg's Bank Inc. This led to a series of legal procedures that lasted for years. In the course of those procedures, the fact that forgery was practised by the bank regularly and on a big scale hardly entered the discussion; the battle was fought instead over the extent to which one could say that those accused had actually given direction to the bank's culpable behaviour.

Although by the end of the 1970s Slavenburg's Bank had grown into a powerful institution with almost 3,000 employees and more than 90 offices, the board of directors continued to behave as if the bank were still a small family firm:

[8] The Solicitor General said in his closing speech at the trial before the court in The Hague that he assumed that the Minister of Justice, in consultation with the Minister of Finance and the Nederlandse Bank, had personally vetoed the prosecution of the corporation (Brants 1988: 43).

There was no question of good administrative or control procedures. [. . .] Meetings were not always held at appointed times, and they often lacked agenda; points that were discussed and decisions that had to be implemented were often never again raised at meetings; for a long time, P. S. held the reins of power, but he withdrew more and more in order to prepare the merger with Credit Lyonnais. When the various black-money practices came to light, the problem was discussed, the regulations were considered, and various prohibitions were issued, but no one checked to see whether the situation had really changed. As long as no news penetrated through to higher levels about the persisting problems, it was assumed that everything had in the meantime been put in order. Directors of the various departments and branches went relatively untroubled about their business.

(Brants 1988: 50–1)

The question arose to what extent such mismanagement, such absence of supervision and leadership, could be understood as 'giving actual direction' as set out in art. 51. The Court of Justice in The Hague went the furthest. The Court assumed that culpable management happens when one of the accused '*knows or should and could have known* as a senior member of the corporation of the occurrence of one or more forbidden forms of behaviour' and had then not intervened although he or she might have been expected to intervene and had the possibility of intervening to that end (Court of Justice, The Hague, 21 May 1985; emphasis added). This went much too far for the Supreme Court, which annulled the judgment and formulated a much more restricted variant of it. One could speak of giving actual direction in the case of prohibited behaviour only when the accused '*was aware of that behaviour*'.[9] In a later judgment, the Supreme Court refined this criterion even further.

Giving direction is culpable only when one is personally aware of the fact that culpable behaviour is taking place, and when one is, moreover, empowered to do something about such behaviour and yet takes no measures to prevent its occurrence. The judgment does not say what and how much one must know, nor does it specify precisely which measures one should have taken. When we examine the further course of the case, it soon becomes obvious, however, that with such an interpretation of the concept, the Supreme Court has little chance of addressing executive officials about the conduct of the bank.

Gonggrijp, the head of the department of foreign credits – the department of the envelope-trick – was completely acquitted by the court in July 1987. It was assumed that as soon as he found out about the black-money operations, he on various occasions prohibited the practice, though only verbally. The court deemed this measure adequate because he was said to

[9] Supreme Court, November 19, 1985, *NJ* 1986, 125.

have received no signals that the practices had continued despite his verbal prohibitions. Ruud Slavenburg, the head of the department of inland credit – the department of the false named accounts and the safe-deposit credits – was acquitted on twenty-three counts and found guilty on only one; he was sentenced to two months' conditional imprisonment and a fine of 25,000 guilders and a year's probation. Veltena, his direct subordinate, was acquitted on four counts. The court deemed it proven that he had early on known of the extent of the black credit, and that he had omitted to tell his boss and had also neglected to draw up adequate guidelines for his subordinates. Eventually he was found guilty on twelve counts and sentenced to four months' conditional imprisonment and a fine of 35,000 guilders with one year's probation. Finally, Piet Slavenburg, the former chairman of the board of directors, the man who had more than anyone else put his stamp on the organisation[10] and was therefore seen by the public prosecutor as the principal accused, was acquitted both by the court and by the Supreme Court of all the charges against him. The Supreme Court found that it was sufficient that the board of directors had prohibited the black-money operations; as chairman he had the right to expect that others would make sure that these prohibitions were observed – as long, that is to say, as no news to the contrary reached him; and it could not be proved that any had: 'In the judgment of the court, [it is going] too far to attribute to the accused a deliberate intention to promote the irregularities under consideration merely because he was chairman of the Board of Directors of the bank *that just happened to be organised as it was*' (The Hague Court, December 2, 1987; emphasis added).

Finally, the whole affair finished with a hefty loss for the public prosecutor's office. Piet Slavenburg and Gonggrijp, each of whom had been supported by a team of lawyers, were awarded 450,000 and 326,000 guilders respectively by the court to meet their costs. Eventually, Ruud Slavenburg, who was found only partly guilty, was awarded more than 68,000 guilders to compensate those costs that involved the counts on which he was acquitted.

The outcome of the Slavenburg affair largely confirms experiences in the United States in similar cases.[11] For political and economic reasons the organisation itself is not brought to account, and it is therefore particularly difficult, partly for moral reasons and partly for reasons of a formal and evi-

---

[10] Piet Slavenburg was blamed above all for his incompetent personnel policy, as a result of which 'people with titles and expensive names' (Den Haan 1987) but few real skills or talents were fetched into the bank while on the other hand management and internal control were neglected. Piet Slavenburg had also introduced a bonus scheme for the directors of regional offices. This scheme was an incentive to boost turnover regardless of costs.

[11] See Stone (1975), Clinard and Yeager (1980), and Stuart Nagel (1975: 349).

dential nature, to address the central figures, the 'key individuals'. In the prosecutions, account is taken of the social position of the accused. If it does ever get as far as a conviction, the conviction seldom leads to a prison sentence. The size of the fines imposed and of the settlements reached is negligible compared with the income of the accused and bears no relationship to the amount at stake in the acts that originally led to the prosecution.[12] The management of Slavenburg's Bank was in a position, with the help of a team of legal specialists, to make optimal use of the procedural and substantive guarantees available to the accused in criminal proceedings.

The shortcomings of ministerial responsibility

Up to now, the emphasis in this chapter has been on the criminal accountability of corporate executives. One could object that in the political sphere, for example in the case of ministerial responsibility for the civil service, the element of blameworthiness is of less importance than in criminal law. For that reason a strictly hierarchical model of responsibility is more appropriate in the case of public organisations. In a liberal democracy, ministers and other political managers often have a sort of risk-accountability. They are, in principle, accountable for everything that goes wrong under their guidance, whether or not they were actually in a position to do anything about it. For politics is *par excellence* the terrain of the ethic of responsibility. As Weber put it: 'The honor of the political leader, of the leading statesman [...] lies precisely in an exclusive *personal* responsibility for what he does, a responsibility he can not and must not reject or transfer' (Gerth and Mills 1946: 95 (Weber 1919: 28)).

Life is often more complicated than doctrine – and Weber was more ready than most to admit that. Thompson notes in relation to political practice in the United States that political leaders mostly accept complete responsibility only *in retoricis*, without attaching any further consequences to the idea: 'Taking responsibility becomes a kind of political ritual that has no negative effect on a leader. Indeed, leaders can often turn this ritual to their advantage' (1987: 43). In the Netherlands and the United Kingdom, one sees that in determining the responsibility of members of the government, blameworthiness also does play a substantial role in practice as well as in rhetoric.

To what extent should a minister be held to account for the mistakes made by his or her department? There is little doubt in either country about

---

[12] An accountant who helped in the investigation of the Slavenburg affair reckoned that the money 'casually' found to have been concealed from the tax inspector amounted to more than 187,000,000 guilders (De Doelder 1986: 13b). Settlements of 5,000 or 10,000 guilders and even a fine of 35,000 guilders look rather thin by comparison.

the initial point of departure, that is to say, a hierarchical, pyramidical model of political responsibility. Officials, the lower echelons, cannot in principle be directly called to account by parliament for their conduct; all official actions are attributed to members of the government, the political apex of the departmental pyramid. Only the ministers are directly accountable to parliament.

This general rule must be specified more closely. At least three different phases must be distinguished in the process of parliamentary accounting: 1) an information phase; 2) a debate phase; and 3) a sanction phase (Elzinga 1989). In both countries, it is constitutionally so that each minister is in principle duty-bound to furnish parliament, on request, with all the information that it wants and requires. Members of the government are also expected to enter into debate with parliament when parliament demands that they account for themselves. The information and debate phase constitute together the explanatory accountability of government (Turpin 1994: 421, 428). In the Netherlands, the extent of this explanatory accountability on the part of the minister is determined by the statutory powers that a minister has: 'The question of whether partial or complete ministerial responsibility applies in the case of a given government action must, unless the law expressly stipulates such responsibility, be answered with regard to the powers that the minister has in relation to that government action' (Scheltema and Lubberdink 1980: 11). That point of departure has in the meantime been generally accepted. It means, for example, that ministerial responsibility applies in the case of everything that goes on within a department. After all, the minister is empowered fully to determine what happens inside his or her department. This is, however, different in the case of nondepartmental public bodies. The minister often has only a restricted say in these 'quangos', where the concept of ministerial responsibility therefore applies only as far as the powers of the minister extend.[13]

The next question, which crops up automatically in almost every case, is as follows: to what extent can the conduct of the officials serving under a minister also be attributed to that minister? Are ministers to be blamed for each and every mistake that is committed in their departments? At this point, we have reached the sanction phase. In this phase, it is therefore not just a question of mere passive responsibility, of whether or not the minister is formally required to appear before the forum of parliament in order to explain himself, but also of active responsibility, of whether or not the minister has behaved appropriately in a substantive sense. Directly linked to this is the question to what extent some sort of sanction is required. At this point, attention shifts from relatively formal, constitutional regulations to

---

[13] For the situation in the UK, see O'Toole and Chapman (1995) and Nolan (1995).

material, political criteria. Passive ministerial responsibility is still to some extent determined by looking up and interpreting laws, statutes, and regulations. Active ministerial responsibility is exclusively a matter of political judgment. In principle it reaches as far as a parliamentary majority wants it to reach. After all, parliament has the last say regarding the substantive conduct of the minister and whether or not the minister should be allowed to stay on.[14] In the debates about ministerial responsibility, both in the United Kingdom and the Netherlands, people tried to formulate criteria in this regard. In those attempts, just as in the case of accountability in civil or criminal law, blameworthiness is a central issue. Broadly speaking, one can distinguish two points of view.

The traditional view of ministerial responsibility holds that a minister in case of serious mistakes of civil servants should take the blame and resign: 'The minister must submit to the judgement of Parliament, and if the failure is a serious one, should resign from office without waiting for a vote of censure' (Turpin 1994: 428). We can call this the *broad* concept of ministerial responsibility. In the Netherlands, people have referred positively to the example of the West German Minister of Home Affairs Hans Maihofer. This minister had twice assured the Bundestag that a certain physicist was not being bugged by the German internal security service. When it became apparent that the physicist was indeed being bugged – and had been for more than a year – the minister resigned. It was obvious to everybody, however, that the minister himself was scarcely to blame; he had been lied to by his civil servants. Another example that has figured in this connection in both the United Kingdom and the Netherlands is the case of the British Minister of Foreign Affairs Lord Carrington, who resigned because his information service not had foreseen that Argentina would invade the Falkland Islands. In both cases, a member of government was officially held politically responsible for crude errors committed by his officials, although he personally was hardly to blame. One important advantage of this approach is that it creates political clarity and can function as a lash with which to whip the civil service into line. If officials make big mistakes they are indirectly punished by the departure of their minister and by the internal unrest that results from such an event. Moreover, the new minister will be sure to take the necessary measures to ensure that the same thing does not happen to him or her. An important disadvantage, however, is that a cabinet can lose very capable ministers in the course of such upheavals.

However, the practice of ministerial responsibility both in the

---

[14] For the situation in the UK, see Turpin (1994: 428–38) and Nolan (1995); and for the Netherlands: *Steekhoudend ministerschap: betekenis en toepassing van de ministeriële verantwoordelijkheid*, Rapport van de externe commissie Ministeriële Verantwoordelijkheid. Tweede Kamer, 1992–1993, 21427, no 41.

Netherlands and in the United Kingdom does not extend nearly as far as this broadly conceived doctrine. In the Netherlands in the period 1945 to 1996, a total of forty-two ministers and state secretaries resigned.[15] Fourteen of them did so because of an appointment elsewhere, four on health grounds, and seven because of political differences inside the cabinet; two state secretaries did so because of departmental differences of opinion and four for personal reasons. Only in ten cases did a member of the government resign because parliament, the government majority, or one of the governing parties, had directly or indirectly made known that it no longer had any confidence in the policy conducted by the minister. In none of those cases was a minister forced to resign by Parliament merely because he was held responsible for what his officials had done. In the United Kingdom the situation is similar. Between 1955 and 1986 there were only six resignations of senior ministers (Profumo; Jellicoe; Carrington and Humphrey after the Argentinean invasion of the Falklands Islands; and Heseltine and Brittan in the wake of the Westland Affair) 'that can be put down to an acknowledgement by the ministers concerned of their responsibility to parliament . . . and in [almost] each case the resignation was connected with the minister's own conduct, not the actions of his department' (Turpin 1994: 432). In fact, the celebrated resignation by Lord Carrington is the only case that fits within the traditional view of ministerial responsibility for the bureaucracy.

If members of the governments in both countries resign because they have lost the confidence of parliament – or think that they ought to have lost it – they do so only when they have at the same time failed in personally supervising their officials or in their conduct in relation to parliament. A rather *narrow* view of ministerial responsibility is therefore maintained in and relation to parliament; members of the government are politically responsible for the mistakes of their officials only when the ministers are actually in a position to influence the conduct of their officials and can personally be blamed for not having made use of that position or for having made a wrong use of it. An important advantage of this narrow approach is that members of the government are less easily brought into political difficulties and that the continuity of a department is guaranteed. Thus one takes account of the fact that as the machinery of government grows in extent and complexity, so the direct actual influence of a minister or undersecretary diminishes. Life and doctrine adapt to one another.

A very important disadvantage, however, is that a large hole threatens to form in the concept of ministerial responsibility for government actions. When one applies the narrow approach, responsibility for the official apparatus is in fact reduced to a responsibility for one's own conduct on the part of the members of a government. 'The system does not appear to provide

[15] These figures for the period up to 1985 are taken from research by Besselink (1987).

adequately for the accountability of civil servants, who nowadays ... themselves formulate policies and take numberless decisions of importance without reference to ministers' (Turpin 1994: 438). This hole is even larger in the case of quango's the quasi-non-governmental organisations which have been largely removed from ministerial control, and whose number and importance has grown substantially, both in the Netherlands and the United Kingdom.

Broadly speaking, in the case of government we see the same problems as with complex organisations in the private sphere. The lines to the top are long, much vital information comes too late or is incomplete, and the delimitation of responsibilities – in the sense of tasks – is vague. Even more so than the private executives and directors, who have in many cases worked their way to the top from within the organisation itself, political leaders are outsiders. Just as in the courts the field of criminal law, so too in parliament there is a tendency to restrict accountability to that business of which the minister has had personal knowledge and that he was in a position actually to influence. This means that in political practices too, the hierarchical model has only limited power of control and preventive effects.

Amending hierarchical accountability

Holding natural persons accountable in accordance with a strictly hierarchical scheme is therefore sometimes a little like trying to grab hold of a piece of soap in a bathtub; whenever you think that you have found someone, first at the top and then a little lower down, who meets all the necessary criteria, he once again slips through your fingers. The semi-autonomous character of complex organisations thus emphatically asserts itself here too – even though in the meantime we have arrived one level further down within the Chinese boxes. In current hierarchical schemes of accountability, the leading levels of an organisation relate to lower echelons in the same way as the controlling outsiders relate to the complex organisation in the case of corporate accountability. The external instructions, laid down in codes, circulars, or general guidelines, of the management or government often lose out to the norms, obligations, and relations rooted in the daily practice of the organisation.

Just like the corporate model of accountability, the hierarchical model is therefore of only restricted use as a solution to the problem of the many hands. There is only a limited number of organisations and situations in which a hierarchical scheme is really useful:

> in case of small, not very complex organisations in which those in charge can find out what is happening at all levels and can also be deemed to be in a position to react quickly and adequately. These are the organisations and operations characterised by what Mintzberg (1979) has called a Simple

Structure and in which there are linear interactions and tight couplings
(Perrow 1988: 332);
   in case of complex organisations that operate in a stable environment in
      which standardisation and formalisation of procedures is possible and
      activities can be performed on a routine basis;
   in all other cases, the responsibility of those in charge remains for the most
      part restricted to responsibility for the formulation of the objectives of the
      organisation and for the drawing up of general policy lines – in short, for
      all those tasks that belong among the direct powers of chief executive func-
      tionaries.

Can the usefulness of the hierarchical model not be increased? I will review
three strategies, each of which takes the hierarchical model as its point of
departure.

1. *Strengthening the hold of the leading bodies.* One could first try to adapt
organisations to ensure that managers can satisfy the requirements of personal knowledge and actual direction to which modern criminal and public
law hold them accountable. That would amount to the reduction of organisations to an extreme form of hierarchy, so that managers can be in a position to administer them in an autocratic way. If Mohammed will not go to
the mountain, the mountain must come to Mohammed; such, is the reasoning here. The chance of that happening is, however, scant. We have
already seen that the most modern complex organisations do not allow
themselves to be administered according to a scheme of absolute autocracy.
One could nevertheless try to reinforce the degree of centralisation and roll
back the autonomy of the lower echelons. Even if one succeeded in this aim
one can still ask whether the cure would not be worse than the malady. It is
altogether doubtful whether such autocratic organisational forms are suitable to administer modern societies and modern, complex production processes. Both in government and in industry, the trend in most western
countries is going in precisely the opposite direction. One works increasingly with project groups and matrix organisations, with self-control and
contract management – organisational forms that all presuppose a large
measure of autonomy at the executive level. Not autocracy but adhocracy
(Mintzberg 1979) seems to represent the wave of the future.
   One might consider whether big complex organisations should not
where possible be split up into small, conveniently arranged organisations
in which controlling from the top is relatively easy. Over the last few years
both in the Netherlands and in the United Kingdom, sections of departments have been transformed into more or less independent agencies
(NDPB's or quango's) with their own directors (O'Toole and Jordan 1995).
These directors have a relatively narrow span of control and therefore count

as insiders who can be addressed as to the conduct of their organisation. For citizens and popular representatives, however, that does not yet mean an end to the problem of many hands. Because most agency heads are for the time being not or rarely addressed directly, but are principally addressed by way of the politically responsible minister, the problem has become bigger rather than smaller. This is because many ministers use the relative independence of the NDPB's as an argument to deny or shift onto others their own responsibility (O'Toole and Chapman 1995).

2. *A reevaluation of hierarchical accountability.* One could also eliminate the difficult point, the question of blameworthiness, by adapting the criterion for accountability. In Dutch civil law, company managers have over the years been confronted with increasingly strict liabilities. With strict liabilities blameworthiness is less of an issue, and often, the burden of proof is shifted to the managers. They are automatically held liable unless they prove they have taken the utmost care. In the case of a bankruptcy, for example, new legislation offers the trustees extensive possibilities to address the managers personally. They have only to show that the manager has clearly acted improperly. Managers can be said to have so acted if, for example, they failed to announce on time that the enterprise was not in a position to pay its taxes and contributions.

With regard to criminal accountability, similar strategies have been suggested. Jörg (1988: 54–56) has proposed, on the analogy of American jurisprudence, to construct the criminal accountability of the managers of organisations as a strict liability. Top functionaries would, according to this reasoning, make sure that they kept their affairs in order if they knew that they themselves, personally, would have to take the consequences of any illegal acts committed by the organisation. Moreover, it may be expected of them that they are fully aware of the regulations that apply in their branch. One could even go a step further and construct a general duty of care on the part of executive functionaries. For example, in cases in which the consequences of the culpable conduct on the part of the organisation are particularly serious, for instance, in the case of serious forms of environmental crime, one could take as sufficient evidence of guilt even very slight forms of personal knowledge and blameworthiness.

Such propositions deserve serious consideration. However, even this strategy is no panacea. To curb 'corporate risks', more is needed than a mere supplementation of our conception of hierarchical accountability. Why, for example, should judges in future deliver harsher and stricter judgments and interpret hierarchical accountability as a general or particular duty of care? After all, such a different interpretation does not change the fact that many managers are outsiders. On a number of points, such a strict liability could only satisfy the need for retribution and, perhaps, for compensation. In a number of fields, the leading bodies of an organisation, however well-meaning, are only partly in control of the course of events. In the long term, the consequences of this strategy, in terms of social utility and power to control, could therefore even be negative. For such constructions can lead to a situation in which many capable but not particularly wealthy people will decline the honour and the risks of the leadership of complex organisations (cf. Coffee 1977: 1107). There is also a threat of paralysis and inertia; the risks of exciting but not completely predictable projects would for many be too great.

3. *Supplementation with other models.* The main objection to the above two strategies is, however, the flattening off and atomisation that is becoming more and more characteristic of modern organisations. The increasing resort to temporary, flat, and vaguely delineated organisational forms – whether under the flag of 'adhocracy', 'sourcing out', or 'business process re-engineering' – will make a model of strictly hierarchical responsibility from the top down for all parts of the organisation less and less easily applicable (Osborne and Gaebler 1993; Peters and Wright 1996).

So we cannot make do with adaptations of existing ideas of hierarchical accountability. Other models are necessary alongside it, or even as primary venue. If one accepts the excuse of the 'manager as outsider', it is a logical step to involve other functionaries, too, in the process of calling to account. The consequence of such a step is that lower, not yet (politically) responsible functionaries can no longer hide behind the broad shoulders of their ministers and bosses. In the next two chapters, a number of such (supplementary) schemes of accountability will be investigated to discover how useful and acceptable they are.

7

Collective accountability: all for one

There are no such things as collective guilt or collective innocence; these terms make sense only if applied to individuals.

(Arendt 1964: 185)

Collective actors and collective responsibilities

Complex organisations are members of the big family of collectives, as each complex organisation consists of a collective of individuals. Collectives come, however, in all shapes and sizes; a group of bystanders at a drowning, a random group of F. C. Den Haag supporters on their way to a football match, an operation team in a hospital, Slavenburg's Bank, or the Department of Foreign Affairs. The first two are examples of what Held (1970) calls a 'random collection of individuals'. That is to say, a collection of individuals that as a result of certain characteristics can be distinguished from the general collection of people, but which has no special method of decision-making. Slavenburg's Bank and the Department of Foreign Affairs, on the other hand, are obvious examples of an 'organised group', a collection of individuals that not only has certain distinctive characteristics but also has at its disposal a clear and independent method of decision-making.

French (1984: 5–18) makes a similar distinction, but adds to it another important element. He uses for the first two groups the term 'aggregate collectivity': a collectivity whose identity is a mere aggregate of the identities of its individual members. A complex organisation is, on the other hand, what French calls a 'conglomerate collectivity': a collectivity whose identity is more than the sum total of the identities of its individual members and whose identity is not directly modified as soon as the membership of the collectivity changes. Officials come and go, but the identity of the Department of Foreign Affairs obviously remains in being. This statement is also true of the procedures for decision-making, the element that Held adds to the equation. Complex organisations are characterised by internal procedures for decision-making that are independent of the individuals who play a role in them (French 1984: 39).

As the complexity of the group structure increases, a collective acquires a more conglomerated character. The group of F. C. Den Haag supporters who at each home game unfurl a yellow and green club flag dozens of meters long on the Central Northern Stand and make decisions about their activity beforehand in the supporters' club is no longer an accidental collection of individuals, a pure aggregate; its members go some way toward fulfilling the criteria set by French for a conglomerate. The same is true of an operation team in a hospital that operates on the basis of an informal but clear and set division of tasks. In both cases there is a procedure for decision-making; moreover, the identity of the group does not change directly when some members of it are replaced.

In the case of complex organisations, as should by now be obvious, we are dealing almost exclusively with conglomerates. The core of the problem of many hands often lies in the fact that the identity and the accountability of the collective is different, or would seem to be different, from that of the individual members. Actions of complex organisations are first and foremost collective actions. It therefore goes without saying that a collective model of accountability must be employed when dealing with the actions of individuals within complex organisations.

The literature about collective moral responsibility-as-accountability is, however, confusing and by no means conspicuous for its conceptual clarity. One must distinguish in the debates about passive collective responsibility between at least two discussions in which different matters are treated, sometimes by the same author. In order to see that this is so, we must bear in mind the scheme set out in chapter 4.

A number of authors would appear to employ the term collective responsibility partly in order to express the idea of an independent moral accountability on the part of a collective, that is to say, an accountability that is not always and not in all respects reducible to pronouncements about the accountability of individual members of the collective. By that I mean questions such as the following. Can we talk of the responsibility of *the* F. C. Den Haag supporters for the bad name that this particular football club has acquired? Could one at the time speak of an independent moral responsibility on the part of *the* Royal Dutch-Shell Group for the survival of the apartheid regime in South Africa or for the suppression of the Ogoni in Nigeria? Or can one speak only of the aggregate of responsibilities of individual supporters and employees? There are different camps in this discussion. On the one side are what I would like to call the *corporatists*; they consider it useful and meaningful to speak of an independent accountability of the collective. Among them are Cooper (1968) and, in relation only to conglomerates, Donaldson (1982), DeGeorge (1983), French (1984: 5–18),

Dworkin (1986: 168–71), and Fisse and Braithwaite (1993:17–31). In the other camp are, for example, Downie (1969) and Benjamin (1976). In the literature, they are reckoned among the 'methodological individualists'. To prevent confusion later on, I shall here call them *personalists*. According to the personalists, there can be no such thing as a collective accountability, here understood as an independent accountability on the part of a collective quite separate from the accountability of its individual members. Each moral pronouncement about collectives can and must eventually be brought back to a pronouncement about individual persons. Held (1970) seems to take a position midway between the two extremes. In chapter 5 I declared myself a member of the corporatist camp in regard to complex organisations. Collective accountability, in the sense of *corporate* accountability, is an idea that can be meaningfully employed – though it does not necessarily exclude *a priori* an imputation of accountability to individual persons.[1]

Alongside and sometimes intertwined with this discussion there is a second debate; this debate not only relates to complex organisations but to collectives of all sorts. The central question in this debate is whether individuals can be held personally accountable for the conduct of the collective to which they belong – their country, ethnic group, party, organisation, or supporters' club – when they themselves have not, or have not in all respects, contributed to the offending events. The most dramatic example of this is, again, to be found in the events of the Second World War: To what extent does each inhabitant of the Third Reich share the responsibility for the fate of the Jews? Or, even more extreme: To what extent can one blame the Germans born after 1945 for the conduct of their parents and grandparents? In fact to do so would be to engage in the collective imputation of *personal* accountability, which is independent from, or can at least be seen as independent from, any possible imputation to the collective as a whole.[2] Walsh (1970) and MacIntyre (1981: 205) would appear to be moderate advocates of such a form of collective personal accountability. I will call them the *collectivists*. Arendt (1964), Levinson (1973), Thompson (1980), and Flores and Johnson (1983) are, following Kant, adversaries of such a broad, not in any way individualised, imputation of personal accountability. Confusingly enough, even those adversaries of what one could call a collective model of personal accountability are reckoned among the 'methodological individualists'. Them I shall call (moral) *individualists*.[3] For they are supporters of a model of strictly individual imputation of accountability in the case of

---

[1] See also chapter 8.   [2] Cf. the scheme from chapter 4.

[3] To make things even more difficult: the term '*methodological* individualism' is also used in the discussions about the *explanation* of collective phenomena on the basis of individual behaviour. Since I am here concerned only with the moral *appraisal* of that collective behaviour, I shall talk only of 'individualism'.

collective acts. Feinberg (1970: 225–51), finally, takes a middle position and, partly on the basis of legal rulings, reviews in a very subtle way a number of forms that such a collective personal accountability might assume.

In short: in the literature, the term 'collective responsibility' (in the sense of 'accountability') can mean at least two different things:

1. An accountability on the part of the collective as a whole for its own behaviour.
2. A personal accountability on the part of all individual members of the collective for the conduct of the whole.

In this chapter 'collective responsibility' is used only in the second sense. The first meaning has already been discussed in chapter 5, in the form of 'corporate accountability'. By a collective model, we therefore understand in this chapter a regulation of responsibility-as-accountability whereby every member of the complex organisation, or of a relevant part of the organisation, can *personally* be held accountable for the conduct of the organisation.

Collective schemes of accountability come in all shapes and sizes. One can in the first place vary the *group size*. Often collective accountability is restricted to the uppermost parts of an organisation, which comes close to hierarchical accountability. A good example in the sphere of law are many big law firms. The leadership of these firms rests mostly in the hands of a partnership to which only a relatively small number of the lawyers is admitted. Each of the partners is in relation to the outside world in principle equally accountable for any possible mistakes committed and any debts accrued by the firm. One could even extend the collective model and hold responsible every member of a given complex organisation. Such a broad collective scheme is not, to my knowledge, employed in law in the case of complex organisations. It is, however, used in the case of some aggregates. For example, when a mortgage or some other form of loan has been taken out by people acting as part of a group, the bank can stipulate that every member of the group is not only liable for his or her part of the debt, but also, individually, for the whole debt.

Broad collective schemes are often employed in political and social discussions. A crude variant of such schemes mostly underlies the bad treatment to which minority groups, foreigners, or prisoners of war frequently fall foul in hostile societies. The conduct of one member of the group, or of the forebears or national representatives of the group, is blamed on every individual person who happens to share the basic characteristics of the group. In the case of complex organisations one also comes across such cases of collectivist imputation of guilt. One example is the destruction by the Dutch action group 'Nightshade', of installations belonging to independent petrol-station owners who sold Shell products; the action was in protest at

Shell's involvement in South Africa. The action group gave as its reason for its campaign the fact that the individual petrol-station owners were responsible by association for Shell's presence in South Africa.

As well as group size one can also vary the *degree* of accountability. The most far-reaching cases are those in which people are held jointly and severally liable in law, such as in that form of partnership in which every member of the collective can be held liable for the total debt, irrespective of his or her own contribution to the partnership or his or her role in the accruing of that debt. Less far-reaching are forms of proportional liability, as for example in the case of an ordinary partnership, in which one can be held liable only for a proportional part of the collective conduct of the partnership. When, for example, a board of directors has four members, each member can be held accountable for a quarter of any damage done. One could also apply this principle to the whole complex organisation and hold each employee accountable for a proportional part of the corporate conduct of the organisation. Something similar happened in the case of the Finnish state bank Postipankki. In 1995 the bank's main office brought in lawyers to start procedures against the personnel of the establishment in New York. It seemed that the New York office had suffered a loss of 460 million markka (approximately 60 million pounds) in the first half of 1995. It appeared that more than half of that amount had been lost in the course of speculation with derivates. Information about the financially risky investment in exotic swaps had, contrary to internal regulations, been consistently withheld from the main office. The bank therefore at first held the entire personnel of the branch in New York responsible for the enormous losses.[4]

With collective accountability, whether moral or legal, the actual contribution of those held accountable plays no role of any significance. The collective nature of the act is to the fore, and no attempt is made to dissect or analyse it in terms of discrete individual actions that vary in force and direction. As soon as one permits such distinctions in the assessment of accountability, one finds oneself moving in the direction of the strictly individual models that are treated in the following chapter.

Internal and external collective accountability

To what extent are collective schemes satisfactory in the light of the three issues of accountability that are on the agenda here? Let us begin with the *practical* problems. Collective accountability has one big advantage over the other schemes, it makes quick work of the practical sides of the problem of many hands. In the case of misconduct on the part of an organisation, every

---

[4] According to a news item in *de Volkskrant*, 1 August 1995.

member of the organisation can be held accountable. One need not worry that the corporation might in the meantime have been disbanded or declared bankrupt; nor does one need to unravel the organisational structure and start looking for the formal or actual executives. One need only look at the pay-roll of the company or at the *State Directory* to know whom one should hold responsible. Victims in need of reparation for damages have a good chance of succeeding, since they can turn to the best-off among the company's officials. Those who are only out for personal retribution will quickly and easily find satisfaction.

Next, there is the *moral* dimension. One can find a cautious plea for a 'broad' collective responsibility in Walsh (1970) and MacIntyre (1981: 205). These two authors base this plea on the observation that too strict an individual imputation of blame or guilt is untenable on epistemological grounds. Individualism, they argue, is based on the concept of a completely abstract and 'pliable' self – all individuals are what they themselves choose to be. But the world is not like that:

> I am someone's son or daughter, someone else's cousin or uncle; I am a citizen of this or that city, a member of this or that guild or profession; I belong to this clan, that tribe, this nation. [. . .] As such, I inherit from the past of my family, my city, my tribe, my nation, a variety of debts, inheritances, rightful expectations and obligations. These constitute the given of my life, my moral starting point.
>
> (MacIntyre 1981: 205)

It is naive to suppose that individuals act in complete isolation from others and that they are in a position to judge autonomously, free from every tie to their forebears, compatriots, and colleagues. As Walsh puts it: 'The truth is rather that, even in their personal actions, men's minds are penetrated by ideas which they share with others, and that, so far from its being true that collective action is but an amalgam of personal actions, collective action is sui generis and distinct' (1970: 8–9).

Individual human identity is constructed from collective elements. For both Walsh and MacIntyre, this empirical observation also has important moral implications. According to them, this historical and social constitution of the 'self' brings with it the fact that individuals can also be held accountable for events or circumstances that came about beyond their will. The postwar generation of Germans cannot absolve itself of a certain degree of moral responsibility for what their parents and grandparents did. Young Irish people can hold their English contemporaries to account regarding the suppression of the Easter Rising and everything that preceded that atrocity. Palestinians can hold Jews in the diaspora to account regarding Israeli conduct in the occupied areas. And individual Dutchmen, as descendants of a race of slave-traders, can, according to Walsh and MacIntyre, be held to account by American blacks.

Is it really justifiable that we should feel responsible, or even guilty, for the deeds of persons or groups to whom we are related? Can others hold us accountable for the deeds of our ancestors, compatriots, co-religionists or colleagues? The answer to the first question is moderately positive, but the answer to the second question is definitely far from positive. The critique by Walsh and MacIntyre of an all too strict and abstract individualism is quite successful from an epistemological and social-psychological perspective. The 'self' is not a fixed and abstract unit that exists in isolation from every social and historical context. Individual identities are constructed from pre-existing elements; opinions are not formed in a vacuum, but on the basis of existing ideas and in dialogue with others.[5] Many people do feel responsible for what their forebears, compatriots, and colleagues have done. It is true that in certain circumstances and under certain conditions, conceptions of collective responsibility, in the sense of *virtue*, are very well defensible. The normative ideal of civil society, for example, offers such a conception. Democratic societies can flourish only when citizens feel a certain active, collective responsibility for the survival of political institutions (Putnam 1993; March and Olson 1995).

A sense of responsibility is, however, somewhat different from feeling guilty; and it must under no circumstances be confused with accountability. Walsh and MacIntyre do not adequately distinguish between responsibility as task, as virtue, and as accountability. Moreover, they do not sufficiently distinguish between internal and external accountability.

A collective conception of active responsibility, responsibility in the sense of task, is very easy to imagine. Many people feel a certain responsibility for the well-being of others to whom they have a given tie. Often this responsibility is even experienced as a moral duty. That is the background to many friendly turns, to instances of neighbourly help, and to the sense of family. Under certain circumstances, one can even be held accountable *for those duties.* Sometimes one has no choice other than to be one's brother's keeper. Dworkin (1986: 198–202) lists four conditions that must be fulfilled in order to transform such a collective responsibility-as-task into a moral duty. First there must be talk of a certain reciprocity in the responsibilities. I am only obliged to help a friend in need when I can be sure that if I myself were in like circumstances, he too would be prepared to do the same for me. In the second place, the other members of the community – one's family, one's circle of friends, or one's neighbours – must understand these collective responsibilities as special and personal obligations. Special, because

---

[5] See also MacIntyre (1988) and the work of Sandel (1982) and Beiner (1983).

they must be distinct from general obligations that one would feel for every individual fellow citizen; personal, because only those obligations are reciprocal that are felt in regard to a member in person and not in regard to the collective as a whole. In the third place, the concrete responsibilities that every member of the collective feels must flow from a general feeling of responsibility for the well-being of the other members of the group. In the fourth place, that responsibility must be felt in similar measure for every member of the group. Brotherhood cannot tolerate a situation in which the welfare of one member of the community is worth more than that of another member of it. One for all, and all for one. Dworkin makes in that connection a distinction between 'bare' and 'true' communities. *Bare* communities are groups that exhibit a certain unity on the basis of genetic, geographical, historical, or social circumstances. However, they are *true* communities only when they also meet these four conditions.

Only within such 'true' communities can there be talk of a collective accountability on the part of the members. Such a collective accountability is, however, still not the collective accountability with which we are here dealing. After all, it is only an *internal* accountability: one group member can address the others, his family or friends, in regard to their collective responsibility toward him. This chapter, however, is about *external* accountability: the accountability of individual members of the group for the conduct of other members of the group, or of the group as a whole, *in respect of outsiders*. Such a collective accountability is, as we shall soon see, acceptable only under very strict conditions.

Walsh and MacIntyre wrongly conclude from their observation, that the 'self' is historically and socially determined and that many people actually feel responsible for the behaviour of others with whom they have certain characteristics in common, that they can also be held accountable in the same way by outsiders. 'Is' thus suddenly transmutes into 'ought'. Why should we be able to subject strangers to a process of accounting – one that frequently entails various sorts of penalties – when it is obvious in advance that there is nothing with which they can personally be reproached? What justifies dropping individual blameworthiness as a necessary condition for moral accountability? What could the young German or the young English person do other than bow his or her head?[6] The implications of the acceptance of such general forms of external collective moral accountability are moreover enormous. It is but a small step from such an acceptance to the

[6] Things would, however, be otherwise were we to restrict ourselves to political rather than moral responsibility. One could definitely hold a young German or British minister to account for the conduct of his predecessors in office. Political accountability tolerates collective schemes better than other sorts of accountability. Members of the government function, moreover, as representatives of political communities. One could certainly hold the German Federal Republic or the United

standard reasoning of terrorists and totalitarian oppressors when attacking defenceless citizens, namely 'blaming the victim': in the end, it is the victims themselves who are the guilty ones. What can we then say, for example, to those who hold today's Jews responsible for the crucifixion of Christ? General schemes of external collective accountability have in the past all too often given rise to much suffering and injustice.

The over-inclusiveness of collective accountability

Collective arrangements of personal accountability are not or barely reconcilable with legal and moral practices and intuitions current in modern western democracies: 'Morally speaking, it is as wrong to feel guilty without having done something specific as it is to feel free of all guilt if one actually is guilty of something [. . .] There are no such things as collective guilt or collective innocence; these terms make sense only if applied to individuals' (Arendt 1964: 185). In imputing accountability the behavioural alternatives, and the nature of the behaviour of the individual members of a collective should be taken into account. Applied to complex organisations: it makes a substantial difference whether someone is a member of the Presidium of the Board of Directors of Royal Dutch Shell Ltd, group director of the African and South Asian region, or director of the subsidiary company Shell South Africa or Shell Nigeria, rather than simply an independent petrol-station owner who sells Shell products. It can also make a difference – think of the question of blameworthiness – whether someone was a strong proponent of investment in South Africa, voted against such investment, or was in no position whatsoever to exercise any influence in the matter; it can even make a difference whether or not in getting his position, or subsequently staying in it, someone had the chance of working for other companies or could only choose between his job and going on the dole.

Collective models are mostly not sophisticated enough to do justice to the many differences that are important in the imputation of guilt, shame, and blame. The chief moral objection to collective models is therefore that they are far too over-inclusive. It is by no means true that all the members of a complex organisation in some measure meet the various criteria of accountability. Often an individual official, by 'simply doing his work', contravenes no specific norm or is in no way conscious of any such transgression. Many functionaries will by virtue of their activities make no causal contribution, or make only a very indirect causal contribution, to the offending conduct

Kingdom, as political and legal successors to the Third Reich and the British Empire, responsible on moral grounds. A similar form of reasoning underlay, for example, the German indemnities paid after the war. However, the latter is an instance of the collective moral responsibility discussed in chapter 5, *corporate* accountability, and not of *personal* accountability, which is the subject of the present discussion.

of their service or company. And even if one makes such a causal contribution, it will often not be blameworthy. Although the conduct of a complex organisation may have a collective character, that does not mean to say that all the members are involved and guilty.

The very fact that individual functionaries can be regarded as morally exculpated, because they were hardly or not at all involved in the offending conduct of the complex organisation, also throws doubt on the *control potential* of collective schemes. From the point of view of prevention, it makes little sense to hold functionaries accountable – and this is a crucial point – who in the future will be able to exercise little or no influence on the eventual course of affairs. It is highly doubtful whether broad models of collective accountability, if applied to complex organisations, will give rise to learning processes and structural changes. After all, those who are held accountable are not necessarily the same people who have in their hands the key to changes and the ability to prevent the undesirable actions.[7] Collective schemes of accountability merely reproduce the problem of many hands: 'When everyone in the collectivity [...] is responsible, citizens have no one to call to account' (Thompson 1987: 47).

An extra complication is that in the case of broad models of collective accountability, 'free-rider' problems can arise. The chance of this happening is greatest when, as is fairly often the case, not every member of the collective is held accountable, but only a few members who happen to be chosen on a relatively arbitrary basis. If the chances of being held accountable are approximately equal for everybody, but are not too great, then it becomes less attractive for members to stick their necks out and address themselves to the problem of how to bring about changes in the structure. The costs entailed will be high, while the rest of the staff will be able to profit from such people's efforts – the chance that anyone would have to undergo such a ticking-off before a forum diminishes – without they themselves having to go to any great lengths. The danger thus arises of a 'logic of collective action': although every individual member will benefit from changes in the structure, it is more advantageous to wait until someone else produces this collective good. Because the same reasoning holds for everybody, no one will lift a finger and little prevention is achieved by holding people to account.

Conditions for collective accountability

However, collective models of accountability should not be rejected in all circumstances. Individual responsibility is, as Feinberg put it, no 'eternal law

---

[7] An exception must perhaps be made on this point for those cases in which *all* members of the collective are held to account (think of the schoolmaster who keeps all his pupils in detention after school because something has disappeared from the classroom). In such a case, the one who has in his or her hands the key to a change in behaviour is also called to account.

of reason' (1970: 241). Contrary to what Arendt said, there are situations in which one can meaningfully speak of a collective, personal accountability. Sometimes the crucial point – here, too, that of blameworthiness – is catered for. Feinberg has discussed the conditions that would have to be met if an application of a collective model of accountability is to be just and sensible (1970: 233–41). These conditions, reproduced in our terms and adapted to our presentation of the question, boil down to the following:

a. *The collective must be characterised by a high degree of* de facto *solidarity.* Such a group solidarity is in most cases closely connected to the presence of a large number of communal interests, of emotional ties to a communal objective, or to one another, and to the fact that the welfare of the group is in a certain sense collective and indivisible. All share each other's misfortune, all share each other's happiness. Examples of such solidarity-based groups are the medieval family and village communities, the mafia, football teams, resistance groups, and terrorist organisations. One might also mention family businesses, small cooperatives, residential communes and some religious sects.

b. *Efficient, professional supervision from outside is unfeasible.* Feinberg describes collective responsibility in criminal law above all as a form of 'mandatory selfpolicing' and restricts it to situations in which an efficient police apparatus is lacking. Given the nature of 'corporate risks', it goes without saying that this element could be extended to other forms of policy, for example administrative or environmental supervision.

c. *Those who are held accountable for the conduct of other members of the collective should be aware beforehand that such a model of accountability will be employed.* One can be held accountable for the conduct of others after the event only if it was obvious beforehand that this would happen. In this way, moreover, one activates responsibility-as-virtue.

d. *Those who are held responsible should have the chance to exercise a certain degree of influence on the eventual outcome.* The possibility of active responsibility, of virtuous conduct, precedes passive responsibility. Herein lies for example the justification of the difference in accountability between the members of a partnership and the administrative staff that are in paid employment. The former have voting rights and sometimes the right of veto, the latter rarely have any such rights.

At issue here are cumulative conditions. In most modern organisations it rarely happens that the organisation and large numbers of its functionaries meet all these conditions. Only certain forms of what Dworkin calls 'true' communities qualify. (Feinberg names as the most important examples the medieval Anglo-Saxon village community and the modern family.[8]) That

---

[8] The liability without fault of parents for their young children in Dutch civil law fits, for example, within these conditions.

means that collective schemes of accountability can contribute only in very restricted measure to the solution of our problem of many hands.

Just as in the case of hierarchical accountability, one could however distinguish a number of paths along which one might try to enlarge the area within which collective accountability is applicable.

1. *Changes in our legal and moral practices.* An important objection to collective models is that they run counter to a long humanistic tradition of strictly individual imputations of responsibility. Moral traditions, intuitions, and practices are not, however, fixed in aspic. They are subject to changes and these changes are, to a certain degree, controlable. In law, there are a number of points of departure for a change in a collective direction such as the system (discussed above) whereby members of a partnership firm are jointly and severally liable; an example of collective accountability within a field of practice that is in the great majority of cases strictly individual in character. In this case social considerations (satisfaction of creditors) receive precedence over moral intuitions. One could tread similar paths in the case of complex organisations. The most important consideration would again have to be the seriousness of the consequences of undesirable conduct on the part of such organisations. One could argue that the moral impurities of such a broad and somewhat blunt and over-simplified collective model of accountability are outweighed by the consideration that, by employing it, the enormous, often irrevocable – and morally most relevant – harm that can result from deviant corporate conduct may be forestalled. But as I indicated above, there is serious doubt regarding the preventive power of such a broad model. So for the time being – it cannot be ruled out that in the longer run we will discover that there is no alternative – the most important argument for setting aside our moral scruples must be declared invalid. Moreover, great dangers attach to the employment on a larger scale of collective models. Such broad models tempt people to seek scapegoats and rattle off processes of calling to account in a peremptory sort of way. It is also possible that the ratio, the degree of seriousness of the consequences of corporate action, fades into the background and that one starts applying collective models in the future to other types of collectives too. Such an escalation would greatly debase the level of our practices of accountability.

2. *Adaptation of the form of organisation.* If complex organisations do not fit well in collective models of accountability, then they should be made to do so – such might be a second reaction to the problem. One could try to split up big complex organisations and thus ensure that they meet the conditions that are here set to collective accountability. Schumacher's 'small

is beautiful' would thus go for accountability too. At first glance, this is an anachronistic strategy; the time of small, conveniently arranged organisations administered on the basis of mutual solidarity and social control would seem to be dead and buried. In the 1960s, however, we saw a revival of thinking in terms of small-scale organisation that admittedly failed to produce the revolutionary changes that many expected it to produce but nevertheless left behind traces of its passage through society – see some of the examples of collectives that I mentioned earlier. According to many organisation theorists, we are in a period of transition from large-scale, hierarchical organisational forms to smaller, horizontally structured forms of networking. The future belongs to the project teams, matrix organisations, and 'adhocracies' (cf. Mintzberg 1979; Toffler 1985; Hood 1991; Osborne and Gaebler 1995; Peters and Wright 1996)). Many of these new organisational forms are directed at stimulating collective and individual forms of active responsibility, at expanding the autonomy and the feeling of responsibility of individual employees and units.

It is, however, doubtful whether some of these new organisational forms will meet the four conditions that were set earlier to passive collective responsibility. The first condition of mutual solidarity will be particularly difficult to meet. An important characteristic of those horizontal, multidisciplinary teams is precisely their looseness. Members come and go, depending on whether or not there is a call for their particular form of expertise. There is no obvious communal interest, let alone an emotional tie that remains even after one has moved on to another project. An important obstacle in the case of such a strategy is moreover the above-mentioned danger of the 'logic of collective action': everybody is accountable after the event, but no one feels responsible beforehand. An adaptation of the form of organisation in the direction of a collective model of accountability therefore demands at the very least a different conception of responsibility-as-virtue. But then one must still ask oneself whether a successful change in mentality is in itself enough to produce an adequate defence against the danger of 'free-rider' behaviour that collective models tend to bring in their wake; to achieve such an end, changes in the structure of the penalties and rewards are presumably necessary. In the concluding chapter, I shall return to this question.

8

Individual accountability: each for himself

... the pursuit of personal responsibility provides the best foundation for understanding the role that human agency plays in good and bad government, and the strongest base for enhancing the accountability that democracy should demand of officials of government.

(Thompson 1987: 65)

The ideal of individual accountability

Collective and hierarchical models of accountability are in a sense *constructions*. For one does not look at who 'really' did it, but, in order to get round the problem of many hands, constructs a form of accountability. As we have seen, neither model is under all circumstances adequate and acceptable, either from a moral or from a controlling point of view. What remains is the third option: strictly individual accountability for the conduct of the organisation. In the case of this individual model, an attempt is made to do justice to the circumstances of the corporate activity. Each functionary is held liable in so far as, and according to the extent to which, he or she has personally contributed to the offending conduct on the part of the complex organisation. With this model, junior functionaries are not spared; the forum does not need to restrict itself to the leading levels of the organisation, but can hold to account each functionary of whom it might be supposed that he or she was involved in the misconduct. Furthermore, the imputation of responsibility will differ from person to person, whether one is at the top or at the bottom of the organisational hierarchy, one is judged on the basis of one's personal conduct. This is the model of accountability that is applied in law and morality with regard to 'normal' individual actions. Every adult is, in principle, held personally accountable for his or her own actions.

Over the last few decades one finds among moral and political philosophers, numerous pleas for the application of strictly individual schemes to actions committed by, and within, complex organisations. Most authors who deal with issues of responsibility within complex organisations have argued for the individual responsibility of soldiers, managers, politicians, and bureaucrats as the ideal means of combating the problem of many hands. Arendt (1964, 1965), for example, concludes her analysis of the Eichmann affair with it; Levinson (1973: 273) distils it from his analysis of the Nuremberg trials and tries to apply a model of individual responsibility to the Vietnam War; Coleman (1982: 102) concludes his analysis of 'corporate risks' with it; Van Gunsteren (1985: 275–6) arrives at it on the basis of a discussion of the possibilities of an autonomous ethics for the public sphere; DeGeorge (1983: 67) and Donaldson (1982: 118–19) recommend individual responsibility as a way out of the problem of corporate responsibility; and Thompson (1987: 65), finally, blows his own trumpet on the basis of his analysis of the problem of many hands in the public sphere.[1]

At first sight this is indeed the ideal model. It is thoughtfully balanced and subtle; justice can be done to the differences in position, power, and behaviour on the part of functionaries; it fits within the western tradition, strongly influenced by Kant, which in the case of punishment and the ascription of guilt takes personal characteristics and behaviour as its point of departure. From a control perspective, too, this model would seem to be more fruitful than the other two. After all, the degree of imputation is related to the actual influence that a functionary has exercised or could have exercised. This means that there is a real chance of learning effects and prevention. No one asks the impossible of functionaries; one is, and will continue to be responsible only for those changes in the structure or in the conduct of the complex organisation that lie within one's own powers. That will produce a big increase in the chance of actual changes. Moreover, the large amount of factual and practical knowledge of the course of affairs that the lower echelons mostly have at their disposal can be put to use. The failing of the hierarchical model, the lack of timely and adequate information and the resulting relative inability of the higher levels to control events, could in this way be overcome.

But there is, alas, no such thing as ideal models. Even an individual model of accountability is subject to drawbacks, side-reactions, and boomerang effects. True, these are not always insurmountable, but they do mean that the individual model at the very least forfeits the status of a panacea. Broadly speaking, I have three principal objections to the recommendations of these individualists.

In the first place, the solution to the problem of many hands does not lie in a one-sided choice for a single model of passive responsibility. As I explained in chapter 6, one can best start by ranking the various models of accountability in proper order. In most cases it would seem natural to begin

---

[1] See also Philips (1972: 462), Flores and Johnson (1983: 543), Fleishman, Liebman and Moore (1981: ix), and Fisse and Braithwaite (1993).

with corporate accountability – the crudest sieve which, under certain conditions, can deal with the biggest iniquities. Alongside it, or rather after it, one can switch to applying hierarchical, collective, or individual forms of personal accountability (or mixtures of two or all of them). The relevance of those personal models will depend, as we have seen, on the internal structure and culture of the organisation, on the actual and formal possibilities of control available to those who are held liable, and on the type of conduct in regard to which people are being held to account.[2]

In the second place, few of the authors I have mentioned provide a more detailed analysis of the possibilities and impossibilities of such an individual model within complex organisations. The plea for individual accountability therefore acquires a somewhat gratuitous character. One finds it for the most part tagged on at the end of an argument. As a result, inadequate attention is paid to the side-reactions or boomerang effects.

Following on naturally from that line of argument is the third objection. None of the proponents of the model of individual accountability has until now paid all that much attention to the implementation of such a model within complex organisations. How can one give form to such an individual responsibility? In which cases, under which conditions, and in which manifestations would it really offer a way out from the problem of many hands?

Mindful of the points of departure of this study, from now on the emphasis will therefore lie on individual forms of responsibility. The first objection has already been dealt with to some extent in the preceding chapters. The following chapters will be largely devoted to the third objection: how is such a model to be implemented? The second objection, stating that inadequate attention is given to the specific possibilities and disadvantages of individual accountability, will be dealt with in this chapter.

The organisation as a Gordian knot

In the case of individual schemes of accountability, the problem of many hands once again makes its appearance in all its many forms. First, the problems of a *practical* nature. The unravelling of corporate action, the reduction of collective conduct to concrete individual acts, is because of the complexity and lack of transparency of many organisations often extraordinarily difficult. How can we find out who did what and when? How can outsiders discover which individual was responsible, and to what extent, for

---

[2] For a very elaborate strategy for the criminal accountability of corporations, which takes a sequence of different models as its point of departure, see the Accountability Model of Fisse and Braithwaite (1993).

the performance or non-performance of certain actions? The conduct of complex organisations usually does not bear a personal stamp.

Such is the case with relatively simple forms of environmental crime, like for example the Uniser affair (Hellinga Commission 1983: 77, 86), or with various forms of economic fraud, such as the Ohio Revco affair, which Diana Vaughan (1983) has analysed. But it has also played a big role in the prosecution of the war crimes that were committed under Germany's Third Reich. At the Nuremberg trials it proved to be extraordinarily difficult to produce the necessary legal evidence to show that individual soldiers, officials, and other functionaries really were involved in the persecution of the Jews: 'the acts themselves were most often performed by those who were in fact never tried by any major tribunal – the ordinary soldier. To find a governmental official guilty demanded the linkage of his activity to that of the final actors themselves, a most complex task' (Levinson 1973: 258). Both the causal responsibility and the element of blameworthiness turned out to be extraordinarily difficult to prove. It was only thanks to the existence of a large number of dossiers and documents that a number of functionaries could be identified and condemned. Levinson provides the following example of this:

> Indeed there is some reason to think that the convictions under the enunciated standards were the result of a fluke – that is, 'the German proclivity for systematic records and the unexpected swift final victory, which placed files of documents in Allied hands'. Without such records, convictions might have been impossible. Thus, for example, the IMT was unsympathetic to Ernst Kaltenbrunner's protestation that he lacked responsibility for the extermination of Jews, because there existed 'very large numbers of orders on which his name was stamped or typed, and in a few instances, written. It is inconceivable that in matters of such importance his signature could have appeared so many times without his authority. And such records were even more essential to the evaluation of lesser officials.
>
> (Levinson 1973: 258–259)

Thanks to this widespread, but relatively accidental, availability of initialled and confidential pieces, the international military tribunals could determine rather exactly the links between a number of concrete civil and military functionaries on the one hand and the extermination campaigns on the other.

But in many cases of corporate misconduct the situation is quite different. Only a few modern complex organisations are administered on the basis of the extraordinarily thorough and voluminous documentation that was usual in the military apparatus of the Nazis. In many cases involving deliberately illegal conduct, people work with shadow dossiers, use veiled and obscure language, or operate on the basis of 'unwritten orders'

(Vaughan 1983: 75). And if there are incriminating documents, it is not easy for outsiders and controlling bodies to lay their hands on them. Many companies and government institutions are characterised by an almost natural tendency to closedness; strict social or disciplinary sanctions often stand in the way of publicly breaking ranks or violating trust. In those companies in which internal dossiers are available, they often give a very restricted or distorted image: 'most written documents in the corporate world constitute simply official versions of reality that often bear little resemblance to the tangled, ambiguous, and verbally negotiated transactions that they purportedly represent' (Jackall 1988: 88).

However, tearing down the paper walls does not end our quest. Within complex organisations there is often a lack of individual continuity. This plays an important role in the cases of deviance that result from negligence. Formal guidelines that were once useful remain in force even if the one who issued them has left and the situation has changed; sensible but unwritten routines are broken off after the arrival of a new superior; a big turnover of administrative staff means that many practical rules of thumb must be rediscovered again and again. New managers subscribe to the traditions and existing practices – or what they think are the traditions and practices – and add their own plans and ambitions, but often leave before those plans and guidelines are tested and adjusted in practice: 'Members of committees [...] change and often the changing ideas of even the existing members combine in surprising ways. The larger the group, the greater the number of changing variables' (Donaldson 1982: 115). Jackall (1988: 88–91) describes how for individual executives a large degree of mobility can be an important, conscious strategy for escaping individual accountability. Managers 'can outrun their mistakes' by not staying too long in the same place. By the time problems arise, they have either moved further up in the company or have left it, so the accountability can no longer catch up with them.

In later chapters I shall look at the question of how one might try, on behalf of outsiders, to tear down the paper walls of complex organisations in greater length. It must be admitted in advance, however, that neither the problem of the paper walls nor the problem of individual discontinuity can be satisfactorily resolved in all cases. A first conclusion must therefore be that, if only for practical reasons, it will always remain necessary to resort to other schemes of accountability, in particular the corporate and hierarchical forms.

Accountability of the whole and of its parts

The tangled character of many complex organisations also has an important *moral* dimension. I am referring to the reduction of collective action to individual behaviour that is relevant in moral respect. Because of the division of labour, hierarchy, and organisational routines, most functionaries often contribute only in slight measure to the total outcome. To what extent is it possible to find separate functionaries who meet all the criteria for passive responsibility? Could it be possible that the whole is more than the parts, that an instance of corporate conduct must in itself be considered as morally unacceptable while at the same time none of the individuals involved can in any way be reproached? At this point, we are back at the previous discussions about corporate and collective accountability.

According to the personalists, for example Downie (1969) and Benjamin (1976), the moral responsibility of the whole is never greater than that of the parts: 'if a collective is *morally* responsible for something it does, its moral responsibility *is* analysable in terms of moral responsibilities of individuals, including some who may not at a given time be members of the collective' (Downie 1969: 68). Moral collective responsibilities always end up being imputed to individuals. This is not at first sight obvious. Think of the three examples that I gave in chapter 4. What about Parfit's 'Harmless Torturers', whose separate actions did not noticeably increase the amount of pain felt by the prisoner, but where the sum-total of their separate actions did? What should we think of My Lai, where Lieutenant Calley could not help the fact that the information that he had received was incorrect, that he had to operate under great pressure, and that his superior later denied having given him specific orders? And what about the responsibility for the special provisions of the Dutch Social Security Act, which, as if guided by an invisible hand, eventually end up being dispensed above all to groups for which they were not intended?

Even more difficult is the question of individual imputation in another hypothetical example, which is a variant of the well-known 'tragedy of the commons'. It is not an example of corporate activity, but it does show how difficult it can be to argue from the collective to the individual. Consider, for example, the case of a village that has at its disposal some communal heathland. All commoners have the right to graze their goats on this land. Unfortunately, there are more goats in the village than is good for the natural equilibrium of the heath. For each individual farmer, however, it is absolutely rational to put his goats to graze on the heath, for there are hardly any other possibilities for keeping goats. Each farmer therefore puts his goats on the heath. As a result, the heath is eaten away, the commons are destroyed, and all the farmers are forced to get rid of their goats. Can one hold individual commoners responsible for the environmental catastrophe that results from their collective behaviour?

Let us in each of these four cases assume that a collective act has been committed that is morally reprehensible. Does that also mean that this collective act can be divided up into morally reprehensible individual actions? In considering this sort of situations it helps to use the distinction that Austin, in his famous essay 'A Plea for Excuses' (1957), made between justifications and excuses. One can speak of a *justification* when the person being held accountable takes the complete causal and moral responsibility for what he has done, but claims that the action was not as such morally reprehensible. In our terms: the action did not meet the first criterion for accountability, for there is no question of a violation of a norm. One can speak of an *excuse* when the person being held accountable does not deny that the individual action as such produced a violation of a norm but gives reasons why he cannot, or cannot completely, be held accountable. In our terms: there is insufficient evidence of a causal link or a blameworthy act. As Austin puts it: 'In the one defence, briefly, we accept responsibility but deny that it was bad: in the other, we admit that it was bad but don't accept full, or even any, responsibility' (1957: 2).

The last two examples, the special provisions and the grazing of the goats, are actions that, *as such*, are not morally reprehensible. Each of the special provisions can be justified on its merits; true, individual social-security workers can be held to account, but they are not morally responsible for the final outcome. Grazing a goat on the heath is in itself not reprehensible; the contrary is perhaps true – without a certain amount of grazing, the heath would become overgrown. It is the extent of the grazing that eventually causes the heath to disappear. The strictly individual accountability of each member of the collective is indeed difficult to establish in these situations. That does not mean, however, that the corporatists are therefore right.

What is left is a switch to (mixed) hierarchical or collective models of personal accountability. So who bears an individual accountability for the whole? Those who introduced the arrangements without thinking about the consequences; or, when the consequences were not foreseeable, those who neglected to evaluate the effects of the arrangements at an early stage and to adjust them as soon as it became evident that the offending consequences would result. In concrete: the members of the cabinet, the officials of the Ministry of Social Affairs, the parliamentary specialists, and the various interest and pressure groups. Or, in the case of the commons: those who took part in the distribution and omitted to put limits on the grazing or to make the grazing in some way conditional (Ostrom 1990; 1992). They cannot justify their behaviour as easily as the individual official or farmer.[3]

---

[3] This does not absolve individual functionaries and farmers from all accountabilities. After a certain period of time, as the consequences become visible for individual social-security workers and commoners, they can be expected at least to raise the collective consequences with their superiors or fellows.

In the first two cases the situation is somewhat different. Administering electric shocks to a prisoner or assassinating civilians is as such, under normal circumstances, not morally justifiable. However, one could find a number of excuses: 'My contribution was too slight to be morally relevant'. 'I knew nothing about it'. 'I did only what I was told to do'. There are in fact a whole number of excuses that are typical for functionaries within complex organisations and that are constantly being used. If they really were all valid, there would not be much room left over for the individual model of accountability.

Ten excuses

More insight into the extent to which corporate conduct is reducible to personal conduct can, therefore, be gained by looking at a number of the excuses that are commonly used by individual functionaries to clear themselves of the charge of individual accountability. The greater the number of valid excuses, the less the value of the individual model for the control of complex organisations. I confine myself to a discussion of ten of the most frequently used excuses. These are not hierarchically ordered as a sort of top ten – I have done no research into the extent to which each of these various excuses is differentially used – but are, as far as possible, classified on the basis of the various criteria for responsibility-as-accountability. The first seven excuses are used above all to demonstrate the absence of any causal connection. The eighth, ninth, and tenth excuse (and sometimes the fifth), are mostly used to throw doubt on the blameworthiness of the action.[4]

1. *I was just a small cog in a big machine.* This is the excuse of the negligible contribution. It more or less comes down to a quantitative variant on the problem of many hands. It may perhaps be that the actual instance of corporate conduct was very bad, but so many functionaries were involved in it that the separate contribution of each functionary was actually, and therefore also morally, negligible. This is the excuse that each of the 'Harmless Torturers' could put forward. It suggests that minuscule, imperceptible or hardly perceptible, contributions to breaches of the norm are not morally relevant. The indefensibility of this excuse is convincingly demonstrated by Derek Parfit (1984: 78–82). Acceptance of this excuse would lead to highly absurd and contradictory conclusions.

To show that it is wrong, Parfit makes a comparison with what he calls

---

[4] As elsewhere in this chapter, I am indebted for several of these excuses and points of view to the excellent article by Thompson (1980, 1987: ch. 2).

the 'Bad Old Days'. In those days, 1,000 torturers each had their own victim. At the start of the day, these victims already feel a slight degree of pain. Each torturer then turns the knob of an instrument of torture slightly higher, and repeats the operation 1,000 times. Each increase intensifies the pain felt by the victim but without the victim noticing the increase. After the knob has been turned 1,000 times, however, the victim experiences great pain. In this example, it would be absurd to conclude from the fact that each turn of the knob does not perceptibly increase the pain that each torturer should be allowed to go free. When we then look at the 'Harmless Torturers', each of whom turns the knob only once in the case of each one of the 1,000 victims, there are two possibilities. One could refute this excuse, to start with, by referring to the total effect of all the immeasurable small increases in the level of pain. To do that, however, we must assume that it is indeed possible to increase someone's pain by an inappreciable extent: 'If we believe this, we can claim: "By pressing the button, each torturer causes each victim to suffer slightly more. The effect on each is slight. But, since each torturer adds to the suffering of a thousand victims, each torturer imposes a great total sum of suffering. Since the victims suffer just as much as they did in the Bad Old Days, each torturer is acting just as wrongly as he used to do"' (1984: 80).

But even if we are not prepared to accept this argument, the torturers still do not go free. For that, we must make an appeal to the total effect of all the torturers. Even when the individual torturers cause no one any particular pain, together they cause a very large amount of suffering to each of the 1,000 victims:

> We can claim: 'When (1) the outcome would be worse if people suffer more, and (2) each of the members of some group could act in a certain way, and (3) they would cause other people to suffer if enough of them act in this way, and (4) they would cause these people to suffer most if they all act in this way, and (5) each of them both knows these facts and believes that enough of them will act in this way, then (6) each would be acting wrongly if he acts in this way.'
>
> (Parfit 1984: 81)

The 'Harmless Torturers' can therefore not exonerate themselves; even the small cog-wheels bear a moral responsibility for the whole machine. In this respect the problem of many hands is perhaps a practical, but certainly not a moral problem.

2. Other people did much more than I did. This is the excuse of inequitable distribution. Solely the big fishes belong in the net; only when no more big fishes are available do the small fishes come in for consideration. It is similar to the previous excuse, yet has a somewhat different tone. The implicit presupposition in this excuse is that in fact only that functionary who contributed the most to the collective conduct is responsible. It is an excuse that is often connected with choosing a scapegoat that is then loaded up with all the blame and sent into the desert in order to do penance on behalf of the collective as a whole. In the context of an individual model of accountability, however, there is scant reason to accept such an excuse. Just as in the case of the first excuse, it remains true that a small contribution to evil is an evil contribution. The fact that one has played a smaller role than others signifies at most that one should be held accountable to a lesser extent; it does not imply an absence of accountability – providing at least that all the criteria have been met.

Having arrived at this point, we should ask ourselves to what extent the individual model is satisfactory from the perspective of *social justice*. In the hierarchical model, responsibility is laid exclusively at the door of those individuals within the organisation who – however relatively – have most power at their disposal. The advantages and disadvantages of responsibility are kept in reasonable balance. Those with the best jobs, highest salaries, and the most powers also run the biggest risks of being called externally to account. In the individual model, all that would seem to be divided up much less fairly. The lower functionaries are also externally liable, without however having at their disposal corresponding powers and freedoms to influence policy making. And what is even more important, they often also have far fewer possibilities to exculpate themselves or to escape their responsibility. In the case of a very strict application of the individual model the danger is real that the 'small organisation man' is subjected to a disproportionately heavy burden, while those at the top get away with whatever they have done.[5] A very strict interpretation of the model of individual accountability can therefore suffer from the same 'intemperance' that marred the collective forms of accountability.

This objection does not yet make the excuse valid, but it does demand the necessary attention. Fortunately individual models, unlike the collective forms of accountability, are equipped with a brake on such overloading. Functionaries are held responsible only as far as their possibilities and powers reach. Such social inequalities would have to be accepted by forums in the course of their deliberations. This factor would also have to be taken into account in instituting internal structures and external processes of accountability.

---

[5] Cf. Fisse and Braithwaite (1993: 50–7).

3. *If I had not done it, someone else would.* This is what Thompson calls 'the excuse from alternative cause' (1980: 909). It appeals to the impersonal character of most positions within complex organisations. For the organisation, it often makes no difference who does something, as long as it happens. Take for example the case of the young researcher who works in the laboratory of a big tyre factory on testing a new product, a new aeroplane tire, which is extremely important for the survival of the enterprise. If he refuses to draw up a report that says that the new aeroplane tyres are under all circumstances safe, while the tests have shown otherwise, then someone else is immediately found who has fewer scruples and is only too happy to take the place of his more principled colleague.[6] So why risk dismissal when to do so would have not the slightest influence on the result?

This argument may perhaps be factually true, but in moral respect it is not tenable. After all, it could be bounced like a ping-pong ball through the whole organisation. Each functionary could employ this excuse, either to stay on in his job or to take the place of somebody else, so that in the end no one is ultimately responsible. The mistake in this kind of reasoning is that the alternative cause, the less scrupulous functionary, will not be responsible for his choice. He is responsible, however, in the same measure as those who stayed on in their jobs – and perhaps even more so, since he should have been warned by the moral scruples of his predecessor. Therefore, this excuse was also unacceptable in trials against war criminals and collaborators, where it was often heard (cf. Arendt 1964; 1965).

4. *Even without my contribution it would have happened.* Sometimes a functionary will argue that it would have made no difference whether or not *he* did it, because his behaviour was not relevant in causal respect. Even if he had acted differently, the challenged event would still have taken place, for example because other functionaries have also performed acts that were in themselves already sufficient to bring about the event. This is the excuse of 'dispensability' (French 1984: 71). Applied to the tyre factory: the falsified test results were not in the long run important in the decision-making, because the management of the factory had bribed those who commissioned the project in the first place and had thus already ensured the safe passage of the project.

This excuse is in itself not without value. If no causal connection can be demonstrated between an action and the challenged event, we will not hold a functionary responsible. However, a problem is that the absence of any

---

[6] Cf. on this point the experiences of Kermit Vandivier, as described in Ermann and Lundman (1982b: 102–22).

causal connection cannot always be demonstrated. It is not so easy to show that the falsified test results really did not play a role in the decision-making. They were perhaps used by the corrupt clients to soothe their conscience and made it easier for the management of the tyre factory to win them over. Furthermore, the extent to which this excuse is accepted will depend partly on the nature of the transaction and on the extent to which the forum allows the eventual consequences to play a part in its judgment. Strict deontologists, for whom intentions are more important than consequences, are presumably inclined to impute a severe degree of blame to those functionaries who deliberately and knowingly neglect their duty or accept bribes, irrespective of whether or not this neglect of duty or bribe-taking has contributed to misconduct on the part of the organisation.

5. *Without my contribution, it would have been even worse.* This is the excuse of the lesser evil. The functionary argues that by remaining in his post he was best able to contribute to moderating the consequences of the challenged conduct. If he had not gone along with it, things would have been much worse. This is a highly treacherous excuse; after all, one can repeat it to oneself whenever a new measure is encountered. However, with each new step one finds oneself on ever more dubious terrain. After a while, it often turns out that one has compromised oneself to such an extent that it is no longer possible to emerge with clean hands.

Hirschman (1970) has analysed how in this way, particularly in organisations whose activities have a relatively broad public impact, a paradoxical and dramatic mechanism can come into operation. In the case of goods with a collective character, a functionary is not just producer but also consumer of those collective goods. If the quality of the goods does not please him, he can, by resigning his post, put an end to his role as producer; he cannot, however, escape his role as consumer. An official at the Ministry of Foreign Affairs, for example, is subject even after his dismissal, but then in his capacity as a citizen, to his share of the consequences of an immoral and bankrupt foreign policy. As long as he stays on, however, he is, unlike his fellow citizens, in a position to exercise a direct influence on the content of the policy. As fewer and fewer like-minded people remain in office and the quality of the performance deteriorates more and more, the positive effects of his staying on, for himself and for his fellow citizens, become relatively ever bigger and it becomes more and more rational for him to stay on in his job: 'The ultimate in unhappiness and paradoxical loyalist behaviour occurs when the public evil produced by the organization promises to accelerate or to reach some intolerable level as the organization deteriorates; then, in line with the reasoning just presented, the decision to exit will become ever more difficult the longer one fails to exit. The conviction that one has to stay to prevent the worst grows stronger all the time' (Hirschman 1970: 103).[7]

Yet the excuse of the lesser evil can, in certain circumstances, be quite plausible; there are certainly situations in which functionaries, by staying on, can prevent a great deal of evil.[8] So this excuse, just like the excuse of the alternative cause (3) to which it bears many similarities, cannot be dismissed immediately. However, the range of this excuse is restricted and for the most part less broad than those who put it forward themselves assume: 'Its weakness has always been that those who choose the lesser evil forget quickly that they choose evil' (Arendt 1964: 186). This forgetfulness in most cases serves functionaries well; with the help of an indirect demonstration – it is never possible to say exactly what would have happened if one had not cooperated – it is possible to justify keeping one's job and one's position of power. In judging this excuse, one should therefore be on the look-out for the presence of less noble motives, and for the great danger of moral inflation in the case of its repeated use.

The judgment regarding the validity of this excuse eventually has to depend on the nature of the functionary's conduct during the period for which the excuse has been advanced and on a consideration of the actual effects of his participation. It is not easy to provide general guidelines on this point. After all, it brings us onto the battleground on which the *Gesinnungsethiker* and the *Verantwortungsethiker* (Weber 1919) or, in British terms, the deontologists and the consequentialists and in particular the utilitarians (Williams 1973), fight out their many duels. I am myself inclined to adopt a position of moderate consequentialism, in so far as we

---

[7] This excuse and all the dilemmas associated with it are clearly set out in a study by Derksen and Van der Sande on the conduct of Dutch mayors during the period of the German occupation (1984: 5–91). Many mayors defended the fact that they remained in office, and, as a consequence, cooperated with the Germans, with the argument that in that way they remained in a position from which they were able to soften the effects of German measures on the civilian population, or even, if the opportunity arose, to sabotage them. People often also argued that by keeping their posts, they could at least prevent a member of the NSB, the Dutch Nazi party, from being appointed, and thus kept out of office men and women who doubtless would have implemented German measures with greater zeal and passion. Without meaning to, however, these mayors became more and more caught up in the policy of the occupiers. Step by step the measures, which they started out by implementing with repugnance in order to prevent even worse things happening, became ever less innocent and resignation an ever remoter prospect.

[8] Derksen and Van der Sande (1984: 34) ascertained, for example, that some mayors who remained at their posts during the occupation managed to take the edge off many German measures and sometimes even to sabotage them.

are dealing with the actions of functionaries working within complex organisations. In the public sphere, for civil servants and politicians, this is in even more so the case (cf. Goodin 1985: 143).

6. *I had nothing to do with it.* This is the excuse of 'null cause' (Thompson 1980: 911). It is mostly advanced within organisations in order to justify a passive and negligent attitude. Functionaries who are asked why they did nothing about the challenged policy, or why they did not distance themselves from it, will tend to answer that it had nothing to do with them or that it could not be reckoned as part of their responsibilities (in the sense of tasks). If they had to worry about what everyone else was doing, they would have no time left over for their own work. There is some truth in this argument. We will not readily hold responsible someone who was not directly involved in the events leading up to the implementation of the offending policy. There must be some causal connection. One cannot hold functionaries to account for all the policies of their organisation on which they were perhaps able to exercise some influence.

There are, however, a number of situations and circumstances in which this excuse does not hold water. In extreme circumstances, in which mismanagement can have serious consequences for citizens or for society as a whole, one can be expected to go further than one's own tasks and powers reach: 'If many officials are not doing their jobs, others may be obliged to do more than their jobs. Even if all are doing their jobs, some officials may be obliged to do more if the circumstances are exceptional' (Thompson 1987: 56). One cannot always pass the buck by sticking to a formal standpoint such as 'it did not belong to my job description'. If one was aware of certain practices, or should have been aware of them, one can no longer simply absolve oneself of blame: 'Omissions, acquiescence, tacit approval, even ritualized opposition – all may gain one a place in the causal chain' (Thompson 1980: 911). The fact that someone neglects to protest internally or raise the alarm externally can be causally, and, at the same time, morally, highly relevant. Moral and often even legal duties include more than just meeting role obligations, even within bureaucratic organisations.[9]

7. *I wash my hands of the whole business.* This is the excuse of the *novus actus interveniens.* According to this excuse, the key to the negative events lay completely in someone else's hands. That person's decision has created a situation for which the responsibility belongs exclusively and unconditionally to him and thus spares the other functionary any blame. The suggestion is in this way conjured up that there is such a thing as a 'fixed pole of

[9] See further under the excuse of role-obligation (9).

responsibility, such that when one person's share goes up, another's must go down' (Thompson 1983: 554).

This excuse has at least two variants. In the first place, it is often used by consultants, policy analists, and advisors. They deliver their advice in complete freedom from all obligations; if a manager follows the advice, the manager is himself responsible; the consultants can be blamed for nothing. This variant of the excuse is not wholly without plausibility, but it is not tenable in such general and absolute terms. Generally speaking, it is true that an advisor carries less responsibility for a failed policy than the managers. However, the extent to which the advisor is absolved of blame will strongly depend on his position in the organisation, on his relationship to the managers, and on the extent to which, on the basis of that relationship, he himself could have foreseen that his advice would be followed. The fewer 'competitors' an advisor has, the greater his authority with the manager, and the fewer inhibitions he has in providing his advice, the greater is his responsibility. In the case of managers who are known to be unstable, the advisor's responsibility could be even bigger than that of the managers themselves.[10]

This excuse is sometimes also used a bit further up in the policy cycle, but then by the managers themselves. The classic example is Pontius Pilate, the Roman governor of Judea, who tried to escape his responsibility for the crucifixion of Christ by leaving the choice between Christ and Barabas to the crowd in front of his palace. They took the decision for him and he could wash his hands of it. Such a resort to a *novus actus interveniens* has over the centuries received little sympathy not just from theologians but also from moral and legal philosophers. The staging of such a decision-making ritual – one could conceivably even let the position of the stars or the flight of the crane decide one's destiny – does not, after all, absolve the manager from responsibility for the performance of the ritual itself. He remains responsible for the delaying and the pushing through of the challenged decisions. Pilate did not have to take refuge in a people's court, he had every possibil-

---

[10] Thompson, who in a separate article has subjected the responsibility of official
    advisers to more detailed research, comes to a provisional set of formal criteria:
        'From the idea of causal responsibility comes the criterion that holds an adviser
        responsible only if his advise would not have acted the way he did but for the
        advice (or its omission). That an adviser intended a certain result may be a
        further reason to criticize him, but such intent is not necessary to blame him for
        the result. An adviser is responsible for the consequences of decisions based on
        his advice insofar as he could reasonably be expected to foresee that they would
        follow from his advice. Finally, although the requirements of role can create a
        prima facie excuse, an adviser is responsible for any foreseeable harm his role-
        bound advice causes when that harm is greater than the harm that would result
        from breaching the requirements of his role' (Thompson 1983: 559).

ity of deciding for himself. This ultimate inescapable accountability on the part of the manager will be even greater to the extent that the outcome of the extra decision-making procedure is predictable, or open to manipulation by the manager.

8. *I knew nothing of it.* This is the excuse of ignorance. It can be used to excuse both negligence and participation. A functionary can claim that he was completely unaware that anything was going on and that therefore he could not have taken action internally or issued a warning externally. It can even be used to excuse active participation in corporate misconduct. Given the complex and barely transparent character of corporate conduct, it can all too often happen that an individual functionary could not have foreseen that his participation, or the policy of the organisation as a whole, would have such reprehensible consequences. As we shall see later, this is one of the important factors that might explain why everyday moral restrictions sometimes carry so little clout in the case of complex organisations.

If it can be established that the functionary held responsible really did not know and, moreover, that it was reasonable that he could not have known, or foreseen, that illicit activities were going on, then that fact absolves him of individual moral accountability. After all, the second criterion, the blameworthiness of the violation of the norm, is not satisfied. However, the sting is above all in the second part of the above-mentioned clause. It is not enough to say that a functionary really did know nothing. *It must also be reasonably apparent that he could not have known anything.* Unless one maintains such a requirement, people could shed their responsibility simply by sticking their heads ostrich-style in the sand. What the head does not know, the heart won't grieve over.

As we saw earlier, in the case of the hierarchical model, such an ostrich policy is not unusual within complex organisations. The Dutch Minister of Economic Affairs, Jan Terlouw, asked his officials to spare him as much as possible of the bad news about the RSV-Concern, so that he would not be forced to account for it. Stone pointed to similar mechanisms in American industry in which the top levels, often not without their own friendly cooperation, are consciously screened by the lower levels from certain types of information (1975: 53, 61–62). In the case of lower functionaries, one can point to the many civil servants, police officers, and soldiers in the Third Reich and in the occupied territories who decided that the best course of action at the time of the deportations of the Jews was to look the other way. We have seen in the case of the hierarchical model that a lack of information can be a real problem for the higher levels of the organisation. Managers are often outsiders. Shortly we shall also see that even lower functionaries, because of the composite character of many organisational actions and because the effects both in time and in place are often far removed, are not always aware of the actual consequences of their contributions. Even in those cases it is still true, however, that there are situations in which one should have realised that something was going on or could have gone wrong. 'In bureaucracies certain patterns of fault are common enough that we should expect any competent official to anticipate them and to take reasonable precautions to avoid them or at least to minimize their harmful consequences' (Thompson 1980: 913).

9. *I only did what I was told to do.* This is the excuse of role-obligation, which in its most extreme form is familiar as *Befehl ist Befehl* (orders are orders). Within complex organisations, functionaries are not free to do and not to do as they wish. They fulfil specific roles and each has his or her own often explicitly defined tasks and powers. Lower functionaries, that is to say, almost everybody within an organisation in one way or another, are subject to commands and assignments by the powers that be. These role obligations differ from everyday obligations and sometimes weigh more heavily. Officials in particular – think of police officers, tax collectors, and prison-warders – must often perform actions that are not permitted to common citizens and that would be experienced as reprehensible in private life or in relations between friends. This excuse implies that as long as they do not actually go beyond their authority and do what they are told to do, they cannot morally be reproached for their conduct.

Since 1945, since the trials in Nuremberg and Tokyo, however, it has become rather widely accepted that this excuse is untenable at least in the case of war crimes and crimes against humanity. Even soldiers in times of war, whose powers and obligations deviate most from those of ordinary citizens, cannot appeal to it.[11] Lieutenant Calley, in whose defence this excuse played a important part, had no success with it. In less extreme situations this excuse is also often found to be unacceptable. A functionary has more responsibilities than just his role-responsibility. In the event of a conflict of

[11] In Dutch military law, there is, for example, the rule that unlawful commands may not be followed if the recipient of them is thereby rendered guilty of a culpable act (art. 140 of the Dutch military code). If the person in receipt of the command assumes in good faith that it is a properly given order and the implementation of the order is, moreover, within his own competency, he cannot be found culpable. In the case of war crimes, however, this ground for exemption does not apply (Van den Bosch 1976: 23; 1981: 42–5). Similar conditions can also be found in most Western countries (cf. Levinson 1973). Israel seems to go further in this regard than any other country. In Israel, there is a law that says that soldiers who receive a manifestly unlawful command must, on pain of prosecution, report it to the competent bodies.

loyalties, the bureaucratic duties must sometimes yield to other duties that do not, or do not directly, flow from the aims of the organisation or the role that one has in it. Complex organisations could turn into unguided missiles if everyone stuck simply to his or her role obligations. At the level of the individual functionary, one can further refute this excuse by pointing to the fact that those role obligations did not come out of the blue. One person-ally chose to take up the function, with all the advantages and obligations that it entails, and one remains personally responsible for that choice and for all the actions that flow from it. Finally, one can point to the fact that each role, however strictly defined, allows the functionary a certain measure of freedom. An assignment can be performed in many different ways. That manner of performance can be morally very relevant and belongs com-pletely to the personal responsibility of the individual functionary. Overzealousness is also a choice.[12]

10. *I had no choice.* This is the excuse of social coercion, a variant on the previous excuse that is important enough to be treated separately. Again, the key question is whether or not the violation of the norm was blameworthy, the third element of responsibility-as-accountability. Crucial in this case is the availability of alternative forms of behaviour. As in the case of ordinary citizens, it is not realistic to expect functionaries to behave as moral heros. We cannot demand of people to exceed certain boundaries; we can at most cheer them on if they do so. In the case of functionaries, such a boundary is reached when we demand that they risk their life, health, or domestic happi-ness in order to prevent organisational deviance. In most Western democ-racies functionaries will usually not be forced by the threat or application of violence to cooperate in illegal or immoral practices on behalf of a bona fide organisation. Much more important are the subtle and often unspoken threats of disciplinary measures, of the forfeiture of chances of promotion, or of dismissal. Often these threats are not even made explicit, and 'trouble-makers' among the employees are driven by the exercise of social exclusion to hand in their resignations. Lieutenant Calley certainly had a point when he said that the refusal to obey a command in the hectic circumstances in which he and his battalion found themselves could have had serious conse-quences for him. However, it will depend on the degree of seriousness of the challenged corporate conduct and on the level of involvement of the func-tionary to what extent we will be prepared to accept such an excuse of social

---

[12] However, the acceptance of this excuse may depend on one's conception of responsibility-as-virtue. Supporters of hierarchical conceptions will accept this excuse in more situations and more readily than others (see also chapter 9).

coercion. In case of war crimes this excuse will be accepted less readily than in the case of doing business with South Africa under the apartheid regime. Moreover, in both cases the counter-argument of 'role-acceptance' can be advanced (Downie 1969: 68); one remains accountable for the fact that one got oneself into such a situation in the first place.

The large number of cases of 'whistleblowers' and other dissident functionaries who had to pay for their behaviour with transfer or dismissal, and the research into manifestations of 'groupthink', shows that this social coercion is a reality in many organisations (Coffee 1977: 1146; Williamson 1975: 146–147; Clinard and Yeager 1980: 66–67; Janis 1982; Ermann and Lundman 1982a: 118; Jackall 1988: 101–133).[13] Many functionaries, in particular the middle managers such as Calley, often come under enormous pressure:

> The middle manager is acutely aware that he can easily be replaced; he knows that if he cannot achieve a quick fix, another manager is waiting in the wings, eager to assume operational control over a division. The results of such a structure are predictable: when pressure is intensified, illegal or irresponsible means become attractive to a desperate middle manager who has no recourse against a stern but myopic notion of accountability that looks only to the bottom line of the income statement.
>
> (Coffee 1981: 398)

Research by Braithwaite into white-collar crime in the pharmaceutical industry produces a similar picture: 'The corporate world is littered with irresponsible companies which have responsible policies. One reason for this is that performance pressures often force middle managers to act irresponsibly if they are to achieve corporate goals' (Braithwaite 1985: 48). Functionaries fairly often end up in double or triple catch-22 situations. Sometimes impossible demands are posed by the service or the company that can be met only by illegal methods, while on the other hand one is also expected not to bring the organisation into difficulties. There is often a strong pressure on people to conform, to engage in loyal 'teamwork', often strengthened by 'groupthink' mechanisms and social pressure that make it particularly difficult to back out of reprehensible activities. On the other hand, one also runs the chance of being held responsible by the outside world, by members of the professional group, or the judicial apparatus, on account of one's loyalty to the organisation or the team. Finally, functionaries at the lower and middle levels do not always have exit-options (cf. Hunt 1982a, 1982b). That means that a resignation, whether or not voluntary, can also endanger one's obligations to one's relatives and family. A number of mutually contradictory duties and loyalties vie for precedence. This has

---

[13] For more on this, see chapters 10 and 11.

important consequences for the tenability of individual accountability in so far as it is applied to complex organisations.

In short, of the ten excuses that are often put forward by functionaries in order to talk their way out of individual accountability, most are not, or only in certain circumstances, tenable. Two of the excuses, however, form a serious threat. The excuse of ignorance (8) can be acceptable, certainly in the case of complex actions and untransparent activities that stretch over the long term and across great distances. The biggest threat to an individual model of accountability, however, is formed by the last excuse, the excuse of social coercion. The hierarchical relationships within complex organisations, the powerful social pressure to conform to the aims and practices of the organisation, and manifestations of 'groupthink' and 'peer-group pressure' can form real obstacles for individual functionaries who intend to act in a morally acceptable way. An obligation to behave heroically is, however, untenable. A second conclusion should therefore be that a certain measure of internal openness, the possibility to voice dissident opinions and the existence of places of refuge within the organisation could be important conditions for adapting individual schemes of accountability to the functioning of normal complex organisations. If these conditions are not satisfied, then individual accountability quickly leads to a situation in which too much is morally asked of people and in which the 'small organisation man' is held disproportionately heavily to account.

The impotence of private morality

The problem of many hands is, however, not just a practical and a moral problem, but also an *issue of control*. The question then also arises as to how far individual accountability is adequate from a controlling point of view. Does it contribute to the prevention of the 'corporate risks'? Does the individual model enlarge the learning capacity and the adroitness of complex organisations? At first sight the answer to these questions is certainly yes. After all, we had already reached the conclusion that passive responsibility – accountability after the event – and active responsibility – taking responsibility – are closely bound up with one another. The chance that one might be called to account for one's individual contribution to the illicit or morally reprehensible conduct of an organisation after the event can exert a strong positive influence on the conduct of individual functionaries beforehand. Clinical-psychological research would appear to confirm this thesis. Accountability will, under certain circumstances, lead to more complex information processing and to more complex decision strategies (Tetlock 1983; Weldon and Gargano, 1988).

The implicit presupposition of the model of individual accountability is therefore that (the chance of) individual accountability leads to the internalisation of norms of behaviour that, in their turn, lead to responsible conduct. Whether this mechanism always works in daily life is a question that can here be left hanging. More important is the fact that a number of indications would seem to show that when, and in so far as, individuals operate within institutional or hierarchical frameworks they are often less sensitive to those internalised moral norms than they would be in their personal life. As Robert Michels put it many years ago: 'The bureaucratic spirit corrupts character and engenders moral poverty' (Michels 1962 [1915]: 191). The moral barriers that hold natural persons back from doing harm to others are often far lower when individuals operate within the framework of a complex organisation than in private life.

An extreme but classic example of someone who was a prudent citizen in his private life, but within the framework of a complex organisation lost his capacity for moral reflection is Adolf Eichmann, as he is described by Hannah Arendt (1965). In her view, Eichmann was neither a sinister psychopath nor a ruthless criminal, but rather a terrifyingly 'ordinary' person without any criminal past, indeed, in many respects a model civil servant – at most perhaps a little on the over-ambitious side. Intuitively Arendt's conclusion that 'the trouble with Eichmann was precisely that so many were like him, and that the many were neither perverted nor sadistic, that they were, and still are, terribly and terrifyingly normal' (1965: 276) is more convincing, however hope-destroying, than the archetypical image of the satanic mastermind. In Arendt's opinion, there is not an Eichmann in every one of us, but the difference between him and us is less large than we would perhaps wish it to be. Her conclusions on this point are confirmed by the notorious research carried out by Milgram. His conclusion was unequivocal:

> After witnessing hundreds of ordinary people submit to the authority in our own experiments, I must conclude that Arendt's conception of the *banality of evil* comes closer to the truth than anyone might dare imagine. The ordinary person who shocked the victim [with electricity] did so out of a sense of obligation [. . .] and not of any particular aggressive tendencies. This is perhaps the most fundamental lesson of our study: ordinary people, simply doing their jobs, and without any particular hostility on their part, can become agents in a terrible destructive process. Moreover, even when the destructive effects of their work become patently clear, and they are asked to carry out actions incompatible with fundamental standards of morality, relatively few people have the resources needed to resist authority.
>
> (Milgram 1974: 6)

The thesis that within authoritarian and hierarchical frameworks most people lose much of their sensitivity for the moral values that help prevent injury to others has been the theme of a number of analyses by philosophers, criminologists, and organisation sociologists (Barnard 1938: 275–278; Nagel 1978; Macintyre 1981: 24–29, 71–75; Van Gunsteren 1974: 5–6; Clinard and Yeager 1980: 63–68; Jackall 1988; Ermann and Lundman 1982a). Similar patterns can be found in the partly autobiographical descriptions of the course of events that led to the Watergate scandal (Magruder 1974: 219–220). It is also confirmed by several psychological experiments. The large measure of obedience that Milgram found in his research was, it seemed, no mere accident. Replica research performed in the United States and elsewhere led to similar conclusions. A strong measure of obedience within authoritarian frameworks would appear to be a consistent and cross-cultural phenomenon (Robbins 1980: 237–239; Meeus and Raaijmakers 1984: 35–40, 185; Kelman and Hamilton 1989).

Some people have objected that in the case of the experiments by Milgram and some of his successors the high degree of obedience must be attributed above all to the way in which the experiments were set up. Milgram looked at how far experimental test subjects in a laboratory, in the framework of a scientific experiment, were prepared to administer electric shocks to third persons. This is an extreme situation that can hardly be found in the course of daily life. In order to find out whether Milgram's results also had external validity, Meeus and Raaijmakers (1984) developed an experimental procedure that closely approximates to everyday conditions in complex organisations. In the course of their experiments, test subjects had to apply torture, but only of a psychological-administrative sort, to an applicant for a job. Supposedly acting on behalf of the government, an institute was required to select candidates for a number of positions. The decisive element in the selection was a psychological test. The test subjects were involved in this selection procedure and had to subject an applicant to the test. It was pointed out to him or her beforehand that the result would be decisive for the approval of the applicant. However, as the test progressed, the test subject was required to make comments and ask questions of an ever more negative character. As a result of these humiliations, the applicant was put under ever greater psychological pressure and he or she eventually flunked and lost the job. The degree of obedience demonstrated, however, was even greater in this experiment than in that organised by Milgram. More than 90 per cent of the test subjects were prepared to go through with the harangue to the bitter end, although it was obvious to them that in so doing, they seriously jeopardised the chances of the applicant. They tried to reduce the conflict of loyalty to which the experience gave rise by conducting themselves in the most official and detached way possible toward the applicants, while they laid the responsibility for the disadvantaging of the applicant principally at the door of the person conducting the experiment (Meeus and Raaijmakers 1984: 221–252).

Why does the internal brake of conscience fail to work when natural persons 'who were usually model citizens in their private lives' (Magruder 1974: 318) act within the framework of a complex organisation? Why are people sometimes not prepared or able to put themselves in the position of the outside world or of the victims? From the (autobiographical) descriptions, the psychological experiments, and the philosophical analyses, it is possible to distil a number of implicit – and tentatively relevant – factors.

> The contribution of an individual functionary to the conduct of an organisation will often be relatively small and unclear in relation to the eventual outcome. Although the sum total of actions can have disastrous or immoral consequences, each individual functionary is often only confronted with relatively slight transgressions. This fragmentation, in combination with the fact that the majority of functionaries rarely has an overview of the whole range of activities developed by the organisation, fails to elicit moral scruples and guilt feelings (cf. Ermann and Lundman 1982a: 43–46, 116–117; Vaughan 1983: 90).

> Another important factor is the fact that the complex bureaucratic structure of many organisations creates a large distance between an individual functionary and any possible victims, or the actual damage, that result from the action. That distance is in the first place physical in nature. Many functionaries do not, or not immediately, get to see, the negative consequences of their decisions, because they were not involved in the actual implementation of the policy or because the damage becomes visible only after a long time or at a large geographical distance (Ermann and Lundman 1982a: 72–73; Stone 1975: 67–68). Moreover, this physical distance, the routine character of many actions, the high degree of division of labour, and the compartmentalised character of the conduct of organisations often produces a large psychological distance (Lachs 1978: 206–212; Jackall 1988: 126–127; Kelman and Hamilton 1989: 18). The individual functionary is hardly aware of the nature and the seriousness of the consequences of his action and is not invited by the structure of the organisation to render account of himself. Both elements can contribute in important ways to the passivity of his conscience.[14]

---

[14] This factor is presumably also important in the case of Eichmann – although it is not explicitly mentioned by any of the commentators. Eichmann was an organiser who did not always act from behind his desk – a great deal of negotiating was necessary – yet even so he maintained some physical and psychological distance from the actual murders. Notwithstanding desperate efforts on his part, the procurator-general did not succeed in proving that Eichmann was ever actually involved in a murder. On the contrary, according to his own admission, he could not bear the sight of the executions and avoided them as much as possible (Arendt 1965: 89; Herzberg 1962: 114–15). Only the distance that his bureaucratic organisation created between him and his victims allowed him to do his work. This

An important factor in the case of Eichmann, according to Arendt, was the fact that he was never, either within his own organisation or outside it, confronted with dissident voices that might have raised doubts in his mind concerning the moral acceptability of his actions. 'As Eichmann told it, the most potent factor in the soothing of his own conscience was the simple fact that he could see no one, no one at all, who actually was against the Final Solution' (Arendt 1965: 116; see also 126, 136, 176). This element can also be found in other, less extreme cases. A permissive climate within the organisation, a large measure of involvement, and strong loyalty to one's superior and one's colleagues are climatic factors that are not particularly conducive to the emergence of doubt and dissident voices (Magruder 1974: 317; Ermann and Lundman 1982a: 47; Stone 1975: 69). The social-psychological experiments also point to the importance of the presence of dissident voices. As soon as test subjects are confronted with group members who break the consensus, their readiness to go obediently about their assignments rapidly fades (Kelman and Hamilton 1989: 158).

Social and cultural factors can also play an important part. Arendt points to the vulgar Kantian notion, at the time widely accepted in Germany, according to which people as citizens should not only obey the law 'but should act as though one were the legislator of the laws that one obeys'. This notion led to a strong degree of identification with the authority, in this case the Führer, and a strong emphasis on extreme devotion to duty (Arendt 1965: 137). Kelman and Hamilton (1989) also strongly emphasise the role that structures of authority and authorisation play in criminal forms of obedience.

The power of judgment can be further undermined by a bureaucratic culture within which a strong emphasis is placed on secrecy and euphemistic language. *Sprachregelungen* (language rules) imposed from above can prevent things being called by their true names and can lead to a dehumanisation of the victims. This makes it easier for people to avoid confronting norms of conscience that may arise when one employs the current terms from daily usage ('murder', 'extermination', 'fraud' , 'burglary') with their negative moral charge (Arendt 1965: 86; Ermann and Lundman 1982a: 87; Kelman and Hamilton 1989: 19).

A lack of insight into the nature and moral status of one's own activities can also be the result of slow habituation and a 'one-step-at-a-time-involve-

---

is a factor that also seemed to lead to significant differences in the experiments conducted by Milgram. Milgram varied the degree of contact between the interrogator and the victim. Apparently fewer – though still many – interrogators were prepared to carry on to the end if there was more contact ('feedback') between the interrogator and the 'victim'. Confronted with the audible, visible, or even tangible consequences of their actions, people seemed in general to apply the voltage for shorter periods of time (Milgram 1974: 32–43).

ment' (Ermann and Lundman 1982a: 46). Assignments whose dubious character is not evident can gradually acquire an ever more fraudulent or immoral character, without one at first being aware of the slippery slope that opens up before one. The individual functionary who dutifully cooperates, however, quickly finds himself in such a compromising situation that it seems as if the way back is closed.[15] In the social-psychological literature, this phenomenon is known as the 'foot-in-the-door' technique (Meeus and Raaijmakers 1984: 159, 273). People who start out by complying with some small request are more prepared to honour a big request than those who are confronted at the very outset with the big request.

In many cases ambition – 'blind ambition', as Dean, one of the 'President's Men', expressed it – has an important part to play. Cooperation and obedience advance one's career. 'Corporate loyalty, obedience to one's superiors, and the desire to get ahead in salaries and bonuses are common justifications, offered for unethical and illegal behavior' (Clinard and Yaeger 1980: 274–275).[16] That obedience is, moreover, in far from all cases blind; not cooperating can in many cases mean the end of one's career and lead to disciplinary measures or dismissal, with all the consequences that such a fate can have for the personal well-being of those involved and their families.

Public organisations, finally, are a special case. Each of these factors can trouble the moral judgment both of civil servants and of private employees. Civil servants and political officials, however, also have to cope with a number of tasks and powers that, depending on their role and function, can differ strongly from the duties and powers of private employees and common citizens. On the one hand, civil servants, in their capacity as executors of public policy, have the power and often even the duty to perform actions that are not permitted to ordinary citizens or private employees. Civil servants draw up laws or implement them, some can give orders or apply force, others grant permits and subsidies, and close down establishments when the conditions are not properly observed; still others decide how much assistance a citizen shall receive. In all these things they are supported by the fact that the government has the monopoly on the use of force. On the other hand, civil servants also have duties that are much more stringent. They are often not permitted to work in ways that are quite commonly followed in business or among citizens. For example, civil servants are not

---

[15] See for a further description and appraisal of such moral snares the above-mentioned excuse of the lesser evil ('without my contribution it would have been even worse').

[16] Cf. Vandivier, in Ermann and Lundman (1982b: 102–22), and Jackall (1988: 49–56) on the importance of 'teamplaying'. See also Finney and Lesieur (1982: 276) on the role of the promotion process as a criminogene factor.

allowed to give friends and acquaintances preferential treatment or to accept gifts in exchange for their services. These extra public obligations, which are at loggerheads with the requirements of private morals, mean in the first place that civil servants are dealing with a more *complicated* system of moral norms. In the event of a moral conflict, civil servants cannot fall back on the familiar values of private morals. They must always take into account their public duties. In the second place, the fact that one plays a public role can, in combination with the special powers attached to that role, sometimes be very *tempting*. Holding public office can sometimes lead to a certain degree of 'moral insulation': 'The combination of special requirements and release from some of the usual restrictions, the ability to say that one is only following orders or doing one's job or meeting one's responsibilities, the sense that one is the agent of vast impersonal forces or the servant of institutions larger than any individual – all these ideas form a heady and sometimes corrupting brew' (Nagel 1978: 76).[17]

These observations give rise to a third conclusion: the structure of many complex organisations and the social and psychological processes that come with it can seriously undermine the preventive force of general models of individual accountability. Mechanisms of calling to account and moral norms that have proved their efficacy in daily life cannot simply be transplanted onto the individual actions of functionaries within complex organisations. 'It seems probable that moral deterioration and loss of personal responsibility is more frequent among executives, especially in political organizations, than among other persons' (Barnard 1938: 278). If one wishes by way of individual accountability also to promote active responsibility, responsibility in the sense of 'virtuous' conduct, then extra conditions must often be satisfied. One of the most important conditions would seem to be that there is room for moral reflection within the organisation. This requires space for dissident voices, calling things by their real names, and achieving clarity concerning the nature and the consequences of the actions of the organisation and the contribution that individual partial actions make toward them.

---

[17] Nagel concentrated in his analysis of the weakness of private morals on the fact that it involved public functionaries and therefore asked himself the question what it specifically is about public office that confronts us with such moral puzzles. In his view, 'The great modern crimes are public crimes' (1978: 75). In the light of the rise of complex organizations as social actors, and the associated rise of 'corporate risks', however, I am more inclined to find the incorporation and above all the bureaucratic organisational structure more important. I would therefore rather say: 'The great modern crimes are corporate crimes'. After all, what is new is not the fact that public norms have another content or effect (think of the work of St Augustine or of Machiavelli), but, as Nagel himself indicates, the scale, extent and institutional character of these 'public crimes'.

The demanding nature of responsibility

Responsibility does not always bring joy in its wake. On the contrary, it goes together both in the passive and in the active form with stress, anxiety, and a certain amount of self-sacrifice. From the passive form, responsibility-as-accountability, some functionaries, as we have just seen, will gain precious little. For the lower levels of many complex organisations, the introduction of a strictly individual model of accountability will mean that their anxiety increases while, in principle, their terms of employment and room for action remain the same. At every step they run the risk that they may later be held responsible and that they will be required to undergo a tiring and often painful process of being brought to account. When personal accountability is rigorously assigned, while organisational relationships remain unchanged, apathy and anxiety are likely to be the result: 'In short, neither men of weak responsibility nor those of limited capability can endure or carry the burden of many simultaneous obligations of different types. If they are 'overloaded', either ability, responsibility, or morality, or all three, will be destroyed' (Barnard 1938: 272). Just as in the case of the other models, individual accountability can all too often lead to reticent behaviour, to the shifting of tasks onto others, and to other forms of risk-avoiding conduct. Many people will no longer be able to summon up the courage to take important decisions or to suggest creative but not entirely risk-free solutions; individual functionaries will as much as possible try to shield themselves against mistakes; and decision-making will be dilatory and happen in strict accordance with the rules.

The workings of the machinery of government in Nepal, as described by Wildavsky (1972), are a good example of the disastrous consequences of an all too strictly enforced system of accountability on the part of functionaries. In theory, the average Nepalese official is extraordinarily ready to help out his circle of clients. However, he does not take the slightest degree of independent initiative. He only acts on the basis of concrete and explicit orders from above. Without those, everything comes to a halt. Because this attitude is present at all levels of the machinery of government, it is extraordinarily difficult to get anything done by the Nepalese authorities – which is a great frustration of many Western development workers and businessmen.

What is the background to this extreme 'bureaucratic' behaviour? Wildavsky seeks an explanation in the history of the Nepalese machinery of government. Right up until the Second World War, at the time of the Rana dynasty, no distinction was made between the government budget and the royal treasury. When an official wanted money for a project, it was fully available, but the expenditure was tied to strict rules and the official was answerable with his own income – and that of his children to the seventh generation – for the legitimacy of the expenditure. The consequences were predictable: 'To most people it seemed better to pass by the opportunity to take initiative if that also meant responsibility for money' (1972: 521). This old Rana tradition has largely been taken over by the modern government administration; as a result, nowadays most civil servants steer clear of showing any creativeness or initiative: 'There can be no spending unless someone wants to take responsibility for it. But history militates against responsibility, that is, against the prospect of taking the blame' (1972: 522). And if any expenditure is made, the main worry is about the legitimacy of the expenditure and not about its efficacy. Individual accountability hangs like a mill-stone around the neck of the individual official and paralyses his ability to act:

> Suppose that in a thirty-year period of service he makes one or two mistakes. His career will be severely damaged. He knows that only by making decisions he can be blamed, thus mortgaging his and his family's future. The easiest thing, the most certain thing, the most rational thing is to maintain his future welfare by doing nothing. If a file reaches him calling for a decision, he can try to find some reason it belongs in another jurisdiction. If that fails, he can find a reason to reject any proposal in it that might lead him to take action. He can seek an ad hoc committee in which all members can avoid personal responsibility or he can find something that makes the matter such that it should go to a higher authority for signature and thus possible blame. Should all these expedients fail, he will try to hold on to the file as long as possible in the hope it will be forgotten or that events will overtake it. Decisions involving responsibility for money are to be avoided most of all.
>
> (Wildavsky 1972: 521–522)

This demanding nature of responsibility is one more reason why the controlling power of individual forms of accountability should not be overrated. Individual responsibility sometimes offers too little, but it can also ask too much.

Research by Adelberg and Batson (1978) seems moreover to suggest that in situations in which resources are scarce, a large measure of passive responsibility can lead to an inefficient distribution of those resources. The two researchers constructed a situation in which test subjects had to distribute scholarships to impecunious students, while there was not enough money to guarantee a reasonable grant to all those applicants who satisfied the formal requirements. It seemed that those who knew that they would have to account for their decisions after the event, regardless of whether this accounting was to be to the students or to the grant-givers, made much less efficient use of the scarce resources at their disposal than those who did not realise that their actions would be scrutinised. The first group tried to forestall any possible dissatisfaction (and any criticism of their own behaviour) by giving each applicant approximately the same amount. However, that procedure led to a situation in which most students received a grant that was so low that they had no real chance of continuing with their studies. The other group, however, felt itself under less pressure to honour the principle of equality and made a clear choice. They gave the applicants who were most in need of support a grant that was large enough to enable them to continue with their studies; the rest got nothing. Instead of everybody getting too little, some received enough. A small measure of accountability thus led to a more efficient use of the funds.[18]

This gives rise to a fourth conclusion: in situations in which functionaries have few resources and little power, a large measure of external individual accountability can be quite counterproductive. Individual accountability should therefore be employed within complex organisations with the necessary degree of care. An all too facile resort to passive responsibility diverts the attention of functionaries to the question of their own self-preservation and their own careers, rather than to the real needs of their clients or their organisation.

Preconditions and possibilities

On the basis of these four conclusions, we can now formulate a number of conditions that are necessary for an individual model of accountability to be adequate and morally acceptable as one of the ways of facing up to the problem of many hands.

a. *Outsiders must be offered a genuine possibility of determining the individual contribution of individual functionaries.*
b. *Within the organisation, individual functionaries must have a genuine possibility of forming a judgment as to the nature and the consequences of the activity of the organisation as a whole and of their own contribution in particular.*
c. *Individual functionaries must have the possibility of behaving responsibly; they must have the opportunity of withdrawing from the internal social pressure and the resulting conflicts of loyalty.*
d. *Individual responsibility should not be allowed to lead to excessive demands on the 'small organisation man'.*

Here too, the question remains: What to do? Which strategies could one follow in order to be able to meet these conditions? We have seen that most of the objections against an individual model have to do with the compli-

---

[18] This mechanism can also be found in the research of Jackall (1988: 77–82).

cated, obscure, and hierarchical structure of complex organisations. The introduction of a greater measure of individual responsibility would therefore have to be paired with internal changes. I will look more closely at three possibilities.

1. *Clarification of the lines of responsibility.* The practical problem of the unravelling of corporate behaviour is to an important extent a result of the long and complicated lines of responsibility. Everyone is responsible to a degree, every functionary or department that is involved in the behaviour forms as it were a single link in one big chain. Without each discrete link, there would be no chain, but each link seems no more than a negligible and interchangeable part of the whole chain. However, to employ another metaphor, one could arrange the structure of responsibility as a series of *sluices* placed one after the other. By means of such a construction the responsibility is not partial but cumulative; each department or functionary is completely responsible for passing on the mistakes made in the policy or production process by the earlier upstream sluices.

James Coleman (1982: 106–107) has called this innovation 'backward policing'. He gives as the most important example the production process in the Honda car factories, which leads to far fewer production errors than in the factories of other car manufacturers. The assembly line at Honda is divided up into a number of departments. At the entrance of each department there is an inspector who belongs to that department. He or she controls the accessories, the wheels, the doors, the seats, and the rest of the equipment that arrives from other departments and has the power to turn them down when they do not meet the standards. The approved and accepted accessories are then processed and sent through to the next department where another inspector is waiting who can, in his turn, refuse the new part. The bonuses that each worker can earn are dependent on the extent and quality of the production of the particular department. In this way, each department, in the form of its inspector, has an interest in ensuring that the in-coming accessories do not have any defects; after all, one is oneself responsible for the next phase. Any diminution in quality is immediately noted and the problem that the top levels of the company, or other outsiders, are not in a position to check the quality of all parts of the production process is to a certain extent overcome. The monitoring no longer takes place from the top down but from back to front, and on the basis of a finished product.

The public sector too could benefit from such a strategy. Regulation would become more transparent and effective if executive organs, those that have to work with the (semi-finished) product, have the chance to raise objections against unsound parts. Such a procedure could also introduce a degree of consolation into the precarious position of many street level bureaucrats, who are often caught between the abstract, unclear, and sometimes downright unworkable regulations set by the powers that be and the concrete claims and frustrations of their clients.

Another possibility of clarifying the lines of responsibility for outsiders (which Coleman also mentions and which in the meantime has begun to find rather general acceptance in business) is the *personification* of products and actions. More and more companies have adopted the habit of marking the packaging of their products with the name of the person who was in charge of a particular product or of checking it. In the service sector, for example in big hotels, banks, and insurance companies, the name of the person who provides a particular service is often expressly mentioned on name-cards, on the telephone, or on letters. This procedure is in the first place intended as an appeal to the employee's sense of responsibility and to increase the level of commitment of the personnel, but it also has the effect that customers are informed of the name of the person they are dealing with in case they have complaints. A similar proposal emanated from the Dutch National Ombudsman in reaction to a complaint about the conduct of the tax service. The Ombudsman suggested that everyone who issues a request should be given an answer that provides the function, name, and signature of the relevant official. The only exception that he made was for standard letters that are sent out in large numbers. Stone (1985: 18) gives yet another, more radical example. The FDA, the American Food and Drugs Administration, has made it obligatory for pharmaceutical companies to institute internal procedures so that it is possible for those people responsible for products to be directly informed of the activities of the FDA that specifically relate to their products. In this way, it is no longer necessary to go via the top, a road that is long, time-consuming, and subject to all sorts of disturbances; instead, one can get in touch with the relevant individual employees directly.

2. *Extension of the personal accountability of civil servants and employees.* When managers are outsiders, insiders become important. One could, for example, make it easier for outsiders to hold lower functionaries accountable for their contribution. As the personification of corporate action increases, more possibilities of that sort naturally arise. Moreover, the research carried out by Meeus and Raaijmakers (1984: 275–284) suggests that the introduction of an element of legal accountability has important consequences for the degree of obedience. When test subjects were asked at the start of the experiment to sign a declaration in which they admitted full legal liability for any disadvantaging of the candidate, 40 per cent refused even to begin with the test and only 30 per cent went the whole way. When

they were asked to do so well in advance and by letter, as many as 70 per cent refused to take part in the selection of applicants and only 20 per cent were completely obedient. If, on the other hand, test subjects received a letter that explicitly mentioned that the institute indemnified test subjects against all legal liability for any disadvantageous consequences that the test might have for the applicants, only 20 per cent refused to take part and the number of those who were completely obedient rose to more than 66 per cent (1984: 285–299).

One possible form that this might take in the public sphere is an accountability of civil servants to Parliament. One could for example consider giving the ordinary, standing parliamentary committees broader powers to question civil servants outside the presence of the minister. The traditional constitutional system of accountability, both in the Netherlands and the United Kingdom, does not recognise an independent accountability of civil servants to parliament: 'the accountability of civil servants is absorbed by the responsibility of ministers to Parliament' (Turpin 1994: 438). However, in both countries the rise of independent executive agencies and non-departmental public bodies – agencies that allow for an increased delegation of responsibility to individual civil servants – has led to a call for the introduction of a certain measure of parliamentary accountability on the part of civil servants (Tuurenhout 1992; O'Toole and Chapman 1995).

How far should this accountability go? Here too it is useful to distinguish between different phases of accounting.[19] In the first place, one could open up the possibility for parliamentary committees to ask civil servants to provide them with factual information about all those technical matters that have been delegated to the civil-service apparatus. More concretely: the legal, financial, and administrative details of policy proposals or of the way in which they have been implemented. Obviously there are limits to this provision of technical information. Just as is presently the case with the ministerial duty to inform, the interests of the state or the right of citizens to privacy can mean that parliament adopts a rather reserved attitude where confidential information is concerned. Even now it often happens that sensitive information in areas such as foreign affairs, national safety, defence, and policing are not provided, or are provided only in camera.

Things become more difficult when civil servants are held accountable for policy choices. After all, at this point we enter terrain that ministers can reasonably be expected to cover. In chapter 6 it was established that the hierarchical model is tenable and useful in case of setting forth general policy

---

[19] It would, for example, also be of some help in creating order in the chaos surrounding parliamentary accountability for the Next Step Agencies, which O'Toole and Chapman (1995) noted.

lines within the organisation. In the phase of decision making when parliament tries to form a judgment about bills, draft laws, and various white papers, the ministers should therefore be the first to be held accountable. They must moreover be offered the chance to defend themselves as well as possible, without fear of being played off against their civil servants. That implies, for example, that civil servants cannot, at that stage, be asked to provide information about their policy advice and have discussions with the minister about the deliberations and decision-making in the cabinet without the consent of their minister.[20] However, in the case of parliamentary evaluation of policy that has already been implemented, things are different. In that phase it is quite conceivable that civil servants too will be asked to give information about the way in which the policy took shape and about the factual and political considerations that played a role in that process.

Does this also imply the introduction of parliamentary sanctions for civil servants? Does official accountability imply that parliament can dismiss civil servants when they are dissatisfied with the information that has been supplied or with the behaviour of the civil servants concerned? Not necessarily. Responsibility and sanctions are, it is true, narrowly connected, but not inextricably so. Processes of calling to account can take place in a meaningful way even if the forum itself does not impose any (formal) sanctions. Offical accountability in respect of parliament must, if the ministerial control of the administrative apparatus is to stay intact, remain restricted to the information phase and the debate phase. It should not extend as far as the sanction phase; that phase remains the domain of the politically responsible members of government. A similar situation already holds at present in the case of parliamentary inquiries in the Netherlands. The parliamentary committee gathers information, interrogates civil servants, and, through its report, sets the agenda for the parliamentary debate. Parliament judges the conduct of the minister, who in his turn can punish his civil servants (and subsequently can be held to account for it by Parliament). There must, of course, be a sanction on not appearing before parliament; in this way, Parliament forestalls that official accountability is all too easily evaded by civil servants.

3. *More room for active individual responsibility.* A major objection to an individual model of accountability is that it asks too much of the lower functionaries. This often validates the excuse of social coercion or ignorance. If forums nevertheless, for example because of the seriousness of the

---

[20] This would only be otherwise if it could reasonably be shown that important public interests were served by a disclosure. More about this in chapter 11.

consequences, hold functionaries to account, that will all too quickly lead to shifting the buck, apathy, and bureaucratic behaviour. There is a great chance that people will seek refuge in shadow dossiers, in informal networking, and in the shirking of responsibilities, as did the civil servants in Nepal. If one wishes to hold lower functionaries personally responsible for the conduct of their organisation, one must at the same time give them the opportunity to make that responsibility come true in the active sense.

It is especially important that individual civil servants or employees get more possibilities, both inside and outside their own organisations, to make their criticisms heard. This would meet with four objections. In the first place, it would make it more difficult for people to advance the excuse of ignorance. An ostrich policy on the part of the organisation, of the top management, or of individual functionaries becomes more difficult if aberrant opinions are allowed expression within the organisation. An important additional effect can be that the preventive force of moral restrictions may thereby be strengthened. What the head does know, the heart will grieve over. In the third place, it can increase the transparency of the organisation. External forums are more likely to act in a preventive way, or can afterwards more easily disentangle the jumble of corporate actions. In the fourth place, this goes against what Fishkin (1982: 14) has called the *cut-off for heroism*. There are limits to the sacrifices that one may ask of an individual; beyond those limits there can no longer be any talk of a moral obligation to act responsibly, one can at most speak of a sense of gratitude for the display of so much heroism. By giving individual functionaries more possibilities to resist the social coercion that emanates from the organisation, one can try to extend those limits.

However, this strategy demands a reflection on the issue of bureaucratic responsibility as virtue. After all, accountability and virtue, active and passive responsibility, hang closely together. An individual model of accountability demands a different notion of bureaucratic virtue. Individual accountability and more room for dissent could, for example, tempt or oblige functionaries to perform actions that now, within the current notions of bureaucratic responsibility as virtue, would be branded as highly 'irresponsible'.

So here ends the passive side of the problem of many hands. The rest of this study will be dedicated to a discussion of the active component of individual responsibility within complex organisations.

PART III

ACTIVE RESPONSIBILITY

9

Virtue: citizenship in complex organisations

The honor of the civil servant is vested in his ability to execute conscientiously the order of the superior authorities, exactly as if the order agreed with his own conviction. This holds even if the order appears wrong to him and if, despite the civil servant's remonstrances, the authority insists on the order

(Max Weber 1946 [1919]: 95)

[A] Civil Servant must ultimately place his loyalty to Parliament and the public interest above his obligation to the interests of the Government of the day.

(Clive Ponting 1985)

The responsible functionary: four cases

What does it mean to act responsibly within complex organisations? By responsible, in the sense of virtuous conduct we understand conduct that is positively prized in moral terms.[1] In chapter 3 we saw that at least five criteria can play a role in the formulation of that positive judgment. Conduct is often called 'responsible' if it shows some sign of an adequate perception of threatening dangers; if in the weighing up of alternative forms of conduct, the possible disadvantageous consequences for others have received special attention; if the decision is made on the basis of an independent judgment; if the conduct is verifiable and consistent; and, fifthly, if attention is given to concrete role obligations.

For functionaries, the role obligations will be of particular importance. After all, a functionary, whether an employee or a civil servant, does not act exclusively as private person, but above all as a member of an organisation. He usually has a clearly defined function and restricted powers and, in exchange for a salary and other forms of reciprocation, fulfils various concrete obligations. In chapter 3 a distinction was made between the *concept* of responsibility as virtue and *conceptions* of responsibility as virtue. Each of the five criteria is after all susceptible to interpretation. With a conception of bureaucratic responsibility as virtue I mean a concrete interpretation of the various criteria, geared to the role of functionary in a complex organisation. Such a notion provides an answer to the

[1] For a similar Aristotelian approach, see also Cooper (1987).

question of how a functionary must deal with the obligations that flow from his or her role.

Often such conceptions of responsibility lie dormant and become activated and formulated in hard cases only, when conflicts of loyalty demand a solution and an individual functionary, or a forum, has to reach a judgment about the functionary's conduct (cf. Harmon 1990). Therefore, I will begin with a description of four cases in which functionaries were held to account for conduct disloyal to their superiors. All four have to do with the question: How far does individual responsibility go? How should a responsible functionary behave in relation to the orders given by a superior and the demands of the organisation when the functionary himself is of the opinion that to carry them out could lead to irresponsible conduct on his own part or on the part of the organisation as a whole? In all four cases (sometimes somewhat adapted or severely abridged, but nevertheless true stories), employees or civil servants were motivated to disobey assignments given to them by their superiors.[2]

1. *The pro-life nurses.* In 1980, after years of discussion, the Dutch Parliament passed a rather liberal abortion law. From then on, under medical supervision and within certain limits, abortion was to be permitted in the first three months of pregnancy. The management and the medical staff of a general hospital in Middelburg then decided that the hospital would make it possible for pregnancies to be terminated in cases where the foetus was found to be very seriously deformed. This decision met with serious objections on the part of a few of the nurses in the department of obstetrics and gynaecology. Two nurses, among them the head of the department, who had been working in it ever since 1963, informed the management that under no circumstances would they cooperate in the termination of pregnancies, of whatever kind. They pointed out that the performing of abortions was against their personal philosophy of life. The management decided that they could not be kept in the – rather small – department and decided to transfer them elsewhere. The two nurses refused to accept the transfer, however. They wanted the hospital to go back on its decision. Moreover, they thought that it was wrong that they should be placed in a disadvantageous position because of their conscientious objection to abortion. They were consequently suspended on full pay by the management and

---

[2] In many treatises on bureaucratic responsibility, much attention is also paid to the conduct of functionaries in respect of outsiders, and in particular to corruption, nepotism, and bribes. Here, however, such themes will arise only in passing. The emphasis here is after all not on the incidental *faux pas* committed by individual functionaries, but on the conduct of the organisation as a whole and on the responsibility that the individual functionary has for it or should have for it.

plans were laid to sack them. Then the two conscientious objectors started a law-suit against their transfer. The judge found in favour of the management. He said that it was up to the management and senior medical staff of a hospital to determine policy, and not up to the nurses to do so. The situation would change only if the policy was found to be socially unacceptable. In the Netherlands, the performance of an abortion on medical grounds, however, is generally held to be permissible – as had also been made evident by the recent approval of Parliament for the draft law (which went even further than the plans approved by the hospital).[3]

2. *The scrupulous customs officer.* The customs officer Jacoby was operating within the area known as the Waterweg, the docks area of Rotterdam. One of his tasks was to check the ships that came into port. This was done in close cooperation with an officer of the port of Schiedam, a neighbouring municipality of Rotterdam, which is also situated on the Waterweg. Each day the two men would sail out aboard a small craft to incoming ships and investigate their cargo and their papers. At a certain point, Jacoby's boss began to suspect that Jacoby's Schiedam colleague was involved in smuggling or some other illegal activity. He therefore gave Jacoby instructions to make secret notes of his colleague's activities and to report daily on them. The customs officer refused, however, because he found it indecent to make secret reports on a good colleague behind that colleague's back. 'That is not the sort of thing you do with your colleagues', he argued. Subsequently, he was relieved of his function by his boss.[4]

3. *Dr Pierce and the Hippocratic oath.* Dr Pierce was employed as a medical researcher at the 'Ortho Pharmaceutical Corporation', an American company that produced medicines. In 1973, she was appointed head of 'Medical Research-Therapeutics', a department that conducted research on non-regenerative medicines. One of the projects being carried out by the department concerned the development of 'Loperamide', a liquid medicine for acute and chronic diarrhoea. The medicine was specially developed for children and other patients who for whatever reason were not in a position to ingest solids. The medicine contained a very high concentration of saccharine – forty-four times higher than the level permitted by American law in sugar-free soft drinks. In the case of medicines, there were no relevant guidelines, but at a meeting in March 1975, the members of the project group, agreed unanimously that the medicine was not suitable for use because of the high content of – potentially carcinogenic – saccharine.

[3] President of the Court at Middelburg, 23 December 1980, *NJ* 1981, 87.
[4] *de Volkskrant,* December 18, 1986.

However, to develop an alternative formula would have meant a delay of several months and have sent the company's costs sky-high.

The project group then came under a lot of pressure from the management of the firm to begin with the clinical tests, i.e. to try out the medicine on patients. After a few weeks, the project group gave in. Only Pierce, the sole doctor in the company and the person on whom the responsibility for the clinical tests rested, refused to agree and appealed to her loyalty to the Hippocratic oath. She deemed it not responsible to try out a medicine with such a high concentration of potentially carcinogenic materials on children and old people.

After she had made clear her refusal to her direct superior, the leadership of the project was taken from her and it was announced that she would be demoted. As an extra penalty, an announcement was to be made within the company of her demotion. Her boss, who until then had had no complaints about her, accused her of irresponsible conduct, a lack of judgment, poor productivity, an inability to get on with marketing-personnel, and inadequate executive capacities. Pierce then resigned because she had the feeling that she was being punished for her refusal to do something that she considered to be unethical.[5]

4. *Clive Ponting and the sinking of the* Belgrano. On 2 May 1982, the British nuclear submarine HMS *Conqueror* torpedoed the Argentinean warship *General Belgrano*. As a result of that action, 368 crew members of the ship lost their lives. The incident marked the beginning of large-scale hostilities in the British–Argentinean conflict around the Falkland Islands; advanced negotiations that might have led to a peaceful solution of the conflict were abruptly and definitively broken off. Almost immediately after the incident became known, questions were raised in parliament about the necessity and wisdom of such a violent naval assault. The government of Mrs Thatcher defended its decision with the argument that the *Belgrano*, given its course and position, represented a direct danger to the British fleet. As the euphoria surrounding the eventual British victory died down and more became known about the actual course of events, doubts about various statements by members of the cabinet increased. The Labour MP Tam Dalyell was especially persistent in asking the government for clarification; however, the government refused to provide much information, on the grounds that to do so would harm the interests of the state.

[5] This case is based on *Pierce* v. *Ortho Pharmaceutical Corporation* (1979), 399 A. 2d. Opinion by Judge Kole, Superior Court of New Jersey, Appellate Division (as described by Beauchamp and Bowie 1983: 299–303).

At the beginning of March 1984, after a very successful official career, Clive Ponting, the main character in this case, was appointed head of the 'Defence Secretariat 5', a top post close to the political leadership of the Ministry of Defence. He became involved in writing draft answers to questions raised in parliament. Not long after that, data about the events preceding the torpedoing were made available by independent researchers who seriously attacked the credibility of the government standpoint. According to them, the *Belgrano* had already been on its way back to its home port at the moment of the attack and had therefore no longer formed a threat to the British fleet. Dalyell then raised a series of new, very pointed questions. Ponting drew up a series of draft answers that contained details on the basis of which it could be deduced that the *Belgrano* had indeed changed course. However, Michael Heseltine, the Minister of Defence, decided not to release the answers and told Dalyell that he had nothing to add to his previous explanations. Ponting, shocked by this refusal on the part of the minister to provide a member of parliament with what was, after all, unclassified information, sent Dalyell a brief, anonymous note in which he encouraged him to press on with his line of questioning. Thereupon, Dalyell raised a new series of questions. The government, however, continued to refuse to answer them. Ponting decided that enough was enough when the Undersecretary of Defence, John Stanley, provided intentionally misleading information to the standing parliamentary Commission of Foreign Affairs. On 16 July 1984, Ponting sent Dalyell an envelope containing two documents: the draft-answers that Heseltine had not wanted to release and an internal official memorandum that contained the information that the parliamentary committee had requested.

Ponting's one-man intervention was to lead to a situation in which the government was forced to let things out into the open and to admit that parliament had been misled on a number of crucial points. However, the source of the leak was quickly traced and the government, furious, decided to prosecute Ponting on the basis of the Official Secrets Act. Ponting defended his conduct as follows:

> I did this because I believe Ministers in this Department are not prepared to answer legitimate questions of MPs about a matter of considerable public concern simply in order to protect their own political position [...] My conscience is clear. In my view, a Civil Servant must ultimately place his loyalty to Parliament and the public interest above his obligation to the interests of the Government of the day.

The Public Prosecutor did not think much of Ponting's behaviour, and nor did the judge. In a rather partisan summing-up at the end of the trial, the judge tried to convince the members of the jury that the interests of the state in this case coincided with those of the government of the day and that Ponting's conduct could not pass muster:

> Ministers take responsibility for policy although they ask Civil Servants to draft documents for their consideration. [...] It is the duty of the Minister to see that the answer is a truthful one. In highly charged political situations one person's ambiguity is another person's truth. If by accident a misleading answer is given it is the Minister's duty to put the record straight. Ministers and not Civil Servants are accountable to Parliament. [...] It is the duty of a Civil Servant not to make policy but to advise on it and to carry out, to the best of his ability, the policy of his Minister providing it is lawful.

The jury was apparently not very impressed by the words of the judge. After a brief deliberation, Ponting was unanimously found not guilty.[6]

Five conceptions of bureaucratic responsibility

On the basis of these concrete cases, at least five competing conceptions of individual responsibility can be constructed. I deliberately say *at least five*, because I do not claim that my list is exhaustive – other conceptions exist or are conceivable.[7] I also deliberately say *construed*, because the five positions can be analytically distinguished from each other. Just like the models in the previous section, they are greatly condensed and simplified. In practice, one would often not be able define them so neatly, and in concrete cases one will see that several conceptions are used alongside one another. Here, however, I have tried to establish a clear separation between them, because, as we shall see later, these positions have important implications. The position that one chooses has specific consequences for the terms in which the debate is conducted, but also for the actual functioning of organisations. Each conception refers to a separate set of norms and is characterised by its own forums (see table 9.1).

The five conceptions are:

1. The *hierarchical conception*, in which the emphasis is on strict loyalty to one's own organisation and in particular to one's own superior. This conception is employed by the judge in the case of the nurses, by Jacoby's and Pierce's bosses, and by the British government and the judge in the Ponting affair.
2. The *personal conception*, in which personal ethics and loyalty to one's own

---

[6] The information on this case is taken from Norton-Taylor (1985).
[7] See for a somewhat similar exercise Harmon (1995).

Table 9.1 *Five conceptions of bureaucratic responsibilities*

Responsibility	Loyalty to
1 hierarchical	superiors & orders
2 personal	conscience & personal ethics
3 social	peers & social norms
4 professional	profession & professional ethics
5 civic	citizens & civic values

conscience are to the fore. This conception can be found in the objections of the nurses.

3. The *social conception*, in which norms of decency and loyalty to one's peers are central. This conception is represented by customs officer Jacoby.

4. The *professional conception*, in which the emphasis lies on professional ethics and loyalty to one's own professional group. This conception can be found in the defence of Dr Pierce.

5. The *civic conception*, in which the emphasis lies on civic values, such as democratic control, and in which loyalty to parliament and the public cause are to the fore. This conception can be found in the position adopted by Ponting.

In the next few paragraphs, these conceptions are further elaborated and discussed. An important question in each case will be in how far they prove to be satisfactory in the light of the problem of many hands.

Hierarchical responsibility: strict loyalty to superiors

One could call the idea that functionaries owe their superior strict obedience, their organisation complete loyalty, and the outside world utmost discretion, the orthodox or classical conception of bureaucratic responsibility. One finds it in academic writings, in textbooks, in legal judgments, in company codes, and in civil-service rules of conduct. Often one uses the term 'neutrality' or 'impartiality' for this point of view.[8] In the public sphere, one finds it under the denominator of 'the primacy of politics' or 'the

---

[8] Cf. for example Ladd (1970: 500), who provides a good representation of the conventional, Weberian conceptions:

'An official or agent of a formal organization is simply violating the basic rules of organizational activity if he allows his moral scruples rather than the objectives of the organization to determine his decision. In particular he is violating the rule of administrative impartiality, that is, the rule that administrative officials "faithfully execute policies of which they personally disapprove"' (Ladd's quote is from Bendix 1952: 132).

separation of politics and administration'. Here I prefer the term 'strict loyalty to one's superiors', because it approximates most closely to the core of this conception. What is expected of the functionary by his superior is, after all, not a general neutrality or quasi-judicial impartiality, but precisely a strict measure of loyalty and a consistently applied partiality; the civil servant or employee must conform as much as possible to the wishes and requirements of the leadership of the day.[9] To put it in extreme form: in the carnival of the beasts, the functionary would go dressed not as grey mouse, but as chameleon.

This classical conception of responsible behaviour is propagated not without reason. It has been a lucid and often effective answer to a number of bureaucratic abuses. Before alternative conceptions of bureaucratic responsibility come up for discussion, we must therefore first ascertain which arguments underlie this conception.

1. *This conception offers the best guarantee for an efficient business management and an efficient government administration.* Complex, bureaucratic organisational forms are developed in order to organise business management and government administration as efficiently as possible. The classical conception of loyalty is indispensable in that process. It is above all the work of Frederick Taylor (1911) and Henri Fayol (1916) that forms the principal background to a discussion of this issue. Both the principles of scientific management as developed by Taylor and the principles of organisation as developed by Fayol prescribe a clear division of responsibilities between workers and management. The manager must be responsible for all planning of tasks and activities, while the ordinary employees are merely responsible for a loyal implementation of them (Taylor 1911: 37–8). Such a strict division of tasks requires a strict loyalty on the part of the employees in respect of the tasks assigned by the managers. Employees need to obey the rules that govern the organisation. In Weber's work, one finds a similar argument for a strict division of responsibilities, but in his case, the division of responsibilities is in the public sphere: 'Without this moral discipline and self-denial, in the highest sense, the whole apparatus would fall into pieces'. Civil servants are after all 'in the political sense of the word, [. . .] irresponsible politicians' (1946 (1919): 95). They have no responsibility of their own in respect of parliament and are accustomed as a result of their daily work to shift their responsibilities onto others. Their training and occupational disability make them unsuitable for a large measure of independence.

---

[9] In the term 'civil servant' this emphasis on service mentality and loyalty is nicely expressed. This term is in its turn obviously related to the Roman *servus publicus* – in the Roman Empire, many public tasks were originally performed by slaves.

The combination of a hierarchical structure with the conception of strict loyalty, so the argument goes, results in one of the most efficient, large-scale forms of organisation. After all, the classical conception ensures clarity at three levels. The top level of the organisation can rest assured that its assignments are implemented punctually and properly and that its policy is not thwarted or derailed by unexpected initiatives from below. The 'rank-and-file' knows what it is up to and is thus released from the need to make difficult choices, and the outside world, the citizens and the consumers, are confronted by a clear and unambiguous policy and have obvious points of address.

2. *This conception promotes the (democratic) control of complex organisations.* The classical conception is also an answer to the problem of many hands. A hierarchical conception of responsibility as virtue is the logical counterpart of a hierarchical model of accountability. The top level of a complex organisation can fulfil its exclusive accountability to the outside world only when the rest of the organisation is unconditionally loyal. If that loyalty slackens, the hierarchical model also slackens. This is a big danger above all in the case of public organisations. If civil servants do not at all times behave loyally toward their organisation and superior, the unsteady equilibrium of the Trias Politica is endangered and the threat arises of a soulless *Beamtenherrschaft*, the development of an uncontrollable 'fourth' civil-service power. One finds this argument in Weber (1946 (1919): 95) and Finer (1941: 336) among other people. Only by putting the emphasis on a strict internal obedience on the part of functionaries to a strong externally accountable leadership would society perhaps still be in a position to put up resistance to the inevitable rise of complex organisations (Weber 1958 (1919): 318–23).[10]

3. *This conception is the best guarantee that the rule of law will be observed.* This argument is *par excellence* applicable to government organisations. Government policy is implemented by thousands of civil servants who are active in often hundreds of different places. If they were not, in doing so, to stick to guidelines and assignments of their department or institution, chaos would reign everywhere. In the private sector, given enough competition, this spectre could be exorcised by the discipline of the market, but in the case of the public services that correction mechanism is not available. Strict

---

[10] Although the terminology in this passage is tailored to public organisations, these arguments are, according to Weber, also applicable to *Privatwirtschaftbetriebe* (private economic enterprises) and *Unternehmer* (entrepreneurs) (Weber 1958 (1919): 322–3).

obedience to the guidelines set up from above is therefore extremely important for the rule of law, certainly in those cases in which the government has
a monopoly over the provision of certain services. Two principles are particularly in need of protection: legal certainty, and equality before the law.
Citizens must know what they can expect and what is expected of them and
they must moreover be confident that they will be treated equally. The
conception of strict loyalty offers them that knowledge and prevents
arbitrariness, nepotism, and corruption.

In the United States, Woodrow Wilson (1887) and Frank Goodnow
(1900), the 'grand old men' of the movement for administrative reform,
were to the fore among those who pleaded for a hierarchical division of
responsibilities for this reason. In their work, the emphasis lay above all on
a strict separation between politics, the formulation of the will and the
objectives of the government, and administration, the actual implementation of that policy: 'administration lies outside the proper sphere of *politics*.
Administrative questions are not political questions. Although politics sets
the tasks for administration, it should not be suffered to manipulate its
offices' (Wilson 1887: 145). This rigorous separation is understandable in
the light of the Jacksonian *spoils system*, which had led to a corrupt, inex-
pert, and venal administrative apparatus.[11]

With this description of the positions of Taylor, Weber, and Wilson, the tone
is sufficiently set. Later writers, in their formulation of the hierarchical
conception, would largely produce variations on the arguments first
advanced by them.[12] They made a distinction, for example, within the strict

---

[11] There are some rather direct connections between the Wilsonian and the Weberian
conceptions. Both authors were directly or indirectly influenced by Bluntschli.
Moreover, in 1904 Weber stayed for several months in the United States and was
quite knowledgeable about the developments in American public administration.
This is also evidenced, for example, in the many references in *Wirtschaft und
Gesellschaft* and in *Politik als Beruf* to the American situation (see also the
introduction by Gerth and Mills to the first English translation of Weber's work,
1946: 15–18). One should, however, bear in mind that Wilson developed the
separation between politics and administration above all in order to roll back the
big influence enjoyed by partisan politicians on the implementation of government
tasks, while Weber had in mind the opposite, namely, rolling back civil service
influences and strategies in political practice.

[12] It would go too far to outline the whole history of the development of the
hierarchical conception. For a survey of it, I refer the reader to Waldo (1948), Hill
(1972: 195–210), and Self (1977: 149–91). One of the most interesting discussions
within this 'paradigm' of administrative loyalty was that between Friedrich (1935,
1940) and Finer (1936, 1941), in which the latter defends the idea of a strict loyalty
on the part of officials while the former defends a conception of official obedience
that goes much further in the direction of some alternative conceptions.

obligation to obedience, between policy preparation and advising on the one hand and policy implementation on the other. In the first case, the functionary had more freedom to take his own initiatives and to air a deviant opinion than in the second case.

This hierarchical conception, which was certainly absolutely dominant in the first half of the twentieth century in most Western countries, has in the course of the decades lost much of its attractive power and force of conviction. For this, a number of reasons can be mentioned:

It fell into discredit after the Second World War, because a large measure of uncritical loyalty to established authority on the part of civil servants, policemen, and soldiers had played such an important part in the persecution of the Jews and in other war crimes – not just in Germany, but also, for example, in the Netherlands (Blom 1983). Under the influence of the Nuremberg and Tokyo trials of the generals and senior civil servants of the Third Reich and Japan, excuses of the *Befehl ist Befehl* sort lost much of their legitimacy – at first in the military sphere, but gradually also within the civil sphere and the civil service.

Partly as a consequence of the Second World War, human rights developed into a major new field of interest. Not only were more and more rights recognised as fundamental, but more and more groups and activities were brought within the arena of basic rights. In the Netherlands, for example, the new civil-service law of 1987 recognised that civil servants, even while still in office, could appeal to the protective working of a number of basic rights. Above all the freedom of expression of opinion has been greatly extended by this new legislation. Broad individual liberties for civil servants and employees are, however, difficult to reconcile with a hierarchical conception of loyalty.

The higher educational level of functionaries has also altered their relationship to their superiors. The postwar employee or official often entered the organisation as early as the age of 16 or 17, after a short secondary-school education. Subsequently, often by way of a series of internal training courses, he was socialized into the mores of the company or of the service. Functionaries today often have a college or university education when they join the apparatus, and, if only for that reason, are some 5 to 10 years older than their postwar equivalents. That means first of all that they are much more difficult to socialise than the relative *tabula rasa* of the past. Much of their higher education has, moreover, a professional and critical character. As a result, the modern functionary often already posseses a series of external, professional norms and values and a critical attitude upon entering the organisation. That can, in particular in the case of staff functionaries, lead to frictions between them and the line managers, who are often more generalist in their orientation.

Not just the functionary but also the modern organisation has changed in character over the decades. The classical, pyramidic form of organisation is often 'flattened' by the application of more horizontal organisational forms such as project and matrix organisations, process reengineering, and various forms of 'adhocracies'. The classical, hierarchical conception of responsibility is, however, not so easily reconciled with these new forms of institutional and individual autonomy.

Just as within the family and society, so too within modern organisations, to quote De Swaan (1982), the command household has been replaced gradually by a regime based on negotiations. The manager or minister must frequently negotiate in order to win his subordinates over. The functionary, just as women and children in the family, has become emancipated. These developments imply that in many organisations in western countries it is becoming increasingly difficult to hold to an uncurtailed version of the classical, hierarchical conception of responsibility.

This conception is, however, not only sometimes *impossible* but in a number of respects even *undesirable*. That fact becomes obvious when we analyse it in the light of the three arguments that support it.

As we have already seen in previous chapters, the thesis that an efficient and effective organisation is best served by a docile and neutral implementation of the assignments handed down from on high is nowadays accepted by only a few organisational experts, and only under specific circumstances. Only when we are dealing with routine problems and processes, or with a stable and simple environment, are tightly managed, mechanistic organisations considered to be the most efficient form of organisation.[13] However, very many organisations at present are confronted with contingent problems, complicated technologies, and a complex and turbulent environment. Under such circumstances, the hierarchical conception is not terribly efficient. It prevents the employment of professional knowledge and local insights, and can lead to dilatory and rather inflexible behaviour. The 'illusion of control by the top' is here emphatically the case. For an efficient business management, many modern organisations are best served by a large measure of autonomy at the lower, executive levels. Many organisations are therefore characterised by professional or ad hoc structures. The hierarchical conception of strict loyalty suits best only one specific form of organisation: the machine bureaucracy (Mintzberg, 1979).

When (democratic) control functions badly or is even completely absent, or when it is a matter of unlawful assignments or of corrupt management, a strictly loyal implementation of assignments can have disastrous consequences. Such is the lesson of the Second World War: '[...] man's tragedy is

---

[13] Cf. for example Burns and Stalker (1961), Perrow (1967), Lawrence and Lorsch (1967), Beer (1975), and Van Gunsteren (1976: 26–44).

not an excess of aggression but an excess of devotion' (Koestler 1979: 15). Considerations of efficiency or effectiveness will therefore, even within machine bureaucracies, not under all circumstances be the decisive factor. Sometimes they will have to give way to considerations of a more civic nature. In extreme circumstances, a docile, efficient organisation can be the very last thing that we need. The classic example here too is Eichmann and his particularly well organised section B-4 of Bureau IV of the Reichssicherheitshauptamt (State Security Headquarters). One can also think of illegal operations by companies, as in the case of Slavenburg's Bank. In extreme situations, the demand for loyalty is therefore currently relaxed or even cancelled and it is expected of civil servants and employees that they themselves will take the initiative in scrutinising the exact meaning of the tasks assigned them. It is, however, doubtful to what extent a thorough socialisation in the doctrine of strict loyalty would permit such a *volte face*. As we have already seen in chapter 8, conceptions of strict loyalty can play an important part in lessening the preventive power of moral restrictions within complex organisations (Arendt 1964; Stone 1975: 69; Ermann and Lundman 1982a: 47; Kelman and Hamilton 1989).

In the public sector, democratic control of official conduct is naturally of the utmost importance. This consideration, however, provides less cause for a conception of strict official loyalty than one might at first glance think. For most supporters of this idea of 'the primacy of politics', it remains unclear for example where exactly this primacy applies: at the top of the civil service, with the political management, with the cabinet, with the cabinet party or parties, with the parliamentary committees, with the members of parliament as a whole, or with the electorate. Most modern supporters of this classical conception seem to lay the emphasis above all on the political management of a department as the central point of reference for bureaucratic obedience. However, such an interpretation of the idea of the 'primacy of politics' is not as self-evident as some pretend it to be. If control by democratic organs is the most important consideration, one would rather expect the loyalty of the civil servant to lie first and foremost with the (majority of the) popular representatives and only secondarily with the political leadership, and only after that with his own official superiors and departmental organisation. It is therefore not easy to see how, for example, conduct such as that of Clive Ponting could be criticised solely on the basis of the argument that it makes democratic control of the actions of the government impossible. But even if one were to locate 'the primacy' in the politically responsible leadership of a department and not with parliament, it is still not self-evident why a civil servant should be strictly loyal to his own organisation and direct superiors under all circumstances. The idea that 'politics' has primacy need not imply a strictly hierarchical organisational culture.

Democratic control of the machinery of government – and also of industry – can in a number of cases benefit from a break-through in the hierarchy at lower and middle levels and from the voicing of dissident or critical opinions.[14] As we saw in the preceding chapters, pre-eminently this classical conception has formed an important obstacle to the timely detection and adequate prevention of misconduct on the part of organisations.

In the public sector, protection of the Rule of Law deserves much attention. That does not automatically mean, however, that all civil servants, under all circumstances, should be obedient to their superiors, loyal to the organisation, and discreet in their dealings with the outside world. After all, this argument applies only to that part of the civil-service body that has to deal with outsiders. By no means all civil servants have direct contacts with ordinary citizens or take decisions in individual cases. For policy-advisers such as Clive Ponting, for scientific researchers such as Dr Pierce, and for consultants and internal accountants, for example, such direct contacts are generally not the case. For those who do have dealings with outsiders, this argument can offer both a basis for and a restriction on obedience. After all, what should one do if strict obedience to (new) guidelines and assignments threatens to come into conflict with aspects of the same Rule of Law? In 'normal' cases, it will not be up to the civil servant to judge such issues, for to do so is after all the task of the administrative courts. In extreme situations, however, citizens can sometimes have insufficient possibilities or too little information at their disposal to bring the matter in good time before the courts.

A final objection in the light of this study is, of course, the fact that the classical conception is at odds with the individual model of accountability. Only the leadership has to account to the outside world for its own conduct and for the conduct of the organisation. Lower functionaries have fulfilled their moral and legal duties when they are loyal towards their organisation and behave discretely towards the outside world (and in so far as they themselves at least commit no serious culpable acts). However, one cannot on the one hand oblige functionaries to carry out their tasks *sine ira et studio* and then, on the other hand, hold them personally accountable for the consequences of that loyalty.

Such are the most important considerations that underlie the classical conception of bureaucratic responsibility. These considerations do not have to lead inevitably and under all circumstances to a classical conception of strict loyalty on the part of civil servants and employees. In the following paragraphs, I want to look at whether competing conceptions of responsibility as virtue are possible and desirable within the limits set by these considerations.

---

[14] Concrete examples of this will follow in the next few paragraphs and chapters.

Personal responsibility: loyalty to conscience

In this conception of responsibility, the emphasis lies on the beliefs and personal values of the civil servant or employee. When a functionary finds that an assignment is irresponsible, loyalty to his own conscience and to his own identity should in the long run be the decisive factor. In the last instance, the individual employee himself, on the basis of his own norms and values, should decide whether or not he wishes to carry out a dubious assignment. Among the important virtues in this conception are self-respect, self-fulfilment, and loyalty to one's own conscience. The case of the Middelburg nurses and the abortion law is exemplary. This conception is not, however, confined to strictly religious objections. For many modern, highly educated employees, personal autonomy is an important value. 'For quite a few young academics working for the government, it is considered as self-evident that they are first true to themselves' (Van Spengler 1988: 25).

In the postwar period one could point to several sources of this conception of bureaucratic responsibility. In the first place, there is the influence of existentialist authors and philosophers such as Camus and Sartre, who, partly as a reaction to the war, put a great deal of emphasis on people's individual, autonomous power of judgment.[15] In the second place, partly under the influence of the ideas of humanistic psychologists such as Maslow and Fromm, a need gradually arose for, and an emphasis was put upon, individual self-fulfilment and creativeness. By way of the supporters of the 'human resources' movement – people such as McGregor (1960), Likert (1961, 1967), Argyris (1964), and Marini (1971) – these ideas have found their way into the sciences of public administration and business management. There is also a close connection to the rise in importance of human rights. One of the underlying ideas is that functionaries, not just in their private lives but also at work, can to a certain extent demand protection of a number of human rights such as freedom of expression, religion, conscience, conviction, and the right to privacy (Ewing 1977, 1983; Van der Heijden 1988). Some authors go even further and claim rights for functionaries that demand a more active support on the part of the organisation or the government, such as the right to self-fulfilment (Harmon 1971; 1981). In many Western countries a long Christian and socialist tradition of conscientious objection inspired by religious or pacifist beliefs also plays a part. In the Netherlands, for example, with its long history of religious and

---

[15] Olafson (1967: 238), speaking of the influence of existentialism on postwar thinking, comes to the following conclusion:

> 'It would not, I think, be an exaggeration to say that for the first time in human history large numbers of human beings have come to think of themselves as autonomous moral agents, capable of raising and resolving for themselves all questions about what they are to do'.

political minorities, an appeal to this conception is a well-beaten track in cases in which functionaries have a principled objection to an assignment or policy. Very many individual civil servants and employees motivate their refusal to work or their decision to resort to whistleblowing with an appeal to their consciences – even when there are no strictly religious or philosophical principles at stake. Also, many conflicts of loyalty are channelled by setting up facilities under the heading of 'conscientious objections'.

A number of important considerations argue in favour of this position. Room for the expression of conscientious objections within organisations is a sign of civilisation. It is an expression of respect for, and tolerance of, philosophical and religious diversity. That room can moreover help in the social emancipation of religious and cultural minorities and can therefore also promote cultural pluralism and social representativity within organisations.

This strictly personal sense of responsibility is, however, scarcely all that attractive as an alternative to the hierarchical conception. This conception can, to start with, quickly give rise to a 'personalisation' of the organisation. Matter-of-fact differences of opinion can more quickly escalate into personal conflicts if self-fulfilment and matters of conscience come to the fore. It is not easy to argue about conscience. Defining issues in terms of conscience turns the debate about responsibility into a morally loaded debate. Doing so often makes compromise very difficult, because the personal integrity of the employee is suddenly at stake. In matters of conscience one can by definition add no water to the wine. Being wronged or 'overruled' can for many be understood or interpreted rather as an attack on one's personal integrity and can in that way become all the more threatening.

The contents of conscientious objections are, for other reasons too, difficult or impossible to subject to a debate. After all, who in a pluralistic society has the right and the ability to voice a judgment about the conscience of another person? On which grounds could you contradict an employee who says that he has a conscientious objection to such-and-such a matter? In a multi-cultural and multi-religious society, there is no generally accepted Archimedean point that can serve us as an anchor. Objections to abortion are in most countries more or less accepted, but why is the same not true for objections to contraceptives, in vitro fertilisation, blood transfusions, or inoculations? It will always be difficult within this conception to set qualitative limits. A limitation to the *extent* of the objection, on the basis of a substantive discussion and a review by third persons, is after all largely out of the question.[16] This undermines the predictability of the conduct of functionaries and therewith the adroitness of the organisation.

---

[16] Formal limits, such as requirements of due care, naturally remain possible, for example in relation to the time at which and the manner in which the objection is first raised.

The taboo nature of the conscience, which is hardly ever up for discussion or debate, also means that it is very difficult to set limits to the *number* of objectors within an organisation. If one objection is recognised, others with the same objections can no longer so easily be refused similar rights. After all, a conscientious objection does not forfeit legitimacy because it is one too many. That is the consequence of a classification under the title of 'conscience'; each quantitative limit is, as a result, arbitrary.

It is evident, moreover, that this conception is at loggerheads with the idea that representative bodies should have the first and the last word in public administration. Civil servants are primarily employed 'to be active in the public service' and not in order to 'actualise' themselves to an even greater extent. The political control of the administrative apparatus would be very difficult if civil servants were to refuse assignments on strictly personal grounds in large numbers. Or – and this would make democratic control even more difficult – if civil servants on their own personal account or on the basis of personal motives were themselves to start playing an active role in forming or implementing policy. There is a real danger of *Beamtenherrschaft* when personal considerations and interests acquire a legitimate place in individual decision-making. One could object that these dangers are reduced when civil servants can be externally called to account, in representative organs, for their decision to deviate from the political guidelines. However, here the apolitical character of this personal conception again takes its revenge. After all, what is the norm against which the political forum can check the conduct of the civil servant and on what grounds can one perhaps condemn that person's conduct? In the last analysis, it is the personal norms of conscience of the individual functionary himself. Norms of conscience do not, however, lend themselves to checking in the course of an open public debate.

Principles such as legal certainty and equality in law, finally, are not compatible with a striving toward self-fulfilment or with the wish to maintain a clear conscience. The classical conception of responsibility often tended in practice to develop in the direction of legalism, of the mechanical application of the rules while at the same time skating over the material objectives and the actual results of the application of those rules. In the case of the personal conception, on the other hand, the danger arises of 'unauthorised discretion', of the conscious ignoring or contravening of the general rules because in the opinion of the functionary the objectives of the organisation are best served by so doing. One step further on, there is also the danger of 'retreatism': the postponing of decisions, the shirking of responsibilities, or the manipulation of rules with an eye to what is convenient to the peace of mind of the functionary himself (Kagan 1978: 90–5).

For these reasons, a general redefinition of the conception of bureaucratic responsibility along the lines of conscience might seriously aggravate the problem of many hands. Clients, customers, and citizens can no longer be sure that employees and civil servants will implement the policies and rules of the organisation in a uniform way. *In extremis:* one's treatment by an organisation depends on the personal values of the civil servant who is handling one's case. In the last instance, the salvation of his soul is decisive, not the consequences for the interests of third parties. Therefore, this redefinition ultimately boils down to an ethic of ultimate ends. Conscience, as Hannah Arendt (1972: 60) observed, is apolitical: 'It is not primarily interested in the world where the wrong is committed or in the consequences that the wrong will have for the future course of the world'.

In a word: in the short term it is unlikely that a return to a classical conception of bureaucratic virtue is possible. For that, the composition and culture of the civil-service apparatus and of employees in business in the western countries have changed too much. The modern civil servant and employee no longer allows himself to be treated in the same way as the Weberian *Beamte.* However, an alternative notion that puts the emphasis above all on personal integrity and fulfilment is, from the point of view of external control and of an efficient and equitable administration, scarcely attractive. With this conception, too, the danger exists that the social power of functionaries is largely withdrawn from public accountability and control. An appeal to the need to protect one's own beliefs can be evidence of a sense of responsibility toward oneself, but is as such still no evidence of a sense of responsibility toward others – the contrary can sometimes even be the case.

Social responsibility: loyalty to peers

There are things in (organisational) life that you simply do not do, not because of your beliefs but in order to preserve your own integrity or to remain a reputable person. One example of this conception is the customs officer and his refusal to spy on his Schiedam colleague. This redefinition is often also put under the heading of personal responsibility (e.g. Harmon 1971: 172–85), but it is analytically distinct from it. Again the question is: what sort of person do I want to be? But here one does not turn to one's conscience for an answer but to one's peers. Within this conception the emphasis lies not on personal, religiously inspired norms, but on social values such as decency, collegiality, and trustworthiness. Loyalty to one's immediate environment, to one's peers – one's colleagues, friends, clients, family, subordinates, and acquaintances – is in the long run decisive. It is not in the first instance a question of whether one can give account of oneself to God and one's conscience, but above all of whether one can look one's own people in the face. The most important virtues within this conception are comradeship, teamplay, and loyalty to one's own group. This notion of individual responsibility is often used by managers in their negotiations with higher echelons or by senior executives when they resign in protest at something (Weisband and Franck 1975).

As with personal responsibility, this redefinition can be of great help to individual civil servants in maintaining their feeling of personal integrity, of self-respect, and of independent choice. Chester Barnard's observations about the functions of informal organisations are a case in point (1938: 60). As such, acceptance of social frames of loyalty can have a civilising effect on organisations. Moreover, it has several advantages over a strictly personalised conception of responsibility. The appeal to integrity and credibility, which are social constructs, means that the official's justifications are not completely immune to public scrutiny. The official's convictions and feelings are still decisive, but at least there is some common ground for debate. After all, one can always conduct a reasonable discussion about what is decent and what not. The interests of third paries can also play a role in such questions, although the circle often remains restricted to colleagues and others in the direct, personal environment of the functionary.

The big disadvantage of conducting the debate in terms of decency and credibility is, however, that group norms and *esprit de corps* are to the fore. There is, ultimately, no external check on the validity and desirability of the standards that are prevalent within the specific peer-group of the disobedient functionary. Social processes such as group-think and peer pressure can in some cases lead, from the point of view of democratic control and the rule of law, to highly unacceptable forms of obedience (or disobedience) within organisations (Janis 1981; Ermann and Lundman 1982; Vaughan 1983; 't Hart 1994). A good example of this is the excesses sometimes committed by the military or police forces (Punch 1981; Kelman and Hamilton 1989). Group pressure and social pressure often play an important part in the perpetration of war crimes, in corruption, and in the illicit acceptance or extortion by police officers of free services of various sorts.

Professional responsibility: loyalty to the profession

Some occupational groups have managed to institutionalise themselves as 'professions'. Doctors, lawyers, and accountants, to name but a few, have long enjoyed a protected status and followed their own professional codes and disciplinary tribunals. Their professional ethics can collide with assignments imposed by the organisation. An example of this is the case of Dr Pierce. Within the conception of professional responsibility, in such cases loyalty to the professional group and to professional ethics is in the end decisive. Professionalism and loyalty to one's own professional rules are among the important bureaucratic virtues. One often encounters an appeal to this conception in the case of conflicts involving company doctors, social workers, engineers, legislative specialists, veterinary services, and (internal) accountants.

This conception is on the rise within organisations, because many professionals work no longer within the free profession but within a complex organisation (Donaldson 1982: 112–15; Abbot 1988: 325). Moreover, alongside the well-established professions such as law, medicine, engineering, and business, other occupational groups have been striving, with mixed success, for professional status; examples of these include consultants, librarians, teachers, social workers, therapists, architects, and systems analysts. Many modern employees and civil servants are in fact semi-professionals. When they arrive in their new posts, they have many years of formal education outside the organisation behind them and are often members of professional associations. Many of these new, or 'minor', professions have also adopted their own professional codes and instituted their own disciplinary procedures (Abbot 1983, 1988; Frankel 1989).

This conception has important advantages over the first two conceptions. It provides the functionary with a certain degree of autonomy *vis-à-vis* his superior and colleagues. It introduces external moral considerations into the organisation, and can thus assist in counteracting phenomena such as groupthink, peer pressure, and crimes of obedience. Moreover, professional norms are intersubjective norms about which one can debate and form opinions. An appeal to professional norms may also promote the effectiveness of the organisation's conduct. Their proximity to the actual outputs of policy making and their technical expertise enable professionals, more so than general managers, to estimate the risks of policy failures or to spot instances of corporate and governmental deviance. At the same time, the reference to professional norms makes this redefinition accessible to public scrutiny and debate. Outsiders, particularly clients and citizens but also political and managerial superiors, can appeal to the executive's professional obligations and standards. They can file complaints, and the possibility exists – though it is at present of little practical import – of lay participation in the development and application of professional codes of ethics (Frankel 1989: 114).

At this point, however, we also come up against various disadvantages. Professional codes often function as an instrument to enhance professional status or to preserve entrenched professional biases, or they are used as a shield against outside interference (Frankel 1989: 111–12). The regulation of internal competition usually prevails: 'In general, obligations toward fellow professionals predominate, especially those that restrain competition for clients, such as pricing policies, rules against client stealing, and the like

[...] The guarantees to client trust that Parsons, Goode and others have seen as fundamental take up a small place in ethical codes' (Abbot 1983: 862).[17] Internal adjudicatory procedures do not always live up to legal standards of impartiality and objectivity, and they can be used by professional elites to prevent the emergence of new forms of professionalism or to hinder the development of new conceptions and standards of professional ethics. Professional frames of responsibility are also problematic in the public sector. After all, what is the democratic legitimacy of these professional, often highly technocratic, norms? They do not lend themselves easily to public scrutiny and democratic control. Moreover, even though the professions often claim to be objective and disinterested, 'self-serving and self promotional interests often intrude into professional activities and prevent the achievement of public goals' (Burke 1986: 155). An appeal to professional responsibility can be used by civil servants to enhance their territory and to fence off legitimate political control. As George Bernard Shaw once remarked: 'Professionalism is a conspiracy against the laity'.

Civic responsibility: loyalty to citizens

An important objection that can be brought against the hierarchical conception is that it is to a certain extent authoritarian and anti-political. It proceeds on the assumption that when employees or civil servants pass through the company gate or up the steps in the morning, they lay aside their citizenship and only retrieve it at the end of the working day, when they leave the organisation behind and go home. In a liberal democracy, however, functionaries are not neutral instruments or *servi publici*. Within both government bodies and business, civic duties and civil rights set limits to one's obligation to obedience and confidentiality. Functionaries remain citizens even during working hours. For that reason, they have a certain responsibility to preserve the community of free and independent citizens. In the conception of civic responsibility, it is the democratic constitutional state itself that sets limits to what you can demand of functionaries. A good example of an appeal to this conception is the case of Clive Ponting. In this conception, the functionary must, in the last instance, be loyal to his fellow citizens and to the institutions of the democratic constitutional state. Disobedience is allowed only when it can be justified by an appeal to general, public interests. One could think, for example, of interests such as the preservation of the rule of law, the enhancement of democratic control, the prevention of a violation of the law, of mismanagement, or of the large-scale waste of government resources.

[17] Cf. also Verkruisen (1993).

It should be noted that this framework comes fairly close to being a modernised version of the orthodox conception. The objectives are the same – only the means differ. Democratic control, the rule of law, and efficient management are still the ultimate goals; it is conceded, however, that certain forms of disobedience to orders issued by one's direct superiors are acceptable as a way of achieving this goal. Loyalty to one's superiors is only provisional, loyalty to the public interest and to the democratic process are the ultimate obligations of functionaries. The main virtues of the modern offical in this conception are not submissiveness but moral autonomy, not detachment and diligence but civility and civic courage. Politics and administration cannot and should not be completely separated. The preservation of the liberal republic and of the rule of law is considered too important to be left to professional politicians. And organisational effectiveness cannot be achieved by managerial rule alone; in modern organisations, a large degree of executive autonomy and individual leeway is indispensable.[18]

This redefinition has several advantages over the others discussed here. It is explicitly framed in public terms. There is no forum that has privileged access to the standards of appropriate behaviour, unlike in the case of personal responsibility. There is no reference to goals or values that lie beyond public debate. An appeal to civic values can be discussed and judged by every citizen. Moreover, since it is explicitly a political and not a moral conception, disagreement is acceptable and need not lead to stalemate or loss of face, as often happens when individual responsibility is framed in terms of conscience or integrity. Finally, the interests of outsiders, notably fellow citizens, have been given a more central place than in the case of the other redefinitions.

It should be noted, however, that this conception of employee citizenship, inspiring as it is, is by far the most demanding. It is demanding for the individual employee since it requires him to be fully up to the demands of citizenship and to disregard the much more concrete personal, professional, or organisational interests. In practice, there is often the danger of social isolation, of ridicule, and of retaliation. It is also demanding from the point of view of the organisation itself, since it introduces external interests and principles into policy making and daily decisions. There is the additional danger of the politicisation of the organisation, of endless discussions and deliberations about public issues, and of partisan policy making.[19]

---

[18] See for a discussion of citizenship in public organisations Frederickson and Chandler (1983); Burke (1986); Stivers (1989); Cooper (1991).

[19] Cf. on the dangers of 'political' conceptions of administrative responsibility the debate between Friedrich (1935; 1940) and Finer (1936, 1941).

Individual loyalty and employee responsibility

This survey of the various notions of loyalty has – so I would hope – both a descriptive and a normative value. In the first place, the five conceptions that I have set out represent important positions in the debates about loyalty and active responsibility within organisations. They are, as it were, the vertices of the arena within which the debate takes place. Also, they are forces that work on an individual functionary in the case of a conflict of loyalties. A strong centripetal force often emanates from the hierarchical and social conceptions of loyalty. They bind the individual to the organisation. The personal, professional, and civic conceptions often work centrifugally. They focus the individual functionary on external loyalties. Between these positions strong tensions can therefore exist in practice. A strong emphasis on professional values can bring an individual functionary into conflict not just with his superior but also with his immediate colleagues in a project team. Personal (conscientious) objections can sometimes be at odds not just with one's loyalty to one's boss and colleagues, but also with one's duties toward one's fellow citizens and one's clients.

In the second place, this survey also yields a number of normative insights. We have seen that the classical, hierarchical conception of official loyalty is for a number of reasons not always tenable in a modern society and in modern organisations. However, several important considerations underlay that classical conception: an increase in the efficiency and effectiveness of organisations and a preservation of democratic control and of the constitutionality of the public administration. None of the four alternatives can, however, fully and independently replace the classical conception. Each alternative has only a restricted measure of legitimacy, because the above-mentioned considerations play only a restricted role in each of them. The danger exists, for example, that we lose sight of those considerations if we allow too much space for the personal considerations and interests of (groups of) functionaries. That is a strong argument for a certain degree of caution in conducting the debates in terms of conscience, decency, or professional integrity. In the light of the social power of complex organisations, civic conceptions of responsibility, in which the debate is conducted in terms of public interests, are preferable. In the rest of this chapter, the fourth alternative, the civic conception of loyalty, will therefore be further elaborated.

Employee citizenship

In a society dominated by complex organisations, the sphere of bureaucracy and the sphere of politics cannot remain entirely separate. Employees and civil servants are also citizens, i.e., members of a political community, with the rights and duties associated with that membership. This employee citizenship can take various forms. In the first place, it can consist quite simply of an extension of the scope of a number of basic rights. Whereas most civil rights were originally intended to offer protection in the sphere of the vertical power relations between government and citizens, they must now also work horizontally in the relationship between private corporate bodies and employees. Alongside the freedom to strike, which they have long had, employees would also have to be able to claim from their employers the protection of other civil rights, such as the freedom of religion, the freedom of speech, the freedom of association and meeting, protection of the privacy of letters and telephone communication. Companies permit themselves a number of infringements of the freedoms of individual employees that in most cases would be deemed inadmissible if the government were to practise them against citizens. Think of the obligation, on penalty of dismissal, to work on religious holidays, the imposition of bans on public speaking, the prohibition on membership of professional associations or of other legitimate organisations, the imposition of penalties without due process, or the uninvited opening of letters, listening to telephone conversations, or spying on employees by means of video cameras (Ewing 1977, 1983; Van der Heijden 1988). Such an extension of the scope of a number of civil liberties is a legitimate and logical supplement to the catalogue of civil liberties recognised by the modern democratic state. The inequality of power between individual employees and complex organisations and the weak position of most employees on the labour market in practice minimises their contractual freedom (Van der Heijden 1988: 22; Gersuny 1994). Most employees cannot afford to give up their jobs in order to regain complete command over their civil rights. *De facto*, their position does not differ all that much from that of a citizen in an authoritarian state. Given the reason behind the classic civil liberties, a horizontal effect on complex organisations is therefore quite easy to defend.

However, employee citizenship consists of more than just the extension of a number of rights. It provides at the same time a basis for external responsibilities.[20] Acknowledgement of the citizenship of employees and civil servants also implies that individual functionaries may and sometimes even must play a role in the preservation of the community of free and independent citizens (Burke 1986). On the one hand, that means that functionaries, as citizens, can be held to account by their fellow citizens for their

[20] See for similar reflections, above all in the public sphere, Fleishman, Liebman, and Moore (1981), Nielsen (1984), Burke (1986), Goodsell et al. (1986), and Cooper (1991).

contribution to the activities of their organisation. The acknowledgement of the citizenship of employees implies that they, just like civil servants, police officers, and soldiers in the public sphere, can no longer so easily hide behind the orders of their superiors. On the other hand, it also implies, as a complement to that external accountability, a legitimation of certain forms of 'civil disobedience' within working hours.[21] If one wants functionaries to behave as responsible citizens, one must also provide them with the space in which to do so.

Citizenship of functionaries implies that the democratic control of organisations need not always happen indirectly, by way of the top political levels or of the company management, but that in some circumstances a direct role is also set aside for lower functionaries. Indiscreet or disloyal conduct on the part of civil servants or employees – think of Ponting or Dr Pierce – can be legitimate when the controlling capacity of the democratic bodies is brought or held to an acceptable standard. The notion of individual autonomy thus arises not just as a normative point of departure, an objective that must be reached, as in the case of the personal notion of responsibility, but also as an instrument, a device for keeping intact the republic of free and independent citizens. Unlike in the case of Harmon (1971) and the other supporters in the 1960s and 1970s of the politicisation and democratisation of organisations, however, it is not a question of democratisation and more individual autonomy *per se*. It is a question of autonomy that strengthens the primacy of politics. That means on the one hand that not all forms of individual autonomy are permitted, but it also means on the other hand that not all forms of indiscretion and disloyalty are excluded, as they were for Weber.

Would the acceptance of such a notion of bureaucratic responsibility mean that as a result the classic notion has lost its right to exist? In my view certainly not. The modern, efficient complex organisation may not be sacrificed to the political activities of its functionaries. To do so would not serve the interests of the political community of free and independent citizens. Where the corporate actor disappears, the citizen too forfeits his rights.

---

[21] This civil disobedience within working hours differs in one important way from 'ordinary' civil disobedience (cf. Rawls 1971; Schuyt 1972). In the latter case, disobedience to the law is an important element and it is always a question of illegal actions that mostly end in criminal proceedings. In the case of employee civil disobedience, the action can also be illegal, as in the case of Ponting, who was prosecuted on the basis of his violation of the Official Secrets Act, but that is certainly no constitutive element. However, there will always be violations of norms – not of a penal nature, but of the regulations, guidelines, and duties within the organisation. In the case of employee civil disobedience, it is therefore in principle a question of private law rather than of criminal law.

In ordinary circumstances loyalty to one's superior should therefore be the 'principal rule'. This rule is, however, not as absolute as in the classical notion; in special cases and under given circumstances, citizenship may take priority. It is sometimes legitimate that civil servants or employees are disobedient.

Employee civil disobedience

When could disobedience on the part of functionaries be legitimate from the point of view of employee citizenship? Which grounds for justification and requirements of due care would have to play a role in the judgment? In judging cases of employee disobedience the three principles that were distinguished by the classical notion can again stand central. As we have seen, there are no differences of opinion with the supporters of the classical notion regarding these points of departure. These three principles are not only the formal *grounds* for breaking the requirement of loyalty to one's superior but are at the same time the most important material *criteria* on the basis of which the disobedient conduct can be tested. For given that they are grounds for justification, they also set the limits to civil disobedience. They are here discussed in order of importance. In discussing them, I shall distinguish between the public and the private sector.

1. *Maintenance or strengthening of (democratic) control.* Loyalty to the public cause is central to the notion of citizenship. That means that employee disobedience is legitimate above all when the survival and the reproduction of a community of free and equal citizens is thereby promoted. In the practice of contemporary liberal democracies, this will mostly mean that the primacy of politics, the primacy of the representative, democratically legitimated bodies in the case of civil servants, or of the external, controlling bodies such as the judicial power in the case of employees, is thereby kept at or brought up to an acceptable level. That means that a large number of forms of disloyal behaviour are not legitimate at all; for example thwarting government or parliament as a civil servant for party-political, personal, or institutional reasons; or refusing to submit to examination by a judge.

It also means that a functionary acts responsibly only when the control, and where necessary the correction, by public bodies of his own behaviour does not become impossible. This will in most circumstances mean that it can be demanded of the functionary that (a) his conduct takes place in the open and (b) he is prepared and in a position to answer for his behaviour on the basis of public considerations. Secretly leaking or selling confidential documents so as to make impossible in advance a policy change desired by a government leader, or to do the same for reasons of personal gain, will hardly satisfy this demand. But refusing certain assignments on the basis of strictly personal, conscientious objections will also be difficult to reconcile with these demands.

Although private organisations too are subject to control by representative and public bodies, in practice the burden of proof for an employee who claims that his or her act of disobedience has been committed with this public interest in mind will presumably be heavier than for a civil servant. Unlike in the case of government organisations, not every obstruction of control by a company need be a matter of weighty public interest. For government organisations, stricter norms apply on this point than for companies. A number of the 'corporate risks' that were discussed in chapter 2 can, however, have such enormous consequences that their prevention readily becomes a centrally important matter of public interest. The notion of employee citizenship can therefore very well be applied to companies when the issues at stake concern the environment, organised fraud, large-scale and risky technologies, or unsafe installations and operations that can result in dangers to the public (for example on ferries, in amusement parks, at public events, or in nuclear or petrochemical installations).

2. *Observance of the principles of the constitutional state.* Among the public interests the principles of the constitutional state will occupy a prominent place. Possible grounds for official disobedience are for example (the threat of) an evident violation of the law or the failure to observe important principles of administrative law such as the principle of equality, due process or the prohibition of *détournement de pouvoir*. Just as in the case of the previous category, these principles not only offer grounds for disobedience but also set emphatic limits to those grounds. Indiscretion and disloyalty are justifiable only when the rule of law is thereby served. The individual functionary too must respect the law or the rights of his or her fellow citizens. The Ponting affair, for example, would have taken a quite different form if Ponting's disobedience had imperilled the lives of the inhabitants of the Falkland Islands or of British troops.

The observance of the principles of the constitutional state will not often be in so many words an issue for employees in business and industry; that element will often remain restricted to an observance of the law. As a result, civil servants will, in practice, be more likely to see a claim honoured than will employees when misdemeanours or the transgression of 'lower' administrative rules are at stake.

3. *Promotion of an efficient and effective administration.* Within the notion of employee citizenship, loyalty to the public cause is to the fore, but that

does not mean that considerations of efficiency and effectiveness should be neglected. On this point too the arguments of Taylor, Wilson, and Weber are still valid. The promotion, or at least maintenance, of an efficient and effective business management should therefore also be an important criterion. This principle, however, occupies only the third place. The promotion of an efficient business management can be a ground for disobedience only when the other two principles are not thereby violated. The notion of employee citizenship does not allow one to prevent democratic control of the organisation, or to violate important principles of law, with an eye to improving the administration or the profitability of one's own business. (The reverse, reducing the efficiency or effectiveness of the organisation with an eye to achieving a greater measure of democratic control or to preventing illegal conduct, is on the other hand quite possible and permissible).

In the case of government organisations, maladministration, waste, and mismanagement have an important public dimension; after all, they involve public means. In many western democracies the big scandals of the last few years were often related to the careless administration or inefficient use of government resources. It is quite easy to imagine that civil servants could in such situations, and under certain conditions, legitimately violate the hierarchical chain of command and turn directly to the top political leadership of their organisation or to the controlling bodies in an effort to raise the question of the waste or the maladministration. In some scandals this has actually happened – as we shall see in the following chapters.

Companies and other private institutions, however, unlike governments, are not financed by public means. Also, they are mostly not directed toward the promotion of public interests. Employees can as a result refer much less readily to the aims of their own organisation if they wish to defend their external forms of disobedience with an appeal to their citizenship. In the case of private organisations, unlike in that of governments, an efficient and effective business management is not by definition at the same time an important matter of public interest.[22]

This principle too can be both grounds for, and a limitation of, disobedience. Disobedience on the part of a civil servant who appeals on these grounds will therefore be acceptable only if it can be shown that the behaviour of the civil servant, in its turn, does not also lead to a large measure of waste or to serious forms of maladministration. The remedy – administrative indiscretion or disloyalty – should not be worse than the disease. Just as

---

[22] In the case of internal forms of disobedience, one could naturally refer to the aims of the company, but in that case, however idealistic one's intention, one could scarcely talk of (external) employee citizenship.

in the case of the above-mentioned grounds, a person's actual behaviour should serve to protect the interests that he or she claims to protect.

A substantive definition of the notion of citizenship in complex organisations along these lines means that the acceptance of forms of employee disobedience need not lead to the anarchy of 'anything goes'. In the case of the personal and social notions in which loyalty to the personal norms of the functionary or to the group are central, such a danger is indeed imaginable. After all, on the basis of which norms and of which criteria would outsiders have to judge the permissibility of disobedient conduct? External review criteria are largely lacking. However, the notion of citizenship and the justification of disobedience with reference to the above-mentioned public interests provide a basis and a direction for public discussion and judgment.

It should be obvious, however, that in judging employee disobedience one should not look only at these substantive grounds. In concrete cases, other, more procedural considerations will also play an important part. After all, we are dealing here with responsibility as virtue. That means, as we saw in chapter 3, that regardless of the substantive notion of responsibility, a number of requirements of care will play a role in the evaluation. Is there an adequate perception of an imminent violation of the above-mentioned general norms? Has consideration been given to the possible consequences of the behaviour for others? Was the decision reached after due deliberation? Did the functionary act on the basis of a consistent and verifiable code? Did the functionary take his (other) role obligations seriously?

On the basis of the above considerations, it is possible to concretise the civic notion of individual responsibility to some extent. As we have already seen, loyalty to one's superior remains the point of departure, but disobedience can under certain conditions be justifiable. In judging the legitimacy of concrete cases of employee disobedience, the following questions will have to play an important part:

1. *Can the disobedience be defended by an appeal to the protection of important public interests? In particular, and in order of importance, does the disobedience serve to:*

    a. *maintain or promote an acceptable level of democratic control of the organisation?*

    b. *promote the observance by the organisation of the principles of the constitutional state?*

    c. *promote an efficient and effective administration?*

2. *Are public forums offered the opportunity to call the functionary to account and to examine his or her behaviour? More particularly:*

    a. does the disobedience happen publicly?
    b. is the functionary prepared to defend his or her behaviour on the basis of the above-mentioned public considerations?

3. *Is it reasonable to assume that one of the interests mentioned is under threat?*

4. *Are the interests that one tried to protect by the act of disobedience more important than the interests that were violated by the act of disobedience? More particularly:*

    a. did the behaviour of the functionary not lead to a violation of the interests that he said he wanted to protect?
    b. has the functionary by means of his behaviour violated more important interests than those that he tried to protect?

5. *Is there is a meaningful connection between the disobedience and the concrete threat to important public interests? More particularly:*

    a. is the act of disobedience a reasonably adequate way of averting the threatened violation?
    b. were there other, less drastic means available for attaining the intended objective?

6. *Did the functionary try as much as possible to restrict the damage that might result from his disobedience?*

In arriving at a judgment as to the legitimacy of employee disobedience from a citizenship perspective, the first question, certainly in the case of public organisations, must in any case be answered affirmatively. In answering the remaining questions, more latitude will sometimes be possible; it is even possible that in some cases they will not be raised. Thus one can imagine that under certain circumstances, for example, within rather repressive organisations, a functionary will not always be able to be directly open about his or her disobedience. If the repercussions threaten to be excessive, but the other requirements are nevertheless satisfied, then at this point the 'cut-off for heroism' comes into effect.

The basic forms: exit, voice, and loyalty

Which forms of disobedience are we dealing with here? It will be obvious that many forms of employee disobedience remain unacceptable, even when one has at heart not one's own personal interest but larger interests. Think for example of the behaviour of the officials of the General Directorate for Industry in the Netherlands in the 1980s. In their zeal to rescue the RSV Concern, they took the side of the enterprise and dragged their feet about informing the other departments, the cabinet and

Parliament, of the big financial risks involved in further investment in the concern. In such cases the conditions formulated above are not satisfied. They took their conduct beyond the field of public control and examination and it turned out that their disobedience violated the interests they tried to protect. An important additional objection was moreover that their behaviour was irrevocable in character. A number of the consequences of their more or less disobedient conduct could no longer be rolled back; the contracts were already signed and the money spent.

It is therefore obvious that in judging disobedience from the point of view of employee citizenship, a distinction must be made between disobedience that consists of acting in the name and in the place of the organisation – what Kagan (1978: 92) calls 'unauthorised discretion', and disobedience that consists of passively preventing and exposing unacceptable forms of policy pursued by the organisation – what you might call 'unauthorised indiscretion'.

The active form of disobedience, unauthorised *discretion*, is highly problematic in the case of complex organisations, because of the irreversible and large-scale character of much corporate behaviour and of the risks that flow from it. The irreversibility of the consequences of the disobedience means that the conduct is withheld from *ex ante* control and review. That is even more problematic in the case of civil servants who in their active behaviour can make use of the monopoly of violence and on whom, as a result of their position, a general duty rests to assure themselves of the democratic legitimacy of their behaviour. For the more passive form of disobedience, unauthorised *indiscretion*, these objections are much less relevant. In the case of passive disobedience, most options still remain open for the organisation and it is in most cases possible, if the passive disobedience is found to be unjustified, to give the functionary an assignment or to have the assignment implemented by others.

What might that unauthorised indiscretion look like? How can functionaries react to the disfunctioning of their organisation? In answering these questions, the elegant threesome developed by Hirschman (1970) is most helpful. Although Hirschman restricts his analyses principally to voters and consumers, his ideas can be effortlessly applied to functionaries.[23] An employee or civil servant who is of the opinion that the performance of his or her organisation, in democratic, legal, or administrative respect, is seriously deteriorating can, broadly speaking, react in one of three different ways. He can quit the organisation (*exit*), he can give voice to his concern

---

[23] See Hirschman himself (1970: 98–105) and, for similar applications, Schuyt (1972: 60–9) and Oversloot and Van Gunsteren (1987).

Table 9.2 *Employee civil (dis)obedience*

	Exit	Voice	Loyalty
Exit	resignation	resignation in protest	working to the rule
Voice		whistleblowing/leaking	internal dissent
Loyalty			obedience

(*voice*), or he can decide to behave loyally (*loyalty*). Each of these three 'types' can combine with either one of the other two yielding the scheme shown in table 9.2.

Exit, in its purest form, occurs when a functionary has had enough and resigns of his or her own accord. In the case of resignation under protest, exit is combined with voice. Working to rule or 'inner emigration' are forms of semi-exit, the combination of exit with loyalty. In these situations the functionary remains a member of the organisation, but otherwise retreats from it as much as possible. An open refusal to work, as in the case of the Middelburg nurses, the Schiedam customs officer, and the American Dr Pierce, fits less well within the scheme, because it is in fact a combination of exit, voice, and loyalty. By virtue of a refusal, the functionary, it is true, quits the organisation in respect of one specific assignment or task, but at the same time remains otherwise loyal and available to the organisation. Moreover, the refusal will mostly happen on the basis of explicit objections. As a result, an element of voice is introduced that causes this form of refusal to stick out above quiet, underground sabotage or indifference. The various exit-options are dealt with in chapter 10.

In combination with loyalty, *voice* can assume the form of internal criticism. The functionary can make known his worries about the merits or the effects of a given policy and can try to convince his superiors and his colleagues of his point of view. When they do not want to listen, or the functionary himself is not satisfied with their answer to the points that he has raised, he can consider giving up his loyalty and decide to come out into the open and 'blow the whistle'. That can happen in secret, by way of leaks to the press or to others, so that the functionary himself remains out of harm's way. The classic example of this is 'Deep Throat' in the Watergate scandal. Ponting also falls into this category, even though in the event he did not succeed in maintaining his anonymity. The functionary can also publicly denounce the policy of his superiors, for example by holding a press conference or publishing a report, an article, or a book. A classic example of this is Daniel Ellsberg with his *Pentagon Papers*. Although both these examples concern pure forms of voice I will speak of 'whistleblowing' only in the second situation. For the first situation, the secret use of voice, I reserve the popular term 'leaking'. Both are dealt with in chapter 11.

The third option, *loyalty*, can also be a form of active individual responsibility within organisations. A functionary can also weigh against each other the consequences of a policy deemed undesirable by him and the consequences of his departure from his post or his criticism of the organisation; and, then, still decide to stay and to carry out his assignments loyally. This is by no means the same as unthinking – 'blind' – obedience. The functionary may have come to the conclusion that the time is not yet ripe, or that the disadvantages of the other options are greater than the advantages. Loyalty can from the point of view of employee citizenship be quite functional. It can lead to the retention of the most critical and active members of the organisation by the organisation and thus, for a while, prevent the start of a negative spiral of exit and further deterioration. A large measure of loyalty also ups the costs of exit and in that way forces functionaries to seek new, creative ways of giving form to their dissatisfaction within the organisation (Hirschman 1970: 79–80). However, such loyalty is dependent on the (estimate of the) extent to which the organisation will meet their criticism. In chapter 12, various possible forms of internal criticism are discussed.

10

Exit: resignation and refusal

> Judicial acceptance of a right to disobey would reaffirm the personal
> responsibility that each public employee must in theory exercise.
>
> (Vaughn 1977: 293)

Passive employee disobedience

The era in which bureaucratic functionaries behaved as described in Max
Weber's ideal-type and acquitted themselves of their tasks *sine ira et studio*,
without scorn or bias, lies behind us – if it ever did exist. The traditional,
loyal functionary is, at least in the Netherlands and the United States, slowly
but surely being succeeded in many organisations by independent-minded,
politically conscious professionals (Eldersveld et al. 1981: 241–7). One way
in which this change materialized is that from the mid-1970s onward, civil
servants and employees have regularly refused assignments on the grounds
of principled objections. We have already considered the cases of the
Zeeland nurses, the customs officer in the Netherlands, and that of Dr Pierce
in the United States. A series of other cases has arisen over the last few
decades in the Netherlands:

A bank employee refused to insure seal-skin coats. He found it irresponsible
that the bank contributed to the maltreatment and persecution of
animals.[1]

A health service employee in Amsterdam, charged with the statistical processing of data, refused to find out how many individuals with an Arabic
surname had used dental provisions. According to the employee the
assignment had a discriminatory import; he thought that the research data
might in future be used to the disadvantage of the ethnic group in question.[2]

Various civil servants working for municipal social services refused to implement a measure that required cuts in social security payments to so-called

[1] *De Volkskrant*, 16 February 1982.
[2] President of the District Court, Amsterdam, 21 August 1986 (not published).

176

'persons living under one roof'. In their opinion, this measure failed the weakest in society disproportionately, threatened their privacy, created inequality before the law, and was susceptible neither of monitoring nor of actual implementation.[3]

A senior police officer refused to work at Schiphol, Amsterdam's international airport any longer. In a seventeen-page report he criticised the equipment, the training, the motivation, and the remuneration of the police on the airport.[4]

These are just a few salient cases that over the years have reached the legal columns or the newspapers. Other examples of assignments refused by employees or civil servants are:

producing a TV broadcast by an extreme right-wing party;
printing anti-semitic, pornographic, or militaristic literature;
guarding nuclear weapons;
taking part in building work in a nuclear power station or on a military base;
transporting nuclear waste, dangerous chemical materials, or war materials;
driving a bus carrying an advertisement for the army;
providing declarations of non-Jewish descent by registration officers;
working with aggressive pesticides;
dumping chemical waste;
providing information about sex in a school;
cutting off gas supplies to defaulters;
working with laboratory animals;
helping with nuclear or genetic research;
deporting illegal aliens.

These cases are relevant because they are instances of 'unauthorised indiscretion'; they involve relatively passive forms of motivated employee disobedience. To what extent are they also expressions of individually responsible conduct given the rise of big complex organisations? At this point, we are back again at the question with which we began part III: what should a functionary do when he is given an assignment that he himself finds irresponsible?

The hierarchical answer: resignation

In the classical hierarchical conception of responsibility there is only one clear and unencumbered answer to this question: 'Take it or leave it.' Anyone who has objections to the nature of his assignments should resign. At work,

---

[3] Civil-service tribunal, Den Bosch, 1 May 1986, *Tijdschrift voor ambtenarenrecht* (Civil service journal) 1986: 165.
[4] *NRC Handelsblad*, 30 January 1986; *de Volkskrant*, 4 February 1986; *NRC Handelsblad*, 19 December 1986.

there is neither space nor time for scruples. The title of David Ewing's book (1983) sums up this standpoint perfectly: 'Do it my way, or you're fired!' In almost every one of the cases mentioned above, the disobedient employee was suspended, relieved of his or her functions, and finally nominated for dismissal.

At first sight, the classical employer's point of view is lucid and convincing. Both the private employee and the civil servant entered their labour agreement or joined the service voluntarily. They are paid by their organisation to promote the aims of the organisation and not to work for their own objectives or self-fulfilment. Moreover, by resigning they can keep their conscience clear in quite a simple way. Nobody forces them to stay. Unlike the ordinary (state) citizen, the functionary has the possibility to choose: he can leave the organisation and find another job.

Such a standpoint is clear and consistent, but on closer inspection hardly tenable as an answer. In the first place resignation is oftentimes not a real option. For many civil servants or employees, the price of a voluntary resignation will be extremely high. Only those functionaries who have special and highly marketable qualifications can easily find another employer, given the rigidity of the labour market in many Western countries. For many others, for example for the somewhat older employees, the labour market hardly leaves any choice at all. For such people, resignation means a choice for long-term unemployment. Moreover, under most systems of social security such a voluntary form of resignation leads directly to a very big fall in income, with all its consequences for a person's family. The classical answer is therefore unsatisfactory if only in a moral sense. It demands such a high price from the functionary – often also in terms of the moral obligations that one has in respect of one's family – that the cutoff for heroism all too quickly comes into effect.

From a control point of view, resignation is not a convincing answer either. The effect of such a step on the organisation involved often bears no relation to the high personal costs. The effectiveness of the exit-option strongly depends on the sensitivity of the organisation to the (threat of) exit by a few, or sometimes even by many, of its functionaries. When the organisation manages to find enough other qualified personnel easily, for example because of a slack labour market, it will experience few incentives to react to resignations on the part of its critical functionaries. It will presumably even be happy to see the back of such trouble-makers with their embarrassing questions and comments. Public organisations are often even less sensitive than private organisations to the exit option (Hirschman 1970: 44). Public organisations can appeal to various forms of financing that are mostly independent of turnover or sales figures. That insensitivity to exit is, paradoxically enough, even greater when public organisations have no monopoly on the services that they provide and when customers, in their turn, can (as a result) defect to private organisations. In such situations, the exit of critical functionaries – often the most motivated and creative members of the organisation – only leads to a worsening of the situation without creating any impulses that might lead to its improvement.[5]

If the answer 'take it or leave it' is consistently applied, it can moreover lead to a very one-sided composition of the public service or company. Only diehards and yes-men (or yes-women) will join the organisation and manage to put up with its ways. The exit-option therefore leads to an ossification of the organisation and to a further reduction of its learning capacity.

In the light of the problems central to this study, the exit-option will therefore not be all that attractive and may often even be counter-productive. After all, we are seeking forms of individually responsible conduct that might lead to *ex ante* prevention of the corporate risks. Individual responsibility of functionaries, both in the passive and in the active form, was especially attractive in that process because in that way use could be made of the insights of insiders. This could, for example, help to circumvent the problem of the internal and external outsiders. The exit-option, however, turns most of the involved insiders into outsiders. As a result, exit in its pure, unencumbered form is not a suitable response from the point of view of employee citizenship, either. It scarcely contributes to a public discussion of the behaviour of complex organisations.[6]

Instead of taking the costly and difficult way of resignation, the frustrated or concerned functionary may also decide to stay on and keep his or her head down in so far as it is possible to do so. The exit-option is therefore exercised not in a physical but only in a psychological sense. This is semi-exit, the combination of exit with loyalty, as for example in the case of go-slows, work-to-rules, or various forms of 'inner emigration'. The functionary remains a member of the organisation, but for the rest withdraws as much

---

[5] Hirschman (1970: 44–54, 74) himself gives as an example of an organisation that is not particularly sensitive to the threat of exit on the part of its functionaries or customers the American Postal Service. Commercial postal and parcel services lure away its best employees and offer big, critical customers a better service. The Postal Service continues, irrespective of this exit, to have the legal task of maintaining a nationwide infrastructure of postal services. As a result, however, there are fewer internal or external incentives to pay proper attention to the quality of these facilities.

[6] From the point of view of personal responsibility, in which keeping one's own hands and conscience clean is central, resignation is a more suitable option (Burke 1986: 177–8). Yet there, too, both normative (freedom of conscience is a basic right) and practical (the pluriformity of organisations) considerations argue for a certain tolerance of conscientious objections within organisations. See also chapter 9.

as possible. He can decide to keep strictly to the rules without any effort and flexibility on his part, or to take up a passive and indifferent position in the hope that in so doing he can at least prevent the worst and thus keep his hands as clean as possible.[7] However, this restricted form of exit has no more than a restricted effect either; it cannot change a reprehensible policy, but can at most moderate the effects of such a policy. Just as in the case of complete exit, it will greatly depend on the nature of the organisation and of the environment whether or not the deterioration in turnover and provision of services will give rise to positive policy changes.

Resignation in protest, the combination of exit and voice, has more to offer. It can be a clear signal, both inside and outside the organisation, that something is wrong. It can arouse outsiders, in particular curious journalists and members of inspection bodies and monitoring organs, and in that way create pressure.[8] However, it is rarely applied because of the rather heavy costs that the person protesting usually has to bear. He not only loses his job but also runs the risk of becoming an 'outcast'. Weisband and Franck (1975: 59) investigated the group of 389 American top officials who, voluntarily and in mid career, left government service between 1900 and 1970. Of them, 355 (91.3 per cent) resigned without any form of public protest; only 34 (8.7 per cent) accompanied their resignation with a public protest. Loyalty not to the public cause or to one's own conscience but to the President and the team was the rule and the dissidents often paid a high price for violating that loyalty:

> [W]hen a dissenter did make his view public, he has invariably been consigned to the political scrap heap. Further, prospects of service in the executive branch are out of the question. Appointments to the judiciary, insofar as these are within Presidential discretion, are unlikely to be proferred. Election to Congress is virtually precluded. Even the resigner's professional life is likely to be irrevocably discounted [. . .] beyond that, the public-protest resigner tends to become the object of a general successful effort – on the part of the Presidency, its agencies and its allies – to destroy his reputation and credibility
>
> (1975: 121–22).

Officials who do not belong to the political staff are not subject to such a strict requirement of loyalty to the President, but in the following chapter we will see that they too are often subject to similar requirements of loyalty and team-play and that the consequences for their personal and profes-

---

[7] This option is often used as a justification after the event when things genuinely get out of hand; it corresponds with the excuse of the lesser evil that is discussed in chapter 8.   [8] Cf. some of the cases discussed by Johnson and Kraft (1990).

sional lives are often equally great. The same goes for many employees in the business world (Jackall 1988). It will furthermore be obvious that this form of responsible conduct loses much of its force the lower the rung that one occupies on the ladder. The chance that, by publicly resigning, one's case will reach the newspapers – a possible measure of the effectiveness of the protest – diminishes the lower one finds oneself in the organisation.

We can therefore conclude that the possibilities of the exit-option, as a form of active responsibility, are relatively slight. Many organisations will not be all that sensitive to the exit of functionaries that can be replaced without too many problems; a number of public organisations will moreover scarcely be inclined to react even to an exodus of their most creative and enthusiastic workers. A braindrain of this sort will in such cases be nothing but counter-productive and the situation will more likely worsen than improve. Therefore, exit is an option that in most situations can function only as a last resort, when all the other options have failed or proved to be unworkable.[9]

The civic answer: a right to refuse

How then can one retain the most valuable employees for the organisation without putting gags on them? It would be worth to consider offering functionaries a restricted but general possibility of refusing assignments on grounds of principle. This could take the form of a general right of functionaries to remain indemnified against dismissal or other disciplinary measures when they refuse to carry out an assignment that in itself, or as a result of its consequences, is in conflict with important democratic or legal principles.

Such a right, formulated in general and public terms, to refuse assignments could not only deal with the problematic character of conscientious objections within bureaucratic organisations, but could also be of some help in keeping the problem of many hands within bounds. After all, it is a form of control in advance; by refusing concrete assignments, functionaries can prevent the often large-scale and in some cases irreparable damage that results from misconduct on the part of a complex organisation. In this way it can lessen the problem of prevention. Moreover, it is also a form of internal control; the functionaries of the organisation are often the first to realise that a policy or assignment is harmful or likely to have otherwise

---

[9] An improvement in the possibilities for politicians and senior officials to resign under protest would perhaps offer some chance of improving the control of public organisations by way of the exit-option. See for some suggestions Weisband and Franck (1975: 181–92) and Hirschman (1970: 119).

undesirable consequences. It can thus help toward solving the problems that result from the fact that not only the external inspections and controlling bodies but also the internal managers and supervising councils are often outsiders.

It emphasises, moreover, the autonomy and personal integrity of individual functionaries – even when they are but small cogs in a large machine. In this way, the development of such a right to refuse can help increase the power of morality within complex organisations. It can contribute to the emergence of a bureaucratic morality in which each functionary knows that he is responsible for the consequences of the partial task that he performs. The introduction of such a right therefore has an important symbolic function. It does not yet offer any direct protection nor does it lead automatically to virtuous action, but it shows that there are alternatives. It is at the very least a way of stripping the excuse of *Befehl ist Befehl* of its last shreds of plausibility.

The instrumental value of a right to refuse lies above all in its signalling function, both within the organisation and outside it. In this way a functionary can make known what is going on to his superior and to the outside world. For his colleagues it is a signal that they cannot make do with the simple execution of the tasks that are assigned to them. If they do – for example, they take over the task of their conscience-stricken colleagues – they know they may be asked later why they chose to obey.

As was already shown in the previous chapter, this public refusal to work is a combination of exit, voice, and loyalty. It is a form of semi-exit; one stays within the organisation, but no longer works on one particular concrete assignment or policy change. Because it is a question of a specific, public form of refusal to work, such a form of exit can be a much clearer and more direct signal than the more hidden forms of semi-exit. The element of loyalty – one stays active within the organisation – prevents the emergence of a number of the disadvantages that a complete exit entails. The individual functionary keeps some access to the internal flow of information and can still exercise some influence on the discussions. The organisation, on the other hand, is not completely deprived of what are all too often its best and most committed members.

The possibility of expressing voice is, on balance, of great importance. A public refusal to work by one or more functionaries is a very powerful expression of disquiet and criticism. The functionary will usually feel obliged to offer an explanation for his refusal. Such an explanation is an important form of 'feedback' for the organisation and should, if only for that reason, but also because of the possibility of testing, be an obligatory part of the refusal procedure. It is important that the element of voice applies not just within but also beyond the organisation. The conscience-stricken functionary must have the opportunity to make public his refusal, and the reasons that underlie it. In that way, the possibility remains open to warn the general public.[10]

A right to refuse could thus be a useful compromise between the often relatively powerless exercise of internal criticism and the one-off demonstration of power represented by the protest resignation. It would moreover also offer more possibilities to junior functionaries, for whom internal criticism or resignation under protest rarely makes sense because of their low status.

Framing a limited right to refuse

A right to refuse is no panacea and has a number of negative side-effects. As we have already seen, from an organisational or democratic point of view there are often good arguments for encouraging the greatest possible measure of obedience on the part of employees and civil servants toward their superiors. If the possibility of refusal is framed too broadly, there is the danger that the problem of many hands again crops up in other forms. Moreover, many complex organisations are in danger of losing much of the decisiveness which they have at their command, thanks to a more or less hierarchical structure and an orthodox notion of employee responsibility.

In chapter 9 we saw that arrangements that are framed in terms of 'conscientious objections' can be risky from the point of view of the effectiveness of the organisation. It turned out to be extremely important that limits regarding the contents of the objections can be set and that not every objection need be accepted 'at face value'. Similarly, a right of refusal should not become a means for resolving internal conflicts or promoting the personal interests and ideological prejudices of individual employees. Considerations of expediency and efficiency must also be able to play a role. In order to have a degree of effectiveness and legitimacy, such a right should therefore be carefully framed.

How might such a general right look? More specifically: (1) What is meant by 'refusal'? (2) What are the grounds for justification? (3) What are the requirements of due care? (4) What are the (procedural) consequences?

Regarding the first question, I can be relatively brief. As I have already indicated in the previous chapter, it is sensible when dealing with this sort of issue to make a distinction between 'active' disobedience: acting and behaving in lieu of the organisation, and 'passive' disobedience: the prevention and denunciation of misconduct on the part of the organisation. I have therefore deliberately spoken of a right to *refuse* and not of a right to

---

[10] See the following chapter for a more detailed discussion of this element of voice.

disobey, as, for example, Vaughn (1977) does. 'Refusal' implies a much more restricted degree of activity (or inactivity) than 'disobedience'. An over-zealous police officer who, without having been in any way ordered to do so, bugs or wire-taps organisations that he suspects of subversive activities, or a social-security worker who gives benefits to a client who is not eligible for them but who, in his opinion, should be object of government attention, are engaging not in a 'refusal to work', but in an act of disobedience. I do not exclude that there are circumstances in which such an active form of dis-obedience is an adequate form of employee responsibility,[11] but I do not want to stretch the idea of 'refusal to work' that far. Here, I look solely at the refusal to carry out concrete tasks in conformity with assignments handed down by superiors.

The *material grounds* on which the refusal can be justified were discussed in the previous chapter. In that chapter I distinguished a number of (sub)questions that can play a role in judging employee civil disobedience. The first question is above all important: Can the refusal to work be defended by an appeal to important public interests? For a legal operation-alisation of these public interests and principles one can use current legisla-tion and jurisprudence in the Netherlands and the United States.[12] Even now a number of general grounds are already recognised to which civil ser-vants and employees with principled objections can appeal. If one combines this current law with the views elaborated in the previous chapter, a number of grounds arise on the basis of which a refusal to work can, under certain circumstances, be justified:

Violation of rules and regulations. This is the classical, universally accepted justification for refusing work, both for civil servants and for employees, that is not grounded in the protection of the conscience of the person com-plaining himself. This will apply in particular when the implementation of the assignment constitutes an illegal act on the part of the civil servant or the employee, for example in the case of fraud, corruption, and other types of white-collar crime. According to Dutch law (Olbers 1984: 151–5), the employee has the general duty to refuse assignments that he knows are in conflict with the penal code. Also, the law on working conditions sometimes offers employees the right to refuse assignments, for example when an instruction to do overtime is in conflict with labour law,[13] or with regula-tions governing driving hours. In the United States, too, employees who refuse to participate in illegal or unethical activities are in most states pro-

---

[11] One can think of police officers, soldiers, or officials in occupied or dictatorially administered areas who deliberately free prisoners, falsify papers, or offer other forms of help to victims of the regime.

[12] See for a similar discussion of American law Vaughn (1977).

[13] See for example HR, 6 April 1979, *NJ* 1979, 492.

tected against dismissal (Dworkin and Callahan 1991: 287). Such a refusal can vary from a refusal to pay bribes, or a refusal to falsify pollution control reports, to a refusal to engage in discriminatory practices (Aron 1992: 213). A separate issue here is the status of the rules. In the case of Dr Pierce,[14] which was discussed in chapter 9, the New Jersey Supreme Court included not only local, state, or federal legislation, but also administrative rules, regulations, and decisions, as well as judicial decisions. The transgression of a professional code of ethics is sometimes also accepted as grounds for refusal. However, that can be the case only if the concrete rule was directed toward the protection of a public interest (Aron 1992: 211–12).

A substantial and specific danger to public health, safety, or the environment. These grounds can also be found in many regulations. The Conscientious Employee Protection Act of New Jersey, for example, allows employees to refuse to participate in 'anything that they reasonably believe to be "incompatible with a clear mandate of public policy" concerning the public health, safety, welfare or the protection of the environment' (Aron 1992: 212). Another example of such a general grounds for refusal can be found in the Dutch law on working conditions. That law expressly gives employees the right to stop working when there is a question of a serious and acute danger to individuals. One also finds such a right in the collective labour agreements in the textile industry ('the threat of calamities that might lead to an acute danger to safety and health') and in the chemical industry.

Abuse of powers or a demonstrable and flagrant conflict with the aims of the organisation. When someone in charge gives an assignment that he is not competent to give, this assignment is, in the Netherlands, legally speaking null and void and civil servants are not required to implement it.[15] One could also imagine that the employees of a foundation that exceeds its authority or of an association that violates its own statutes could not without further ado be accused of a simple refusal to work if they refused to cooperate in such an act.

A demonstrable, large-scale waste of public funds. In the light of the recent series of scandals involving large-scale overspending or waste of government support or subsidies – think of the RSV scandal – one can imagine that a civil-service tribunal would not readily sanction the sacking or reprimanding of an official who under such circumstances refuses an assignment. On this point, one could refer to the many whistleblowing provisions that explicitly mention these grounds for justification.[16]

---

[14] *Pierce v. Ortho Pharmaceutical Corp* (1980) 84 N. J. 58.
[15] Centrale Raad van Beroep (Central Court of Appeal) 17 February 1971, AB 1972, 11. [16] See the following chapter.

This list is by no means exhaustive. In legal and administrative practice, other principles exist that might be able to play a role as the occasion arises. Think for example of the obligations that a given public office can entail, of the rules of the democratic process, or of the right of animals to proper treatment. However, the list is also limited. There is only a limited number of grounds for legitimation. This prevents the opening up of a Pandora's box, as would happen in the case of a general rule framed in terms of conscientious objections.[17] By no means all the cases of refusal to work mentioned at the beginning of this chapter could be subsumed under one of these categories.

It should be clear that a refusal to work is not legitimised purely by virtue of the fact that one formulates one's objections in such a way that they can be subsumed under one of these categories. The refusal must also satisfy the more formal *requirements of due care* if it is not to lead to dismissal or some other disciplinary measure. Refusal to work on the basis of generally recognised public interests can still lead to a charge of non-performance, or wrongful conduct. For a formulation of these norms of due care, one can turn to the five remaining (sub)questions in the previous chapter. Here, too, one might refer also to the existing literature and to case law, in particular in the field of the right to strike and civil disobedience. When judging concrete forms of refusal to work, the following questions should also play a role:

> *Did the refusal take place publicly and was it reasoned?* The refusal to work on grounds of principle differs from an ordinary refusal to work not only because it must be argued on the basis of public interests, but it is in a certain sense also a public act that requires an answer. That is particularly so in the case of civil servants. Public forums, such as representative bodies, arbitration committees, civil service tribunals, and courts of law, must be offered the possibility of calling the functionary to account and of weighing his arguments and testing his behaviour. It is necessary therefore, that functionaries must make their objections known to their superiors in writing and that they must give reasons for those objections.
>
> *Is it reasonable to assume that one of the named interests was likely to be violated?* The functionary must be able to show, in the light of the information and circumstances known at the time of the refusal, that a violation was indeed to be expected. That expectation must be objectivised to a certain extent; the functionary cannot make do simply with reproducing

---

[17] This does not mean that within organisations there is no room at all for conscientious objections (as defined in chapter 9). However, the framing of such a provision goes beyond the framework of this study.

his strictly personal point of view. It must be obvious that a reasonable thinking person in the same position would have been able to come to a similar conclusion. New Jersey's Conscientious Employee Protection Act, for example, requires that there must be a 'reasonable belief' (Aron 1992: 212). Vaughn (1977: 265, 284) even goes one step further and demands that the conviction should have arisen in 'good faith'. This latter requirement is in my view redundant. If one proceeds on the basis of the requirement that a reasonable person, on the basis of the circumstances as known at that moment, could have reached the conclusion that an assignment is irresponsible, then that should be sufficient. One need not enter into the possible motives and integrity of the person complaining. The content and plausibility of the objection, and not the motives of the person complaining, should in the course of the review be to the fore.

Is there a reasonable connection between the refusal and the concrete threat to the named public interests? The refusal must in the first place relate to relevant assignments or activities. The functionary must be able to show that the refusal of the assignment will indeed contribute to averting the concrete threat. In the second place he must be able to show that other, less drastic means of averting the threat were not (or no longer) available. The refusal must be not only a relevant remedy but also a remedy of last resort.

Does the refusal not lead to a violation of the interests that one claims to be protecting? The remedy must not be worse than the disease. An official of the social service who refuses to make any payment whatsoever, because he thinks a new ruling infringes upon his clients basic social rights, is acting inconsistently. Therefore, he should not have his objection honoured. It is unacceptable that the interests that the functionary claimed to be protecting should end up being damaged as a result of his refusal. In that respect, the number of objectors can also play a role. If the example of the Schiphol guard were to be followed on such a massive scale that any real protection of travellers were to become impossible, that fact would in itself be a relevant consideration in judging the legitimacy of any later such refusals.

Does the refusal not lead to the violation of weightier interests than the interests that the functionary was trying to protect by means of his refusal? This is the requirement of proportionality. The public interest that is served by the refusal must be weighed up against other public interests that are violated by the refusal. For example, it is highly questionable whether the refusal of a customs officer – think of the case of Jacoby – to give information about a colleague who allegedly takes bribes can pass muster. In the case of a serious crime, the right to privacy of a colleague will in most cases lose out. Moreover, it must be evident that the public interest that is served by the refusal weighs more heavily than the interests of the organisation or the personal interests of individual citizens who are harmed as a result of the refusal. To champion a legitimate but relatively unimportant public interest, or to strive to avert a relatively unlikely and remote threat which produce a serious violation of the rights and interests of individual clients or of the effectiveness of the organisation will scarcely be found to be careful.

Did the functionary try to limit the damage that resulted from his refusal as much as possible? If damage to legitimate interests actually does result from the refusal – and in many cases it will not be possible to avoid such damage completely – then it may be expected of a careful functionary that he will try to restrict that damage to a minimum. For example, depending on the circumstances, the functionary can be expected to make his refusal known in good time and in an adequate way to his superior, to hand over the relevant dossiers, and to hold himself available loyally to carry out tasks that are not directly connected to the challenged assignment.

This list is likewise not exhaustive; it is conceivable that in legal practice a refusal to work could be considered to be without due care for other reasons. The formulation and further elaboration of these requirements of care is typically a task that must be left to precedent. The list is moreover not fully cumulative. As I already indicated in the previous chapter, it is conceivable that the questions will not all have to be raised or answered affirmatively. If the threat is extremely acute, it will for example not always be possible to announce the refusal publicly, in writing, and in good time.

Subsequently, what *consequences* would have to be tied to the refusal to work? Unlike in the case of conscientious objections, an extended discussion and substantive review of the objection would be appropriate, for example by means of an independent arbitration committee or labour court. After all, one can exchange ideas and reach judgments about public principles without having to creep into the skin of the person complaining at the same time. Principal objections thereby lose their absolute, intractable character. The fact that objections can be talked about will presumably promote the general readiness for compromise and improve the atmosphere in the organisation. It will also prevent functionaries with principled objections from going 'underground' and withdrawing their disobedience from discussion and review. Moreover, the person complaining is in this way offered a forum. One thus provides the possibility for hearing both sides of the argument and the chance for starting up a general discussion about the functioning of the organisation.

A review by an independent forum is also in order to protect the organisation or the general public from overzealous, negligent or malafide employees. In the course of that review, one may therefore also set substantive limits. In the first place, one no longer needs to take every objection at face value. Precisely because one appeals to fundamental and public principles, a reviewing body can itself arrive at a substantive judgment about the relative importance and the threat to the invoked principle. A weighing-up of the issue against other interests and principles therefore always remains possible. Moreover, each principle sets its own limits. Considerations of expedience can also play a role in the procedure. Limits can be set that relate to the interests of the organisation where the person complaining works, such as the importance of an effective and efficient administration. The number of objectors can also play a role in the matter.

If it turns out that the assignment was indeed unauthorised, that people's health is threatened, or that the organisation comes into conflict with the law as a result of the assignment, the refusal would be correct and the functionary should enjoy a broad measure of protection against dismissal. That protection would in the first place mean a reinstatement to the same or to an equivalent position, in the case of functionaries who had suffered dismissal or suspension. One can also think of other equitable remedies, such as the restoration of seniority and fringe benefits, or the payment of reasonable litigation costs and lawyer's fees (Aron 1992: 213; Barnett 1992b: 446). In some American states compensation of the actual, non-economic, damages is also possible. If the objections are declared groundless, all that remains is to resume cooperating or to resign voluntarily. Compulsory resignation would be appropriate if it could be proved that the refusal was groundless, negligent, or careless.

11

Voice: whistleblowing and leaking

Havelaar waited that evening. He waited the whole night. He had hoped that displeasure at the tone of his letter would perhaps achieve what he had tried in vain to achieve by means of gentleness and patience. His hope was groundless! The Governor-General left without having heard Havelaar. Another Excellency had retired to the motherland!

(Multatuli 1973 [1860]: 291)

Whistleblowing and citizenship

BCCI, RSV, Uniser, Challenger, Slavenburg, Savings and Loans – the list of fiascos and scandals in which complex organisations have played a principal part is long. For many people, these scandals come again and again as a surprise. The general public often lacks the expertise and insight to evaluate the signals. Controlling organs, both within the organisation itself and outside it, do not always manage to foresee the derailments in time. Many managers, some of them deliberately, are outsiders in their own organisation. But such ignorance never affects everybody. For some within an organisation, a scandal definitely does not come out of the blue. In many cases, personnel at the preparatory and executive levels know at an early stage that things are going wrong. However, that information does not reach the right place, or it does not reach it in good time.

How can one ensure that information about imminent fiascos, mismanagement, and transgressions of the law is received in the right place and in good time? One way is the introduction of whistleblowing provisions, legal measures aimed at the protection of employees and civil servants who go public with information about misconduct by or the disfunctioning of their organisation. In this chapter, I will consider the extent to which such an approach deserves imitation from the point of view of employee citizenship. I will first present a few examples of whistleblowing so as to give us an idea of the issues at stake:

Eduard Douwes Dekker, Assistant-Resident of Lebak in the Dutch East Indies, noted with sorrow how the local regent and the other native chiefs cowed the local population and regularly contravened the regulations. On 24 February 1856, he sent an official account of what he had seen to the

Resident of Bantam, accompanied by a request for strict measures to be taken. When the resident refused to take any action, Douwes Dekker sent his complaint to the Governor General of the Dutch East Indies. Eventually, in 1860, he made the affair public in the book *Max Havelaar*, under the pseudonym Multatuli. This novel is still regarded as a high-point in Dutch literature.

Daniel Ellsberg, who was employed in various confidential functions at the Pentagon, the US State Department, and the RAND Corporation, discovered in the course of writing a memorandum for McNemara, the Minister of Defence, that various American governments had lied to Congress about American involvement in the Vietnam War over the years. In the course of 1969 and 1970, he sent the relevant secret documents, the so-called 'Pentagon Papers' – a total of more than 7,000 pages – to a number of senators and later also to the press.[1]

Dan Gellert, a pilot working for Eastern Airlines with more than twenty-five years' experience, discovered a mistake in the automatic steering while flying a new prototype. He told the test department, but the model was nevertheless passed as fit for flying. When four months later, in December 1972, one of the new airplanes crashed and more than 100 passengers died, he sent his findings to the management. However, the management took no action. Gellert then sent the report to the National Transport Safety Board and appeared as witness in the hearings about the accident.[2]

Willem Hoevenagel, head of general affairs at the Dutch ABP, the big pension fund for civil servants, observed with mounting concern a number of dubious transactions on the part of the director of the investment fund, A. Masson. In June 1983 he could not take it any longer. He wrote a black paper that he sent through civil service union channels to various members of the Dutch parliament. This black paper marked the beginning of the ABP scandal, and later played an important part in the criminal prosecution and conviction of Masson on counts of fraud and corruption.[3]

These are but four among many cases (see Glazer and Glazer 1989). Some whistleblowers have become public figures or have been perpetuated in films and books. Examples include Daniel Ellsberg, 'Deep Throat', Karen Silkwood, Frank Serpico, and Hugh Kaufman in the United States, Clive Ponting in the United Kingdom, and Max Havelaar in the Netherlands.

The element common to each of these cases is that a member (or ex-member) of an organisation, without having received an assignment or

---

[1] See for the background of this case Ellsberg (1972: 9–41) and Schrag (1974).
[2] Gellert's story can be found in the *Civil Liberties Review*, September-October 1978: 15–19 (reprinted in Westin and Salisbury 1980: 106–10). See also Ewing (1983: 145–52).
[3] *NRC Handelsblad*, 28 and 29 November 1986; *de Volkskrant*, 28 November 1986.

consent to that end from someone in a position of authority, reveals information or in some other way goes public with the aim of drawing attention to an abuse of which he gained knowledge by virtue of his work within the organisation.

Two observations are pertinent in passing. In its broad sense, the term 'whistleblowing' includes almost every case in which someone publicly warns about abuses. Here the term will not be used so broadly and we will restrict ourselves exclusively to members of an organisation going public. Moreover, it is important that those in power should not have given any assignment or consent. We are interested above all in revelation as a possible form of civil employee disobedience. That also means that the external forms of whistleblowing, in which the information is taken outside one's own organisation proper, are central to this chapter. Whistleblowing can, however, assume both internal and external forms.[4] Often one will first blow the whistle internally, within one's own organisation, and go public only if that initial step yields no result.[5] For example, Douwes Dekker first warned the Resident, then the Governor General, and only then went public with his *Max Havelaar*. The more internal forms of whistleblowing, which are much more likely to be expressions of loyalty, will be discussed in the following chapter.

In assessing whistleblowers, the way in which the whistleblower went public will often be of considerable importance. Sometimes 'whistleblowing' label is restricted to those cases in which one goes fully public and abandons all anonymity. In that way, whistleblowing is distinguished from 'leaking', where one remains anonymous. This distinction will not be closely observed here, because we are concerned in the first place with a description of the phenomenon. However, it will play a role when the requirements of due care are discussed. Many whistleblowers – for example, Ellsberg and Ponting – begin with a leak to parliament or the press and only then, sometimes against their will, drop the cloak of anonymity. Even after all these years the identity of 'Deep Throat', who leaked about Watergate, is still a well-kept secret.[6]

It should be clear, moreover, that the term 'whistleblowing', like the

---

[4] It should be obvious that 'internal' and 'external' are relative notions. If a complex organisation is built up of a number of sub-units – and when is that not the case? – where there are holding companies or decentralised government bodies, for many members of the sub-unit the outside world will begin with the next layer of administration.

[5] See the steps in the process of whistleblowing that Stewart (1980) distinguishes.

[6] One ought, by the way, to realize that far from every leak is at the same time a case of whistleblowing. Many leaks are not inspired by worries about attacks on public interests, but by people's own personal interests or by considerations that have to do with office politics (Bovens, Geveke, and De Vries 1995).

comparable terms 'civil disobedience' or 'principled objection' discussed in the previous chapters, is not an absolutely neutral, strictly descriptive term but already carries within it a certain degree of benevolence. After all, by describing a given case of indiscreet conduct as 'whistleblowing', the speaker indicates that he proceeds on the assumption that the functionary concerned is acting from noble motives. Others, for example the supporters of the classical notion of responsibility, and those in authority who are involved in the case, will quickly talk of 'snitching' or 'alarmism' or even, if they become really exercised, of 'treason' (Laframboise 1991).

The plight of whistleblowers

Most whistleblowers get caught up in conflicts of loyalty. Their direct superiors and often their colleagues, too, expect them to implement the actual policy of the organisation loyally, to maintain solidarity with the 'team', and to be discreet in relation to the outside world. For bureaucratic organisations as Weber (1980 (1920):573) noted, official secrets are especially sacred. On the other hand, many whistleblowers feel obliged, with or without an appeal to their consciences, to honour other loyalties, for example to parliament, to the formal aims of the organisation, to the customers, or to their own professional group. In many cases, whistleblowing also implies an accusation against one's superior or one's colleagues – they have failed in regard to their obligation of supervision or have behaved improperly in some way.

The position of whistleblowers is therefore precarious. As in most groups with a strong degree of social or hierarchical control, the price for publicly breaking ranks is high. Complex organisations have at their disposal a broad range of formal and informal sanctions that in such cases can be imposed either publicly or in some more subtle way. Douwes Dekker was reprimanded by the Governor General, relieved of his post, and transferred – whereupon he himself resigned. Ellsberg and Ponting, once their identity became known, were dismissed and subjected to criminal prosecution. The pilot Gellert was banned from flying by Eastern Airlines when he sent a second report to the National Transport Safety Board. Only after years of litigation did he succeed in getting the ban lifted. In other cases, whistleblowing has led to psychiatric investigation, degradation, the loss of chances of promotion, suspension, fines, and other disciplinary measures; whistleblowers have also often been the victims of social ostracism and harassment.[7] The chance of such sanctions can bring the whistleblower into

---

[7] See for an empathetic description of the fate of a number of American whistleblowers Glazer (1983) and Glazer and Glazer (1989). See also Nader, Petkas, and Blackwell (1972), Parmerlee, Near, and Jensen (1982), and Ewing (1983: 133–42). For Britain, see Norton-Taylor (1985: 124–8).

conflict with a third group of loyalties – those to one's self, to one's kin, or to the others who are dependent on the whistleblower's wage or salary.

In the United States, Congress has come to the aid of whistleblowers, partly as a result of Watergate and the important role that internal leaks – such as those by 'Deep Throat' – played in the bringing the affair to light.[8] The Civil Service Reform Act, which was passed by Congress in 1978, prohibited federal institutions from dismissing or otherwise punishing civil servants who bring information about mismanagement into the open. Since then, the protection for whistleblowers has been increased enormously. More than twenty-five federal laws have provisions for whistleblowers, in both the public and private sector. In sectors especially susceptible to risk, such as mining and nuclear energy, or in the case of environmental pollution or fraud, employees who complain to controlling bodies about unhealthy, unsafe, or fraudulent situations receive extra protection against dismissal or discrimination (Dworkin and Callahan 1991: 269–274; MSPB 1993: 34). In 1989 the Federal Whistleblowers Protection Act further strengthened the position of official whistleblowers. Also, nearly forty states have passed statutes to protect whistleblowers (Near and Miceli 1995).[9] Other western countries, too, are increasingly establishing special whistleblowing provisions.[10]

Later in this chapter I shall investigate how protection has taken shape in the United States and how the relevant legislation is functioning. First, however, I will consider the precise meaning of such protection. Why should one actually tolerate such forms of disobedience?

Justifying whistleblowing

At first sight there do not seem to be many arguments in favour of permitting whistleblowing and even fewer of actually promoting it. Breaking

---

[8] Another big influence on public opinion was the book by Nader, Petkas, and Blackwell (1972). A big influence on the decision-making process in Congress was the report by Senator P. Leahy, *The Whistleblowers: A Report on Federal Employees Who Disclose Acts of Government Waste, Abuse and Corruption Prepared for the Senate Comm. on Governmental Affairs*, 95th Cong., 2nd Sess. 42–44 (1978). A description of a number of early cases can be found in Peters and Branch (1972); background analyses can be found in Westin and Salisbury (1980), Westin (1981), and Bok (1981; 1982: ch. XIV).

[9] For an overview of state whistleblower protection statutes, see Barnett (1992b), Aron (1992), and Dworkin and Callahan (1991).

[10] Thus for example the state of South Australia adopted its own Whistleblowers Protection Act (no. 21 of 1993) in 1993. In Europe there are still hardly any explicit provisions. See for a survey of the situation in the European Union, Public Concern at Work (1995).

confidentiality is far from always salutary and is often done out of motives that are anything but pure. It can be inspired by resentment, by self-interest, or by political considerations. And how do we stop provisions for whistleblowers from becoming an operating base for quarrelmongers, self-appointed moral censors, or spies (Laframboise 1991)? Moreover, the effectiveness of complex organisations surely depends on a very high measure of loyalty and discretion on the part of its functionaries. If employees expose each assignment, remark, or development which does not please them, this would soon lead to the paralysis of the organisation and confusion in the outside world. In order to work quickly and efficiently, peace and quiet and a certain degree of resolution are indispensable.

If civil servants blow whistles, there is an added reason to be careful. Whistleblowing activities can be inspired by party interests and 'fourth power' aspirations. They can lead to unwanted forms of politicisation of the public service, and even to the *Beamtenherrschaft* so feared by Weber. It is therefore not up to civil servants but in the first place to popular representatives – and after that perhaps to the courts – to decide whether the policy will pass muster. Moreover, what remains of confidence? Whistleblowing can, by accident or design, lead to the revelation of information that for political or strategic reasons should stay secret. When information is involved that has been entrusted by citizens or companies to the organisation (for example in the case of a hospital, an insurance company, or the tax office), or when the personal life of colleagues or superiors is involved, whistleblowing can strongly undermine the privacy of third persons or cause irreparable damage to reputations.

Discretion and loyalty should therefore be paramount. This is a good point of departure, but it is by no means an absolute truth. One can argue for a degree of tolerance of whistleblowers and even for some support on the basis of three sorts of considerations.

First, there are considerations of a constitutional nature: whistleblowing is a *form of free speech*. If only from the point of view of basic rights, whistleblowing deserves a certain measure of protection – even if that speech takes place during working hours or concerns matters that have to do with the work itself.[11] The protective effect of basic rights no longer stops short of the factory gate, the service entrance, or the porter's office. In the United States, public sector whistleblowers have been accorded constitutional protection under the First Amendment to the Constitution (Aron 1992: 219). In the Netherlands, the civil service law, for example, now admits only one restriction on the freedom of speech for civil servants: only when the proper

[11] See for pleas for protection of whistleblowers from a constitutional perspective Ewing (1977); Westin and Salisbury (1980).

discharge of a person's function or the proper functioning of the public service can in all reasonableness no longer be ensured will the official be expected to restrain himself.

Secondly, there are pragmatic, instrumentalist considerations: whistle-blowing can be an important *source of information,* an additional instrument for the control of complex organisations and for the prevention of 'corporate risks'.[12] Within this perspective, whistleblowing need not be directed toward external, public interests *per se;* it can also aim to facilitate the internal provision of information. After all, employees often have a large amount of factual knowledge about the goings on in their (part of the) organisation at their disposal and may therefore be aware of abuses and failures at an earlier stage than the relative or absolute outsiders at the top of the organisation or in the inspecting bodies. Moreover, fraud and violations of the law are phenomena preponderantly associated with the lower and middle levels of management (Coffee 1981: 397). In the recent past, whistle-blowing activities have been able to play an important part in bringing to light various abuses. I have already pointed to the role of Hoevenagel in exposing the corruption at ABP and to the role of 'Deep Throat' in the Watergate affair. Another example is the investigation into the black-money circuit at Slavenburg's Bank, an affair which broke thanks to the scruples and the secret files of one of the book-keepers at the bank. When the proper channels work too slowly, distort the contents of messages, or block the process of transmission, whistleblowing can be an unorthodox but adequate means of passing on vital information at an early stage to executive or controlling bodies.

The combination of these constitutional and pragmatic considerations yields a third consideration of a political-moral sort: whistleblowing as an *expression of citizenship.*[13] The protection of whistleblowers stresses the personal responsibility of functionaries, not just for the well-being of their own organisation but also for the safety of their fellow citizens and the functioning of the political community. Not only is whistleblowing important as a source of information for outsiders but it is also an important signal to the insiders. Criticism demands an answer, a justification of the existing situation, and thus forces the organisation to think about its policy. The permitting of dissident voices is one way of turning managers into participants. Moreover, as a result, others with the same scruples can begin to feel strong

---

[12] An argument in favour of whistleblowing from an instrumentalist perspective can be found in Stone (1975: 213–16).

[13] See for a justification of whistleblowing that is principally based on considerations of ethics and citizenship Nader, Petkas, and Blackwell (1972); see also Bok (1982: 210–29).

enough to make their own objections known.[14] Protection is thus also a pre-condition for negating the excuse of *Befehl ist Befehl* – not just after the event, from the easy moral high ground of the spectator, but also before-hand, in the actual situation of someone in a subordinate position. Furthermore, dissident voices break through the excuse of ignorance that colleagues could otherwise rightfully advance. The various social-psychological studies on employee obedience show, as we have already seen in chapter 8, that the presence of dissidents and critical voices led to a substantial decrease in people's readiness to take part in the experiments (Kelman and Hamilton 1989: 158). Thus, with the help of the various forms of voice, the preventive power of moral restrictions within the organisation can be amplified and outside the organisation citizens and public bodies are enabled to judge the activities of the organisation. In this way, the institutionalisation of whistleblowing can act as an instrument for bringing about a change in mentality: a shift from an 'Eichmannian' to a 'Camusian' model of responsibility (Schuyt 1972).[15]

The effects of whistleblowing

In the framework of this study, one question is of particular importance: can whistleblowing contribute to the prevention of corporate deviance and to the solution of the problem of many hands? Over the last ten years much research has been done into the personality characteristics of whistleblowers and the circumstances under which whistleblowing is most likely to happen (Dozier and Miceli 1985; Miceli and Near 1985; Near and Miceli 1986). Much less is known so far about the actual effects of whistleblowing on the conduct of organisations (Perry 1992; Near and Miceli 1995). The little research that has been done yields a mixed picture.

The thesis that whistleblowing can remedy the lack of timely and adequate information about misconduct on the part of complex organisations would seem to have been borne out. Research into the effects of the Civil Service Reform Act showed that a considerable number of federal civil servants said that they were aware of cases of fraud, waste, mismanagement, and abuse of powers (1980: 45 per cent; 1983: 25 per cent). In approximately half of those cases informants estimated the losses at more than $1,000; 15

---

[14] Johnson and Kraft (1990: 865) describe for example how the actions of Hal Freeman, an official in the American Office for Civil Rights who resigned under protest because of the refusal of the leadership to deal with complaints about discrimination by people with AIDS, gave others the courage to speak out.

[15] The latter model was described by Schuyt as follows: 'I remain responsible for the consequences both of my obedience and of my disobedience' (1972: 393).

per cent even thought that in their institution more than $100,000 was lost through wastage (MSPB 1984: 12–22). In practice, however, it seemed that approximately 70 per cent of those civil servants put their knowledge of improper administrative practices to no further use. For a number of them, fear of retaliation was the most important reason. A first condition for the effectiveness of whistleblowing is therefore that the whistleblower, as the harbinger of bad news, should not need to fear retaliation by the organisation directly.[16]

The majority of those questioned (53 per cent) kept quiet, however, not so much for fear of reprisals as because they were convinced that nothing would ever be done with the information they provided (MSPB 1984: 31–5). That brings us to a second important condition which, because it is so obvious, can be easily overlooked: whistleblowing activities as such do not lead to an improvement in the flow of information. Facilities for whistleblowers have an effect only when the processing of the information is fast and effective and the potential whistleblowers know that this is so. Whistleblowing is meaningful only thanks to a public that hears the whistle loud and clear and is in a position to do something about it (Bok 1980: 3). Whistleblowing stands or falls with an alert and active press, with an active popular representation, or with an alert leadership at the head of the organisation. Johnson and Kraft (1990: 868) even suggest that 'a favorable political environment' is the most essential factor for the successful policy impact of whistleblowing. The whistleblower himself can, moreover, by effective political behaviour, contribute to the creation of such an environment. Of great importance for the effectiveness of federal whistleblowers is for example that the whistleblowers seek out current political agendas and politically appropriate constituencies (Perry 1992: 94).

The expectation, on the basis of Hirschman's work, that whistleblowing would also lead directly to a change in behaviour within organisations has not yet been confirmed by research into federal institutions (Perry 1992: 92–3). No clear linkage between voice and organisational performance could be established. Perry suggests that this might have to do with the dissentient nature of some whistleblowing disputes, the ambiguity of performance norms, and the limited effect of individual action on organisational performance.

Whistleblowing, therefore helps only when whistleblowers are listened to. However, if one listens to whistleblowers too often, the effect on the provision of information and on the solution of the problem of many hands might eventually be negative. In introducing whistleblowing provisions, one

---

[16] This condition is not only a matter of intuition but would seem to have been confirmed by experiments, though not unambiguously (Dozier 1988: 1, 2, 42).

must therefore take account of four possible *boomerang effects* of a too broadly conceived or insufficiently balanced form of protection.

1. *A decrease in intra-organisational openness and pluriformity.* Too much room for whistleblowers can be counterproductive. Many executive functionaries will consider going public with unfavourable confidential information a form of 'treason'; dirty linen should not be washed in public, whatever the cost. When that can no longer be achieved by isolating the dissidents, organisations or departments will seek other ways of protecting themselves against these 'fifth columns'. Depending on the nature and the range of the whistleblower clause and the culture within the organisation, there is always the danger that this will not happen by stemming waste and fraud but by limiting the internal flow of information and by the use of veiled language, secret codes, and a drastic classification of data. The risk therefore arises that the provision of information by the 'formal' controlling organs, both within and beyond the organisation, is further obstructed (Coffee 1977: 1147). Some organisations might also pay special attention to qualities such as loyalty and conformism when selecting new members. In either case, the protection of whistleblowers leads to a lessening of, rather than an increase in, internal flexibility and the external provision of information.[17]

2. *An escalation of internal conflicts.* Whistleblowing, particularly when it is done ruthlessly and without consultation, carries with it the danger of polarisation. This is the risk of trench war that we already encountered in our discussion of conscientious objections. If – and precisely because – the individual functionary places all his bets on the cards of integrity and moral principle, the road to negotiations and compromise can be cut off. Two separate, incompatible values conflict with one another: loyalty to the group and its norms versus loyalty to one's own integrity and personal convictions. That can, both for the organisation and for the individual functionary, end in an all or nothing situation; a victory for the one means a loss (of face) for the other. If the whistleblower knuckles under or is put in the wrong, this means either that he denies his personal principles or that his complaint was not serious – which would imply that from the point of view of the organisation he had acted immorally, i.e., he had acted disloyally and indiscreetly.

---

[17] Similarly counterproductive effects can also be found in the American Government in the Sunshine Laws. Too much openness of administration can strongly restrict the flexibility of negotiations and provide an extra stimulant for resort to the corridors and the smoke-filled rooms. See for a highly informative study of the boomerang effect of the American Government in the Sunshine Laws the work of McLaughlin and Riesman (1986).

If the organisation gives in, then it admits that it has acted immorally or it demonstrates, if it is not prepared to acknowledge its immoral action, that the group norms that were apparently so strict do not actually mean all that much. In many cases such an impasse will end in apathy and cynicism or even (including after a verdict on the basis of whistleblower clauses) in the departure of one of those involved – mostly the whistleblower – because work relationships have broken down for good (Argyris and Schön 1986).[18]

3. *Ritualisation of dissident opinions.* Whistleblowing is a means that works only if used in moderation. This limitation flows from the observation that the whistleblowing can only be effective if it can be dealt with. Whistleblowing can, like any form of 'voice', be carried to exaggerated lengths. If too many people reach too often and too quickly for their whistles, the public tends to go numb and deaf, and people no longer listen or take the warning seriously even when an emergency really does arise. This is the 'cry wolf' syndrome (Wohlstetter 1962). And if one continues blowing even after the message has been received, one obstructs the taking of adequate measures. The organisation must be given the opportunity to put things in order without being unduly disturbed in the course of doing so.[19] If undue use is made of the whistle, there is also the danger that whistleblowing will degenerate into a ritual; a form of 'token-protest' that is politely heard out, after which one returns to business as usual. In such cases, there is also the chance, especially in the case of internal forms of whistleblowing, of what James Thomson (1968) has called the 'domestication of dissenters'.[20] Notorious worriers and pessimists can be saddled with the role of 'official' dissident or devil's advocate – a process that at first sight seems to satisfy everybody, but which actually changes nothing. The top management can boast of its tolerance without having to really change its policy, relations between people remain polite and pleasant, and the whistleblower has the chance to vent his feelings and soothe his conscience. His position has become clear – but also predictable: 'This predictability means a fatal loss of power for him; his position becomes discountable. The dissenter is allowed to recite his piece on condition that he engages in "role-playing" as "a member of the team". In this way, he is made to give up in advance his strongest weapon: his threat to resign under protest' (Hirschman 1970: 115–16).

---

[18] A number of useful tips to help managers prevent such an impasse arising on account of whistleblowers can be found in Ewing (1983: 165–89) and Seymour (1988).   [19] Cf. Hirschman (1970: 31–3).   [20] Quoted in Hirschman (1970: 115).

4. *Whistleblowers as tell-tales and inquisitors.* Whistleblowing has up to now been presented as an activity that deserves if not admiration, then at least legal and moral support. As an instrument of control, however, whistleblowing can be used both to good and to bad ends. In totalitarian societies it can, in the form of anonymous tip-offs to people's committees, militias, and the intelligence services, be an important means of repression.[21] Even in more open societies the official use of whistleblowers can leave a bitter taste. One of the first proposals to protect whistleblowers was made in 1951 – at the height of the McCarthy witch-hunt – by the then senator Richard Nixon. Nixon wanted to encourage civil servants to give confidential information about colleagues and citizens with real or putative communist sympathies to the congressional committees of investigation. Whistleblowing can furthermore also be imposed or enforced from above; for example in the form of spies and monitors specially employed by top management. In the United Kingdom one sometimes speaks in this connection of 'Raynerism', after Sir Derek Rayner, a confidant of Margaret Thatcher, who in the context of a special 'scrutiny programme' was given far-reaching powers and a team of monitors to act as a sort of Grand Inquisitor by combing through service after service in search of waste and inefficiency. Here too the cure often is worse than the ailment, because it can lead to an extra degree of closedness and rigidity at lower levels; moreover one comes up against important objections from the points of view of privacy and basic rights.

Whistleblowing provisions: some American experiences

Whistleblowing is therefore not always salutary and does not always happen out of the purest motives. It can, because of the way in which one discloses the information or because of the scant importance of the violation of the norm noted by the whistleblower and the relatively large amount of damage that results from the revelation, be disproportionate. Whistleblowing can

---

[21] One need think only of the role of anonymous tip-offs in the persecution that took place in the People's Republic of China during the Cultural Revolution and (though to a far lesser extent, for by that time the regime had forfeited much of its legitimacy and power of intimidation) during the suppression of the popular protests of 1989. In the Soviet Union, too, complaints by whistleblowers were an important source of information for the authorities. Interestingly, the emphasis in that case lay not so much on political offences as on corruption, inefficiency, and other economic violations. Readers' letters to party newspapers were a particularly popular safety valve. The fate of individual whistleblowers in the Soviet Union was for the rest as difficult and frustrating as in the West, if not more so. See Lampert (1985).

also be inspired by selfish interest, by resentment, or by party-political considerations. Such practical objections deserve careful attention. Protective measures must not become an operations base for troublemakers, moral sticklers, and (industrial) spies. By restricting the number of grounds for justification and by establishing requirements of due care and a procedure hedged in with the necessary guarantees, a threshold must be thrown up against frivolous or malicious forms of whistleblowing. At this point, it therefore makes sense to change perspective. Now that a managerial and political-theoretical analysis of whistleblowing has turned out to be moderately positive, it is time for a more legal approach. How could that protection best be arranged?

The experiences in the United States with the protection of federal civil-service whistleblowers can teach us a number of lessons on this point. Initially, up to the mid-1970s, civil-service whistleblowers could in some cases find protection in the First Amendment. In *Pickering* v. *Board of Education*, the Supreme Court decided that the interest that a civil servant, in this case a schoolteacher, had in publicly criticising his employer had to be weighed against the interest that the government as employer had in the efficient functioning of its services.[22] The whistleblower could also in some cases appeal to the Freedom of Information Act. However, the protection offered by these provisions was restricted and moreover far from always effective. Whistleblowers were as a rule immediately dismissed; only in a few cases, and mostly only after long legal battles, were they taken back into service or did they receive compensation.

In the course of the 1970s, public opinion as well as Congress strongly urged an improvement in the position of whistleblowers. President Carter, who had campaigned on the ticket of an ethically clean public administration, stood by his election promises and submitted the Civil Service Reform Act. Congress adopted this act as law in 1978, and afforded an even more generous protection to whistleblowers than the Carter government had itself proposed.[23] This law explicitly prohibits federal institutions from taking disciplinary measures or other sanctions against a civil servant or a would-be civil servant on the grounds of justifiable forms of whistleblowing. Under the latter, the law understands the following: 'a disclosure of information by an employee or applicant which the employee reasonably believes evidences (i) a violation of any law, rule, or regulation, or (ii) mismanagement, a gross waste of funds, an abuse of authority, or a substantial and specific danger to public health or safety'. This not only offers

[22] *Pickering* v. *Board of Education* (1968) 391 U.S. 563.
[23] Publ. L. no. 95–454, 92 Stat. 111. A discussion of this question can be found in Vaughn (1982) and Eastwood (1984).

whistleblowers significantly more protection than the First Amendment but it also provides them with a greater degree of clarity. Instead of a weighing-up of interests (in which the interests of the employer seemed in practice to weigh very heavily) the law offers a restricted number of specific criteria that the whistleblower must satisfy if he or she is to gain the protection of the law.

In the first place, there must be a 'disclosure of information'. That disclosure can be made to anyone, unless the information falls under particular obligations of confidentiality (in which case it can be disclosed only to specific intermediaries). It must, however, concern the disclosure of factual information in one form or another; sheer criticism of government policy does not in itself qualify for protection.

The requirement that the whistleblower should 'reasonably believe' that the information evidences misconduct consequently throws up a barrier to trouble-makers and pseudo-whistleblowers. The whistleblower need not prove that misconduct actually took place, but he must be able to show that every right-minded person in his situation might have come to such a conclusion and that he has moreover acted in good faith.[24] Protection will furthermore be withheld from him if he brings material into the open that either violates the privacy of others or is in some way classified; for the law sets yet another condition: 'if such disclosure is not specifically protected by law and if such information is not specifically required by Executive order to be kept secret in the interest of national defense or the conduct of foreign affairs'.[25]

What is meant by 'misconduct'? Through the agency of Congress, the Civil Service Reform Act received a much broader meaning than the Carter government had originally intended. It is obvious that the law speaks in the first place of 'a violation of any law, rule, or regulation'. However, maladministration also includes 'mismanagement', which in its broadest definition is 'wrongful or arbitrary and capricious actions that may have an adverse effect on the efficient accomplishment of the agency mission'.[26] Also, 'a gross waste of funds'[27] and 'an abuse of authority' is meant by it.[28] The least room is actually offered by the last form that the law distinguishes; after all, there must not only be talk of 'a danger to public health and safety', but this danger must also be 'substantial' and 'specific'. General criticisms of the

---

[24] According to Vaughn (1982: 626), it can be inferred from the text and the history of the law that a 'good faith requirement' is also entailed in this requirement of reasonableness.   [25] 5 U.S.C. § 2302 (b) (8) (A).   [26] 5 CFR 1250. 3 (e).

[27] The definition of this hardly adds anything to the idea itself: 'unnecessary expenditure of substantial sums of money, or a series of instances of unnecessary expenditures of small amounts'. (5 CFR § 1250. 3 (d)).   [28] 5 CFR 1205.3 (f).

Ministry of Health are not protected, but concrete complaints about the malfunctioning of the cooling system in a nuclear reactor are.[29]

What does the protection consist of? If an official has the impression that he has been dismissed, demoted, transferred, fined, not nominated for promotion, or in some other way disadvantaged because of his whistleblowing activities, he can make a complaint to the Office of the Special Counsel (OSC) of the Merit Systems Protection Board (MSPB), a sort of ombudsman for civil servants. The Special Counsel is obliged to investigate every complaint and can, if he finds the complaint to be well grounded, recommend that the penalty be made undone. If this does not happen, he can put the matter before the MSPB, which then delivers a binding judgment. He can also ask the MSPB to take disciplinary measures against those in authority over whistleblowers who have been subjected to unfair punishment.

The OSC functions also as a special administrative channel along which official whistleblowers can unload their information. By means of this provision an attempt has been made to put an end to a situation in which whistleblowers can call attention to their grievances only by way of (negative) publicity in the media. It offers an opportunity for dealing with criticism as much as possible within the confines of the state authority, without causing too much harm and loss of face to those involved. When it is a case of information that is classified or falls under a legal obligation to secrecy, the Special Counsel, together with some other specially designated counsellors, is itself the sole permitted channel for whistleblowers. The OSC makes possible a discreet and, if requested, anonymous form of reporting information to the competent bodies. If the Special Counsel is convinced of the seriousness of the case, it can force the institution involved to carry out an investigation and to bring out a report within sixty days.[30]

The Civil Service Reform Act was the show-piece of the federal reform movement and the symbol of the struggle against fraud, corruption, and waste by the government. The law has greatly helped to strengthen the legitimacy of whistleblowing in the United States. The adversaries of protective measures, who warned of the large-scale dislocation of government institutions that would result from the activities of genuine or pseudo whistleblowers, have so far not been proved right. The problems with the law turned out to lie elsewhere. As is often the case with symbolic legislation, the Civil Service Reform Act seemed to have improved the actual position of whistleblowers only to a limited extent. In 1980 and 1983, the MSPB carried out survey-research into the functioning of the law. The results of

---

[29] The example was highlighted during the handling of the law in the Senate (Vaughn, 1982: 628).   [30] 5 U.S.C. § 1206 (b) (1)-(3).

that research were by no means all that optimistic. The law had not reduced the fear of reprisals among federal civil servants. The effect, however, was to the contrary. The MSPB asked its respondents whether they had got to know of illegal practices or of the wasting of government money in the course of their work. In 1980, 20 per cent of those who answered this question affirmatively, said that they had not passed on the information for fear of reprisals by the organisation; in 1983, this percentage had almost doubled, to 37 per cent. The percentage of employees which did pass on such information, but claimed to have been punished as a result, rose slightly from 20 to 23 per cent (MSPB 1984: 31). The conclusion of the investigation was that 'the Civil Service Reform Act "whistleblower protections", by themselves, have not met all the stated expectations of Congress [...]. There is no evidence that the protections have had any type of ameliorative effect on employee expectations or experiences relative to reprisal' (MSPB 1984: 7).

The criticism by Congress of the structure of the law and above all of the behaviour of the OSC was less veiled. Patricia Schroeder, democratic representative for Colorado, called the protection an unmitigated failure. Two years' research on the basis of week-long hearings, reports by the auditor's office, and numerous conversations with whistleblowers and their lawyers had shown that the whistleblowers law offered too few guarantees. The procedure was intricate and lasted far too long, the evidence of unjustified reprisals turned out in many cases to be difficult to acquire, and the OSC often behaved indiscreetly in the presence of those in authority over the people complaining. The independence of the OSC in relation to the MSPB and the federal government was absolutely inadequate. It turned out that the OSC thwarted whistleblowers rather than help them; more than half of the complaints were set aside without any investigation whatsoever. When investigations were carried out, those involved behaved more as judges and later even as employers rather than as ombudsman; since 1981 not one single whistleblower got his job back with the help of the OSC.[31] Partly as a result of an initiative by Schroeder, an amendment of the law took place, resulting in the Whistleblower Protection Act of 1989, which had as its objective the strengthening of the position of whistleblowers in relation to the various procedures. More attention was paid to keeping the names of whistleblowers secret and the burden of proof was lessened and in some respects transferred from the whistleblower to those in authority. The OSC has received an independent status, separate from the MSPB; whistleblow-

---

[31] 99th Cong., 2nd Sess. H 7864–7870 (September 22, 1986). See also Dworkin and Callahan (1991: 282–3).

ers can henceforth get round the OSC and appeal to the MSPB directly and independently. Furthermore, it has become possible to appeal to federal judges and more bodies have been brought under the law.[32]

However, the effect of this amendment to the law has up to now been restricted. In 1992, a new survey-research was carried out into the effects of the law (MSPB 1993). The number of federal employees who said that they had personally observed or obtained direct evidence of illegal or wasteful activities had fallen to 18 per cent. Of them, however, 50 per cent had reported their observations and evidence. That represented a considerable increase over 1983 (30 per cent). The researchers suggest that this greater readiness has to do with a more favourable climate in relation to whistle-blowing on account of the amendment to the law and other provisions. The legislation and the publicity regarding it are said to have strengthened the legitimacy of whistleblowing. In other respects, however, the effect of the law was apparently much smaller. In the overwhelming majority of cases, people confined themselves to making an internal report. Only in one single case did a person complaining go to Congress (2 per cent). The popularity of the special whistleblowers' organ, the OSC, remained highly restricted. Only a very small percentage (less than 1 per cent) turned to it. Just as in 1983, more than 50 per cent of those who had reported nothing gave as their most important reason the fact that they expected nothing to come of a complaint. It also seemed that fear of retaliation was still an important reason for not making any report (33 per cent). In 1992, too, that fear also appeared not to have been groundless; more than one third (37 per cent) of those who had entered a report said that they had experienced or had been threatened with some sort of reprisal as a result. This figure was a lot higher than in 1983. The reprisals were largely a matter of shunning by co-workers, verbal harassment, and poor performance judgments. It was, however, encouraging that the more formal and serious forms of retaliation, such as transfer, suspension, grade-level demotion, or reassignment were all expe-rienced by a smaller percentage in 1992.

Framing whistleblowing provisions

The protection of whistleblowers in the United States has not remained restricted to federal civil servants. Over the last few years, facilities have also been created for civil servants in a number of states and for employees in the private sector. On the basis of those examples and with the discussion about employee citizenship in chapter 9 in the back of our minds, a few sugges-

---

[32] Publ. L. no. 101–12 (April 10, 1989), 103 Stat. 16, the Whistleblower Protection Act of 1989.

tions will follow for legal facilities for whistleblowing within complex organisations. Just as in the previous chapters, in so doing a distinction will be made between grounds for justification, requirements of due care, and procedural consequences.

Both employees and civil servants are often subject to general or particular requirements of confidentiality. Organisations must be able to rest assured that their industrial secrets or sensitive information relating to people's privacy will not get out into the open. The first question is therefore (again), what sort of activities or situations are so serious that they will be able to justify a violation of those requirements of confidentiality. A nonrestrictive list of possible *grounds for justification* includes the following:

Knowledge of penal offences: From a citizenship perspective, it is extremely important that the community is protected against criminal activities of organisations. In the light of the problem of many hands, the disclosure of information about penal offences will therefore often weigh more heavily than the duty to maintain secrecy. This will naturally not apply in equal measure to all penal offences and all functionaries. Whistleblowing aimed at the prevention of a threatened crime against a person is more likely to be accepted than in the case of simple transgressions of the laws governing the hours of trading. In the Netherlands every citizen, and therefore every employee and civil servant, has the duty in the case of serious violent crimes to report penal offences. For less serious misdemeanours, there is no such duty, but merely the power to do so if one so wishes. Civil servants also have a special duty to report serious offences committed by officials, such as embezzlement, forgery, the destruction of evidence, the acceptance of bribes, the abuse of authority, the breaching of the privacy of correspondence, and the theft or embezzlement of goods that one is required to administer as an official. This duty to report has precedence over the legislative requirements of confidentiality of civil servants and over the need to protect the personal sphere of life.

Conflict with other legal requirements. The American Civil Service Reform Act admits extremely broad grounds for justification: the 'violation of any law, rule, or regulation'. Civil service whistleblowers are protected not only if they report penal offences, but also if they report the transgression of any other legal requirement. This is quite consistent from the perspective of the Rule of Law. The government should itself be a paragon of law-abiding. In the case of companies, this requirement of legality is less strict and it is conceivable that the obligation to secrecy sometimes takes precedence. In such cases, much will depend on the seriousness of the transgression and on the interest that the requirement is designed to serve. Most of the American state statutes that protect employees in the private sector 'do seem to require that the issue be relatively serious' (Barnett 1992b: 443).

A substantial and specific danger to public health, safety, or the environment.

Just as in the case of refusal to work, the aversion of a threat to popular health, safety, or the environment can form the grounds for turning one's back on ordinary labour duties, both in the public and in the private sector. Almost all general whistleblower legislation in the United States mentions 'danger to public health and safety' as a separate ground for justification. Unlike in the case of a refusal to work, that threat need however not be acute – after all, in acute situations whistleblowing usually no longer makes any sense and the only thing left to do is to refuse. One should, however, as in the Civil Service Reform Act, be able to demand that the threat be substantial and specific.[33]

A gross waste or unauthorised use of public funds. In the light of the role that whistleblowers have played, or could have played in revealing various recent financial scandals, it seems appropriate to limit the duty to maintain secrecy. Consideration must also be given to include large-scale forms of mismanagement under this heading. In the Civil Service Reform Act, mismanagement is incorporated as a separate ground. This is, however, an extremely open term and in practice, at least in the case of public organisations, an operationalisation of the term will presumably often boil down to waste or to one of the other grounds. A nice compromise can be found in the Whistleblowers Protection Act 1993 of South Australia, which speaks of 'substantial mismanagement of public resources'. This ground will especially play a role in the public sector, but need not be restricted to that sector. Employees should also be able to appeal on these grounds when their organisation squanders or misuses government money, for example when non-profit organisations receive subsidies or when destitute companies receive government support.

The misleading of controlling or supervising bodies. We have seen that provisions for whistleblowers could play a role in the improvement of the information in and about complex organisations. Whistleblowing can help prevent representative and supervisory bodies, particularly Parliament or Congress, from being misled about the activities of public organisations and office-holders. It would seem appropriate to consider this as a separate ground for justification. Both in the public and in the private sector, whistleblowing can play a very important role in preventing or tracking down fraud and other forms of financial irregularities (Vinten 1994). In the European Union, research is now being done into the extent to which provision for whistleblowers can help in combating the large-scale fraudulent use of European Union money (Public Concern at Work 1995). Internal accountants, who are often torn between their professional ethics and their loyalty to the firm, will be particularly well served by the possibility of an appeal on such grounds.

---

[33] See also the requirements of due care, which are dealt with later.

As in the case of the justificatory grounds for a refusal to work, this is by no means an exhaustive list. Life is often more creative than theory. In legal and administrative practice, additional grounds will presumably be developed. Thus, in the public sector maladministration, incompetence, or negligence are sometimes mentioned separately.[34] Generally speaking, the grounds for justification in the public sector are broader than in the private sector, certainly on the point of 'maladministration'. In the case of public organisations, maladministration is by definition a matter of public interest; in the case of most other organisations, it remains restricted to an issue of internal management or a worrisome point on the agenda of a shareholders' meeting.

As in the case of a refusal to work, it is not enough to demonstrate that one of these grounds for justification is at issue. In judging a concrete case of whistleblowing, the manner in which the individual employee or civil servant acted will be of very great importance. The whistleblowing must, given the circumstances, also have been careful. For a formulation of a number of *requirements of due care* we can refer to the (sub)questions in chapter 9 and to the jurisprudence and legislation that has become available in this field. On that basis, it would seem appropriate for a forum, when assessing a case of whistleblowing, to review the following questions one by one:

> *Did the whistleblowing take place publicly and was it reasoned?* As the principled refusal to work, whistleblowing, at least from the perspective of employee citizenship, is a public act that requires a response. The whistleblower must be prepared and able to answer for himself on the basis of the grounds set out above. That means that the functionary may often be asked to come out into the open, with his or her full name, and give his or her reasons, preferably in writing. This also means that leaking, i.e., going public behind a screen of anonymity, is in principle not justifiable. This is not just a matter of citizenship and verifiability – the presumption also exists that whistleblowing becomes more effective when whistleblowers identify themselves at the outset (Near and Micelli 1995: 792). This requirement cannot, however, be absolute. In very repressive organisations, situations are conceivable in which the whistleblower cannot be reproached for remaining anonymous until the point at which he or she was discovered.
>
> *Is it reasonable to assume that one of the interests that the whistleblower says he or she wants to protect actually is in danger of being harmed?* As in the case

---

[34] For example in the Whistleblowers Protection Act 1993 of South Australia.

of a refusal to work, and on the basis of the example provided by the Civil Service Reform Act, whistleblowing can be considered to be careful only when the functionary can show that any reasonable person would in the same situation, on the basis of the facts available at that moment, be able to come to the conclusion that what was happening constituted a case of (or threat of) misconduct. On this point, the seriousness of the threat, as well as the extent of the transgression, will also have to be taken into account. Most of the statutes that protect whistleblowing therefore require that the whistleblowing be based upon a 'reasonable belief' that something improper was occurring or was about to occur. Some statutes go further and also require whistleblowers to make a personal investigation to determine the accuracy of their charges before they make any disclosures (Barnett 1992b: 443). Personally, however, I consider this too heavy a demand; most individual functionaries lack the insight and the means to establish fully whether or not their allegations are correct.

Were other, less far-reaching means available to the whistleblower? A functionary is not acting with due care if he, in the case of a threatened violation, immediately starts whistling furiously. It must be obvious that, given the circumstances, there was no way available of raising the matter internally. However, there should be no obligation to raise the matter in the first instance internally, as is required in some American state statutes (Barnett 1992b: 443). The functionary must, however, be able to show that the internal channels were so clogged up or corrupted, or that the threat was so acute that there was in all reasonableness no other way available. It also must be evident that the threat could not be averted along other, less harmful ways – for example, whistleblowing is not appropriate when competent controlling bodies were already dealing with the matter.

Do the interests that the whistleblower was trying to protect weigh up against the interests that he harms as a result of his whistleblowing by means of his disclosure? How does the seriousness of the abuse match up to the damage that would result from the whistleblowing? In the case of some facts and data, it is necessary to act cautiously, since revelation could do great harm to legitimate interests of the public service, of the company, of colleagues, or of some third person. In arriving at a judgment about the carefulness of an act of whistleblowing, a central question will therefore have to be whether the interest that the whistleblower intended to serve by means of his revelation weighs up against the possible damage to those legitimate interests caused by the breaking of confidence. Again, the remedy should not be worse than the disease. A situation must not be allowed to arise in which it can reasonably be foreseen that revelation might possibly do more harm than good to the interests that someone is claiming to protect. In the second place, the whistleblowing should not be allowed to lead to a situation in which other legitimate public interests that are more important than those that the whistleblower was trying to protect are actually harmed. In the public sector, the importance of the disclosure must weigh up against interests such as foreign relations, the economic and financial interests of the government, the tracking down and prosecution of punishable offences, inspection, control, and supervision by or because of public bodies, or the right of every citizen to privacy. Especially when the security of the state is at stake, or when confidential business and manufacturing data are in danger of being revealed, the whistleblower has a particularly heavy obligation to prove the legitimacy of his action. Only under special circumstances and, preferably, on the basis of the protection of those same interests, will it be possible to justify the disclosure.

Has the whistleblower tried to restrict the damage that resulted from his disclosure as much as possible? If damage is nevertheless done to legitimate interests as a result of the whistleblowing, a careful official or employee may be expected to do his best to restrict that damage as much as possible. In that way, it can be demanded of the whistleblower that he make no more data public than is necessary to substantiate the threat, that he do his best to protect the privacy of those involved and of third persons, and that he refrain from making unnecessarily hurtful comments and imputations.

Did the whistleblower turn to the appropriate body? It is an important issue, finally, to whom the whistleblower should or might turn if he or she goes public. From a citizenship perspective, it would seem appropriate that the whistleblower would turn to public, controlling bodies. They can be representative bodies, such as parliamentary or congress committees, or supervisory bodies such as inspectorates, the Public Prosecutions Department, or the General Auditor's Office. Some laws, such as the Whistleblowers Protection Act of South Australia, have indicated very explicitly and in considerable detail which information belongs with which body. Such a detailed specification would not, however, seem to make much sense, since it might in practice put up a large barrier. After all, it requires whistleblowers to have a considerable knowledge of the law and of the many specific sections of the government apparatus. The same is true of the construction of a special council adopted in the Civil Service Reform Act, and in some state arrangements (Barnett 1992b: 444) – it should in my opinion not be imitated either. The OSC is too removed from practice and the procedure is extremely laborious, as a result of which many bona fide whistleblowers are deterred from taking action. One could, however, require the whistleblower to be aloof and unresponsive in his or her relations with the news media. Media attention, however effective, often causes much damage to legitimate interests and offers few possibilities for a substantive and procedurally careful consideration of the matter in hand.

Do these requirements demand too much of whistleblowers? Can one keep to them in practice? I think that one probably can. Most of the cases mentioned at the beginning of this chapter (Douwes Dekker, Ellsberg, Gellert,

Hoevenagel), for example, would fall within these limits and could reckon on receiving protection. In all the cases mentioned, grave public interests were at stake: the misleading of democratic bodies, public security, the prevention of breaches of the law, fraud, and corruption. In most of the cases those concerned first travelled the internal, least drastic path, and only later went public with their criticisms. Most of them turned to an appropriate body and not, or not immediately, to the press. Moreover, they made themselves personally known – at least to the body to which they turned – and made themselves available to appear as witnesses and to give account of themselves. Each one of them gave reasons for his concern and based those reasons on data and documents from which one could reasonably deduce a threat to legitimate interests.

The protection that whistleblowers should be able to reckon on is quite similar in most of the existing schemes. It consists of a broad level of protection against 'adverse personnel action, discharging, disciplining, or otherwise penalizing' (Barnett 1992b: 443). Under it falls any form of 'adverse action regarding promotions, transfers, assignments, performance evaluations, suspensions and terminations, or any other negative change in whistleblowers' terms and conditions of employment that can be linked to whistleblowing', or a threat to take any such actions.

The limits of the law

Why do whistleblowers deserve protection? Experiences in the United States suggest that if whistleblowers are – with a certain degree of moderation – allowed to operate, an important new source of information within complex organisations about corruption, mismanagement, and improper behaviour will be opened up. Necessary, though by no means always sufficient, conditions (Near and Micelli 1995) are that whistleblowers be offered a certain degree of protection against reprisals by their organisations and that one really does pay proper attention to the messages that they bring. However, whistleblowers also deserve attention and protection on more principled grounds. Whistleblowing not only enhances the quality and the transparency of (public) administration, but is also a form of speech and deserves if only for that reason a certain amount of support. Protection of whistleblowers can also contribute to the preservation of a 'civic culture'. It is a necessary complement of the model of personal, individual responsibility which, certainly after the Second World War and the Nuremberg trials, underlies large parts of the legal system in western countries. If one does not expect functionaries to knuckle under unthinkingly and indiscriminately to assignments handed down by the powers that be, one should also give them the opportunity to behave responsibly.

Experiences in the United States with whistleblowing provisions call into question the assumption in Britain and on the European continent that it is self-evident that the requirements of confidentiality should always take precedence over other considerations. One can also stimulate whistleblowing instead of tacitly tolerating it (in the form of leaks) or tolerating it only in exceptional cases. The fear that protective measures will provide an operating base for troublemakers, self-appointed moral censors, and (industrial) spies has not up to now been realised in the United States. The legitimacy of whistleblowing has increased, but this increase has not led to a rise in indiscretions, pseudo-moral blathering, and letters to the editor.

The problems with the whistleblowing provisions would appear to lie on a completely different plane. They do not seem in practice to offer enough protection to dispel the fear of reprisals on the part of civil servants (and employees). This is to a certain extent the result of extremely complicated procedures. The Civil Service Reform Act is so long-winded and full of safety clauses that not only troublemakers and spies but even bona fide whistleblowers are effectively kept at bay. I would personally recommend not choosing the method of special 'whistleblowing councils' but rather adopting a relatively big-hearted approach in designating the bodies to which whistleblowers may turn.

It is doubtful, however, whether a generously conceived whistleblowing arrangement really would increase the enthusiasm of employees and civil servants for reporting organisational deviance. A legal protection can never be entirely satisfactory. An arrangement imposed and executed from the outside will sometimes be too dilatory or too general to straighten out completely the fundamental differences in power that exist within hierarchical organisations. Research into the effects of the Civil Service Reform Act shows for example that in the period 1983–1992, the more official forms of reprisals have shown a distinctive decline; however, at the same time there was an increase in the more subtle forms of reprisal (MSPB 1993: 22). A majority of the civil servants questioned was very sceptical about the support that the legal protection would be able to give them in the event of reprisals. Here, we once again come up against the limits of the law.

Such a far-reaching form of voice will in practice therefore often be available only to functionaries for whom exit is a real option and no threat. For example, there appeared to be a clear connection between the number of service years that a civil servant was able to claim and whether or not that civil servant was prepared to report abuses. The civil servants with thirty years service or more – and therefore not far off from a good pension – were significantly more likely to blow whistles than their younger colleagues (MSPB 1984: 26–30).

Moreover, provisions for whistleblowers do not remove all the boomerang effects that were mentioned earlier. External whistleblowing, however well regulated, always carries with it the risk of an escalation of internal conflicts. External whistleblowers therefore often end up along paths from which no one emerges unscathed: 'Much whistleblowing is ineffective in creating change, and, in worst case scenarios, it benefits no one and harms many, including the whistleblower who may suffer retaliation' (Near and Micelli 1995: 703).

All this means that legal protection of whistleblowers can never be the sole instrument for improving the internal and external information flow. Whistleblowing is above all an emergency brake that is not suitable for use in routine situations. Other measures, such as suggestion boxes, 'hotlines', 'open-door policies', open forums, dissident channels, and internal ombudsmen, will also have to be thought through and where necessary dealt with. In the following chapter I shall give an initial impetus to such a project.

12

Loyalty: responsibility as a by-product

The fundamental change [...] is to reduce the disparity between interests of
the corporate actor and interests of those natural persons who occupy positions within it.

(Coleman 1982: 110)

Responsibility as a by-product

Refusal to work and whistleblowing are like bee-stings. They are often one-
off actions, for the stings are frequently deadly for the employee himself.
Legal remedies can be only partly of help, as the asymmetry between
complex organisations and individuals also applies internally. Refusal to
work and whistleblowing can also be very painful for the organisation.
Public dissidents destroy the unity of the team and sow discord and confusion. Whistleblowing and refusal to work force responsible conduct on the
part of the organisation. An uncompromising and one-sided striving
toward virtuousness can, moreover, harm the 'good' cause to a great extent.[1]
For these reasons, the law, with its antagonistic procedures and external
bodies, is presumably not the best means of coping with the issues of
responsibility sketched here.[2] Therefore, a form of protection which is more
than merely legal is necessary. The structure and culture of complex organisations will themselves also have to change.

For the continuity and stability of the organisation, it is moreover important that the overwhelming majority of the functionaries stays loyal. One or
two alert dissidents can provide an incentive to change, but the loyalty of the
silent majority ensures that the organisation stays in operation and that the
knowledge and manpower that is necessary to effect the changes remain
available.[3] Therefore attention must be given to non-legal and loyal forms
of individual responsible conduct. That attention must be directed in particular toward modifications in the structure of organisations that might

[1] See also Argyris and Schön (1986) and Elster (1983a: 38–9).
[2] Compare Fleishman et al. (1981: viii).
[3] See for a comparable argument in relation to consumers, Hirschman (1970: 24–5).

215

help to stimulate responsible conduct on the part of individual functionaries without imposing this conduct on them. In other words: how can one
arrange organisations in such a way that loyalty produces responsible
conduct? Is it possible to change the organisational structure in such a way
that loyalty to the organisation and active responsibility (from the point of
view of employee citizenship) coincide – so that responsible conduct arises
of itself, as a natural by-product?

At this point, we leave behind political philosophy, sociology, and law, and
step into the arena of 'organisational design'. That is an area on which the
accent has not expressly lain in this study, but which is of great importance
for the solution of some issues of responsibility. In the field of organisational design various developments have come about that are well worth
considering. Some relate above all to the question of giving shape to the
structure of responsibility, others are interesting because they create space
for internal forms of 'voice' and other forms of organisational learning.

Tinkering with the structure

Many a researcher, having reached the final point in his analysis of the
issues of responsibility that can arise in complex organisations, concludes
with a call for a change in mentality. Functionaries would, according to this
approach, be nurtured into responsible citizens through various forms of
schooling and training.[4] Such calls are noble but not all that convincing. It
is naive in the context of complex organisations to put one's trust exclusively in the force of moral arguments and good intentions. If one wants to
change the conduct of individual functionaries, one must also change the
conditions under which those functionaries act, i.e. the material and
psychological incentives that they receive from the organisation. First
comes structure, only then the morals.[5] At the end of chapter 8, I discussed
a number of changes that might bring the structure of complex organisations more into line with individual models of responsibility. Among other
things I mentioned the clarification of the lines of responsibility by means
of backward policing, the creation of points of accountability by means of
a personification of products and activities, and the introduction of internal procedures that make possible an immediate notification of new

---

[4] See for example Glover (1970: 196) and Harmon (1971: 185): 'What is being
proposed essentially is that public administrators learn how to become more
democratic'; or a number of authors in the volume edited by Fleishman, Liebman,
and Moore (1981).

[5] That is to say, at the level of the individual functionary. For the highest levels, where
changes in the structure can be set in motion, this does not apply. Moral or political
considerations can play an important part and precede the structural mutations.

regulations to those functionaries responsible for the relevant products or processes.

I would like to suggest a number of other changes in the structure of organisations that will help to stimulate responsible conduct on the part of functionaries or of the organisation as a whole – not by asking functionaries to act against the organisation, but by allowing internal loyalty and external responsibility to run parallel to one another.

More autonomy within organisations. Coleman in his 1982 study suggested the franchise construction as a possible answer to the problem of many hands. A number of big American restaurant and hotel chains, for example McDonald's, Holiday Inn, and Hilton, as well as many European department stores and supermarkets, in reality can hardly be said to form one single organisation any longer. They consist of a number of separate companies that are grouped around a central body. They share the name, have a similar organisational shape, and often offer the same range of services and products, but otherwise they are largely independent as far as business management is concerned. The degree of autonomy can differ from branch to branch. Some are administered from a central point, others are entirely free to determine their own policy and operate completely at their own risk. Some facilities are centrally regulated, others are perhaps adapted to local circumstances.

The franchise is interesting because it might be able to bring the problem of many hands back to more manageable proportions. In the first place there is a practical respect: one can address the owner or manager of the local branch about many things directly, without having to make the long and frustrating detour by way of the main office. Because the local concessionary has a relatively large freedom of action, he will find it less easy to make excuses and moreover will be able to respond more quickly and more effectively. Power and accountability therefore coincide to a considerable extent. This makes the direct individual accountability of the branch manager in moral respect, too, more acceptable and increases the chance of learning effects and responsible conduct. Such a construction of the organisation in fact forms the mirror image of the situation of the Nepalese civil servants described in chapter 8.

One condition for this is, however, that the sub-unit can freely negotiate the conditions within which it must operate. At this point, problems frequently arise. Often those who acquire the franchises are connected to the franchiser by way of 'stranglehold contracts' or by way of technical, economic, or social ties. For example, the central unit has a monopoly on the supply of a number of essential products or services, or the holder of the franchise is closely tied by 'golden' bonds to the chain on account of the working capital that it makes available. In this way 'the price for an independent set-up [. . .] is high and in most cases beyond people's pockets' (Gerding 1986: 148).

An orientation to tasks instead of to products. We have already seen that, as organisations grow and the chain of actions becomes longer and more complex, not only does it become more and more difficult to hold anyone to account about defective products or improper actions, but individual functionaries feel less and less called upon to do anything about such failings. End-products pass through too many hands for them to be able to evoke feelings of responsibility. Stone (1975: 190–1) suggested that this could be put right in part by switching from an orientation toward (end) products to an orientation toward tasks. He proposed making it obligatory in risk sectors, such as the pharmaceutical and chemical industry, or in the design and manufacture of cars or airplanes, for companies to appoint special internal inspectors explicitly charged with checking the safety of the product (or of parts of it). Such a procedure might return the responsibility for any failings to individuals who can be addressed internally and in some situations even externally on account of those failings, and who therefore have an incentive to prevent such failings in future.

However, an important condition for such a construction is that these internal inspectors have enough powers at their disposal to carry out such tasks according to the expectations of those who set them.[6] Such inspectors should, for example, be able to carry out independent investigations, to reject products, to switch off machines, and to nominate employees for dismissal. One might also think of the construction that is used in the Netherlands in the auditing of accounts. Once auditors have given their approval to the annual statement of accounts of a corporate body, they are personally responsible for the accuracy of the data. One could follow similar procedures in the case of the reporting of clinical tests or in environmental reports. Inspectors can refuse to declare the product safe or express some reservations. This can induce government to take the product out of circulation or consumers to boycott the product. An orientation of this sort toward tasks could take various forms. Stone spoke of obligatory inspectors; one could, however, also imagine a situation in which organisations independently assign such tasks and powers to internal employees, or in which they – following the example of the auditors – hire external experts for that purpose.

Real aims, feasible tasks. Research by Braithwaite (1985) into fraud and embezzlement in the pharmaceutical industry showed that excessively

---

[6] It is therefore doubtful whether it makes sense to oblige companies, as Stone did, to appoint such inspectors. After such a start, will they not always remain outsiders in the organisation?

heavy targets and excessively high production norms are an important source of irresponsible conduct. The management of a company sometimes makes such high demands on the personnel that they can achieve their aims only by means of negligence, various forms of cheating, and breaches of the law. In some cases a high degree of inappropriate conduct is deliberately calculated in by the management of the organisation, for example because they want to produce at whatever cost (Paine 1994: 107–8). In such situations structural changes are of scant avail, and whistleblowing or a refusal to work can be called for. However, there are also cases in which top managers are not conscious, or not conscious enough, of the unreasonableness of their demands. A regular check on the part of the management of the feasibility of its aims, quotas, and targets can sometimes yield results on this point. Braithwaite (1985: 49) gives the example of IBM, which does set its sales managers targets, but at the same time makes sure that these are such that they can be achieved in conformance with the law. For example, checks are made to see whether a majority of the sales managers are in a position to achieve at least 100 per cent of the target figure; moreover, the quota is adjusted if the economic climate worsens. In this case, morals therefore take precedence over structure; the attitude of the top management of the organisation determines the structure of system of the incentives and thus also the attitude of the lower and middle management.[7]

  Clear responsibilities and direct attention. Braithwaite also did research in the United States into the five mining companies that had the lowest accident rates, in the hope of tracking down positive structural factors. However, the structure of the five companies appeared to differ greatly; the five had only one or two general properties in common. In the first place, it appeared that in these mining companies too the attitude of the management was extremely important for the safety climate and the sense of responsibility in the organisation. The safety inspectors could usually count on a clear formal and informal support from the management. However, the eventual responsibility for safety lay in all cases not with the person in overall charge of safety but with the line managers themselves. In all companies it was clearly established which line managers were responsible for which part of the production process. The assignment of these tasks took place in an emphatically decentralised way, even in the most centralised company. At central level, however, the number of accidents for each section and each manager was carefully recorded. If managers no longer satisfied the norms, they were directly called to account by their superiors in the company. There were also in most cases special procedures that were directed toward prevention and toward the promotion

---

[7] See also the research cited by Braithwaite (1985: 49, note 27).

of learning effects, such as the obligation to put down security procedures in writing, the institutionalisation of regular individual contacts between supervisors and employees, the obligation to keep extensive security dossiers on individual employees, and obligatory reporting and hearings in the case of accidents.

Integrity strategies. In many organisations, responsible conduct is defined as compliance with the law. The responsibility of the organisation remains restricted to the provision of guidelines and the supervision of their observance. This supervision is mostly left to the legal department. Transgressions are mostly conceived as personal aberrations, the chance result of a rotten apple that must be removed from the barrel. In increasing measure, however, the realisation dawns that the organisational structure and culture play a very big role in the emergence of organisational deviance. Many of the chapters in part II also testified to this fact. The consequence of that observation is that the prevention of deviance and, better still, the stimulation of responsible conduct is not a question of individual scruples but must be reckoned as part of the daily work of the management. Paine (1994) describes how over the past few years various companies have successfully opted for an 'integrity strategy'. The core of this strategy is: 'honesty lasts longest'. She describes how the management of various companies, by making integrity and responsible behaviour the core aims of the organisation, have succeeded in bringing about structural improvements in the quality of the conduct and in the products of their organisation – while at the same time preserving or even increasing profitability. To that end, a mixture of instruments is used that is partly described in this chapter: codes of conduct, ethics training, internal channels for voice, ethics offices and ombudsmen, and the abolition of sales contests. In this strategy, however, more important than a choice of specific instruments is the fact that 'company leaders are personally committed, credible and willing to take action on the values they espouse'. This means, for example, that 'the espoused values are integrated into the normal channels of management decision making and are reflected in the organisation's critical activities' (1994: 112). It is also crucial that those core aims play an important part in the selection and assessment of managers and employees. They are judged not only on their production and sales figures, but also on the way in which they reached them.

Internal forms of voice

A large measure of loyalty can prevent an early exit of those functionaries that the organisation urgently needs to get back onto the right track (Hirschman 1970: 76–105). This loyalty is, however, in most cases neither unconditional nor implied. If employees have exit options, they will remain loyal only if they hope for an improvement in the situation and if they expect that they themselves can exercise some influence in achieving such an improvement. 'As a rule, then, loyalty holds exit at bay and activates voice' (1970: 78). It is therefore appropriate to look for ways of making better use of these loyal forms of voice.

By introducing alternative communication channels into the organisation one could retain the advantages of whistleblowing without having to pay the price of bad external publicity and disrupted internal relations. Internal channels for expressions of dissent and concern diminish the chance of employees going public with their criticisms and complaints (Barnett 1992a: 949). By stimulating internal forms of voice, employers can moreover get extra feedback about the functioning of their own organisations. This offers employers the chance to act discreetly at an early stage and thus to prevent the affair spreading and leading to harmful publicity for the organisation. In essence, internal whistleblowers 'are informal internal auditors' (Dworkin and Callahan 1991: 300).

Internal forms of voice will also be much more satisfying for individual employees. Research suggests that most whistleblowers have a long service record, a reasonably good position within the organisation, and a large measure of loyalty (Dworkin and Callahan 1991: 300–1). The great majority of them have first tried to go the way of internal criticism and they go public only when they are not familiar with internal complaints procedures, or when they fear that internal complaints will not get very far or will lead to reprisals. 'They believed initially that they were behaving in a loyal manner, helping their employers by calling top management's attention to practices that could eventually get the firm in trouble' (Near and Miceli 1985: 10).[8] The majority would far sooner stick to internal remedies. Moreover, there are many indications that the chance of reprisals and disruption of relations is much greater in the case of external forms of whistleblowing (Dworkin and Callahan 1991: 302). From the point of view of the problem of many hands, it is, finally, important that internal forms of criticism can play a role in putting an end to phenomena such as 'groupthink' and can help to strengthen the power of private morality within organisations (Kelman and Hamilton 1989: 158, 332–58).

Internal voice therefore deserves to take preference over external forms of voice. What forms might this loyal voice assume?

The appointment of an internal ombudsman. Various scholars (Ewing 1977: 166–70; Stewart 1980: 98; Braithwaite 1985: 46; Leech 1991) have proposed appointing an internal ombudsman who could function as an inter-

---

[8] Research by Glazer and Glazer (1989) points in the same direction; in almost all of the more than 60 cases they investigated, the whistleblowers first tried to deal with the affair internally.

mediary for complaints and as a buffer between the individual employee and his or her superior. In the course of the last few decades, more and more organisations have introduced a system of internal counsellors to whom employees can turn with their personal complaints; for example, about sexual harassment, discrimination, or other forms of negligent treatment. One could consider making such counsellors available for complaints that relate above all to the failure of the organisation in the light of its own aims or to the violation of generally accepted public interests. Or one could appoint a separate ombudsman or director for such complaints. In this way an extra information channel to the top is created in the hope that bad news will get through sooner and without distortions. However, important conditions are that the individual employee or civil servant can count on the discretion of and careful treatment by the ombudsman and that the ombudsman himself enjoys such good access to the management and such a high internal status that any complaints recognised by him are taken seriously within the organisation.

In the Netherlands, the Lockheed affair led to the appointment of a permanent internal counsellor by the Ministry of Defence (De Hosson 1995). Civil and defence personnel can approach this intermediary with complaints about any irregularities in the contacts between the defence sector and private companies, such as bribes, fraud, forgery, and any other undesirable financial transactions or entangled interests. The internal counsellor subsequently takes over the matter. He carries out his own investigation on the basis of dossier research and interviews. This happens as informally and discreetly as possible. Finally, the counsellor delivers a written report on the matter to the top management. This advice is confidential and does not mention the name of the complainant. Such a procedure has several important advantages. The original whistleblower is taken seriously and at the same time given the necessary protection. The organisation gets to know about irregularities with a minimum of internal unrest and external publicity. If necessary, the intermediary takes over the role of the whistleblower and himself becomes an internal whistleblower. However, it is important that the intermediary has access to all relevant dossiers and individuals and that he or she is supported by the top management. To safeguard the anonymity of the whistleblower, it can be useful for the intermediary to have a right to exemption from giving evidence.

The introduction of 'hotlines' and 'open doors'. One can also try to create a direct form of access to the top levels of the organisation. David Ewing (1977: 178–80) gave the example of New England Telephone, a company that makes it possible for, and stimulates, employees to speak directly with top managers about questions concerning their work. That contact can take place by letter, but also verbally – as one might expect – by way of special, direct telephone lines. When an employee rings one of these 'hotlines', he gets the chance to set out his complaints and he can reckon on receiving a direct answer. If the matter is too complicated for that, then the staff takes up contact with the responsible functionary. If the employee so wishes, he can remain anonymous.

In the wake of the Civil Service Reform Act discussed in the previous chapter, in the United States 'hotline' facilities have also been introduced by a large number of federal bodies. These are supervised by the Inspectors General, which are independent presidential appointees. As in the case of the federal provision for whistleblowers, special attention is paid to information about waste, fraud, abuse of powers, and breaches of the law. During office hours, and sometimes also day and night, special, free telephone numbers are available in every ministry that one can ring with one's complaints, anonymously if one so wishes. Although it has been estimated that no more than approximately 20 per cent of the telephone calls to such lines can be considered as substantial complaints, most organisations think that such provisions are a useful and effective way of preventing mismanagement and misconduct.[9] It will perhaps not come as a surprise to learn that the success of these systems seems in practice to depend to an important extent on the speed and carefulness with which complaints are processed. As a result, in some cases strict time schedules, varying from one to three months, have been set for dealing with the complaints.

Another mechanism is the 'open door' policy. This was developed by IBM, but has in the meantime also been applied within other organisations and in the public sector (Ewing 1977: 181–2; MSPB 1993: 28–9). If an employee has complaints that cannot be resolved in the course of a discussion with his direct boss, he can write to a higher manager of his own choice. This higher manager must then answer quickly and personally. Moreover, the policy is to look at the matter first from the point of view of the employee and to investigate it thoroughly by listening to all sides of the argument. There is also a 'speak up' provision for employees who would rather remain anonymous and a 'suggestion plan'. The latter has a system of rewards and is a sort of modern variant on the suggestion box. In this way one can keep complaints in-house and the top levels of management can benefit from the information and knowledge that is available at the lower levels of the organisation. An important condition for the successful functioning of such an 'open door' policy is that the treatment of the complaints and the protection of those who make them is carefully organised and that measures are immediately taken in the case of reprisals.

---

[9] Such are the conclusions of an initial investigation by the federal government into the functioning of such facilities (MSPB 1986).

Individual loyalty and organisational learning

Because of the layered character of complex organisations – the Chinese boxes of chapter 2 – many of the objections that characterise the external forms of whistleblowing can also apply to the internal forms of voice. On the level of the directorate, the section, or the department, a complaint to higher levels in the company or a decision to drop in on the secretary-general or the CEO can also easily give rise to conflicts and to an atmosphere of mutual distrust and suspicion. Also, the internal ombudsman may offer nothing but paper protection. Speak up provisions, suggestion programmes, and open doors can, through ritualisation and routinisation, give rise to new information black-outs. By way of conclusion, therefore, a few proposals will follow concerning ways of improving the internal flow of information that relate not so much to the organisational structure as to the style of decision-making:

The introduction of 'model O-ii' forms of learning behaviour. Addressing organisations or individual functionaries will lead to prevention only if they learn from past mistakes. In chapter 5, I pointed out that it is risky to draw a direct parallel on this point between individuals and organisations. An anthropomorphic, uniform approach obscures the problematic character of the learning behaviour of organisations. How then could one improve that learning capacity?

Argyris and Schön (1978) made a distinction between model O-i and model O-ii learning behaviour. The first model is characterised by 'single loops'. Within a given set of aims, an attempt is made in an instrumental manner to remedy the failings of the organisation. The norms and aims of the organisation and the assumptions on which the policy is based are not up for discussion. This leads to stability and continuity in the organisation, but in the long term and in a turbulent environment it can give rise to ossification, to inadequate reactions, and to a continuous repetition of the same mistakes. In model O-ii learning systems one tries, alongside this single form of learning behaviour, to stimulate 'double loop' learning. In so doing, the policy goals and the tacit presuppositions and hidden assumptions that exist within the organisation are also put up for discussion and where necessary adapted. In that way, an attempt is made to prevent defensive routines, contradictory assignments, prejudices, and unspoken animosities from muddying the view on reality. The question is how such model O-ii forms of learning in organisations can become firmly established. In so far as Argyris and Schön have dealt with the implementation of model O-ii approaches, the emphasis lies above all on therapeutic interventions from the outside. By way of role-playing, group discussions, and training, the management is expected to become conscious of the limitations of its policy theories and routines and to try to learn an open and reflective – Argyris and Schön even speak of a 'dialectical' – style of management. However, precisely what forms the transition to modes of plural learning should take and whether this can happen without the help of external consultants remains rather unclear.

The social-psychological work of Janis (1982) could perhaps be of service here. Janis' examples are restricted above all to policy formation in the fields of foreign policy and national security, but his analyses and recommendations are applicable to various processes of decision-making within complex organisations, both in the public and in the private sector ('t Hart 1994). His description of 'group-think', the phenomenon whereby decision-making in groups with a strong internal cohesion can be obfuscated by conformism, social coercion, and a need for unanimity, runs in many respects parallel to the description that Argyris and Schön give of the learning blockages that can arise when only model O-i learning behaviour is permitted in organisations. Janis does make a number of concrete recommendations for preventing groupthink.[10] Some of them can be of help here:[11]

> When managers institute a project group or committee that is charged with developing a new product or mapping out a new policy, it is best if the top management allows itself not to be tempted to express preferences and expectations. It is better at first to restrict oneself to formulating the problem and the conditions within which the solution should be sought. According to Janis (1982: 263), this promotes a situation in which the members of the committee weigh up the various alternatives in an atmosphere of openness and impartiality.
>
> When a committee consists of representatives of various departments or services, it is recommendable that they regularly, and on an informal basis, consult with one or more members of their own department. This forces them not only to formulate the proposals clearly but it also opens up the possibility of using unexpected criticisms and new suggestions at an early stage in policy formation.
>
> It can also make sense to let expert outsiders take part in the deliberations occasionally and to ask them for judgments or advice. This is of course important above all in the design or preparation of complicated production processes or risky products and operations. If the members of a department or a team have worked on a problem for a long time, there is

---

[10] See also in this connection 't Hart (1994: 284–94).

[11] Janis (1982: 262–71) made a total of nine recommendations. We will return to some of them in the course of our discussion; others are too closely tailored to the formation of American foreign policy to be of direct use here.

a substantial risk of professional or organisational blindness, or the temptation to seek an enforced consensus. An unprejudiced 'second opinion' delivered by a respected expert outsider can lessen this sort of risk. One condition would of course be that such outsiders get a genuine chance to speak their mind, preferably before a definitive – and often hotly contested – compromise has been reached.

When a decision has been arrived at, it can sometimes be sensible not to go public with that decision immediately but first 'to sleep on it' and not to take a final decision until the next meeting. According to Janis, at this 'second chance meeting' the participants should be asked to raise their remaining doubts and objections one more time and to check them one by one.[12] This is above all important if the decision was taken under hectic conditions and if risky operations with consequences that are far-reaching and difficult to appraise are at issue, but also in cases when agreement has been reached all too quickly and too easily.

Working with devil's advocates and Cassandras. Another piece of advice, from the sphere of foreign policy (George 1980: 169–174), deserves special attention because it can be employed in a broader context to promote the learning capacity of organisations and the carefulness of their conduct. I have already explained at considerable length the importance of places of refuge for dissidents and the need to keep open channels for critical voices. One could even stimulate criticism artificially. This could be done by appointing one or more members of the group as a devil's advocate when important decisions are at issue. Such a devil's advocate would have to oppose the proposal that has the most chance of being adopted and do his or her best to destroy its chances of adoption. Devil's advocates could also be used to defend unpopular positions.

This is a technique that quickly becomes ineffective when carelessly applied. On the one hand, there is of course always the danger of the 'domestication of dissenters' that we also saw in the case of whistleblowers, although that is perhaps less likely to happen in the case of deliberately designated dissidents. More likely is the danger that the argument advanced by the devil's advocate becomes a mere formality, an obligatory routine that is performed to convince oneself and the outside world of the carefulness of the procedure, without seriously considering whether or not to go back on the decision. An important condition is also that the devil's advocate has a certain standing within the group; not only because this increases the like-

---

[12] Janis (1982: 271) gives the example of the president-director of General Motors who closed a meeting, in which unanimity existed in regard to some major decision, with the words: 'Gentlemen I propose we postpone further discussion of this matter to our next meeting to give ourselves time to develop disagreement and perhaps gain some understanding of what the decision is all about'.

lihood that his arguments will be taken seriously, but also in order to prevent him suffering personally as a result of putting forward his views too sharply, or to prevent him sucking up to the majority or to the boss for fear of treading on people's toes or upsetting them in some way. It can therefore also make sense to rotate the job regularly.[13]

A variant on this proposal can be found in the work of Janis (1982: 269). He proposes to appoint or hire a special 'Cassandra' figure in some situations. He restricts this recommendation to the interpretation of the intentions of hostile powers, but one could also apply it to risky operations and difficult decisions in the civil sphere. These modern Cassandras would have the job of sketching disaster scenarios in as convincing a way as possible, or delivering a sombre but plausible interpretation of the available data. In this way, people could be prevented from closing their eyes as a result of wishful thinking and other forms of self deception to the risks that are connected to the behaviour of the organisation.

Multiple advocacy. Alexander George (1980: 191–208) goes a step further. He suggests that information black-outs, blind spots, and false consensus can sometimes be prevented or got round by resorting in the course of policy formation to a system of multiple advocacy. Various departments or subgroups are charged with bringing out advice independently of one another about the same problem. The idea behind this is the same as in the case of the Cassandras and devil's advocates: 'This management model accepts the fact that conflicts over policy and advocacy in one form or another are inevitable in a complex organization [...] The solution it strives for is to ensure that there will be multiple advocates within the policy-making system who, among themselves, will cover a range of interesting viewpoints and policy options on any given issue' (George 1980: 193). By not glossing over and smoothing out those various points of view and proposals, but instead emphasising them and allowing the alternatives to compete with one another, George hopes that the quality of the provision of information and of the consequent decision-making can be improved.

The difference with the other proposals is above all its structural and large-scale character. That is also evident from the conditions that George sets. Thus it is extremely important that the various departments have roughly the same intellectual and material facilities at their disposal and that their status is roughly equal. This is in order to prevent certain alternatives from being proposed for the wrong reasons. For the same reason, there should be enough time left over for debate and negotiation. Those who take the decisions get an important but detached role in this process. Their task

---

[13] See also George (1980: 169–74) for a more extensive discussion of the advantages and disadvantages.

is that of judge. They must at first abstain from comment and make sure that the procedure runs properly and smoothly; only after all parties have been heard should they take their decision.

With these recommendations and suggestions I have wandered rather a long way from my original point of departure. Analyses of a philosophical, sociological and legal nature have given way to organisation design and to tips about good management. This area is by no means without its dangers. After all, analysis and prescription are not two sides of the same coin. Often the analysis of problems demands different skills and insights than does the process of coming up with workable solutions. The temptation is often great to hold a mirror up to the problem and to suggest solutions that are the diametrical opposite of the structures that seemed to cause the problem in the first place. If hierarchy was the problem, then a more egalitarian organisation; if loyalty was the problem, then more autonomy; if secrecy, then more openness. Thus, one runs the risk, to use the same cliché yet again, of losing the next war while engaged in a desperate attempt to avoid repeating the mistakes of the previous one. Organisational advice is, moreover, unlike legislative proposals or political theories, difficult to express in general terms. What may promote responsible conduct in one organisation, can give rise to indifference or misconduct elsewhere. With organisational advice, the detachment of the theorist quickly turns into a liability.

Epilogue: the quest for responsibility never ends

BCCI, *Challenger*, RSV, Slavenburg – these were some of the corporate and governmental fiascos that prompted this study. I have explored some of the main issues of responsibility that these sort of scandals call forth, concentrating in particular on individual accountability and employee citizenship. I have also suggested some adaptations of the models of accountability, of the notions of responsibility, and of the organisational structure, that in the future might contribute to the prevention of corporate and governmental deviance. Scandals and fiascos, however, happen at all times and, what is even more annoying, each time has its own fiascos (Bovens and 't Hart 1996). Legal regulations and organisational structures are transient. Within organisations, counter-strategies will be developed that undermine legal provisions. Organisational innovation will make the problem of many hands return in different forms. In the next decade, three developments are of particular importance in the quest for corporate responsibility:

> *The rise of large, multinational corporate groups.* In this book, a rather conventional image of corporate actors, as unitary legal entities, has been used.

Increasingly, however, corporations have merged into incredibly complex corporate groups: 'the contemporary large business, [...] typically includes scores or hundreds of corporations collectively conducting a common business under common control' (Blumberg 1993:341). These corporate groups come in a potentially infinite variety, as structure, ownership and form of control can differ widely (Antunes 1994). Many of these corporate enterprises no longer have a specific national identity, but operate in many different jurisdictions at the same time. This multinational and 'many-headed-Hydra' (Teubner 1993) character of corporate groups adds new, formidable dimensions to the problem of many hands. Moreover, the rise of these multinational networks of majority and minority holdings and cross-holdings 'creates the potential for a wide range of abuses' (Hadden 1993: 358). These networks can be used to construe misleading accounts, to avoid liability and taxation, or to evade regulation.

The fragmentation and debureaucratisation of complex organisations. The complex organisation not only merges into increasingly complex networks, it also crumbles internally, because of process innovation, reengineering and decentralisation (Davenport 1993; Crook, Pakulski and Waters 1992). Many modern organisations, both in the private and in the public sector, are trying to increase their flexibility with the help of information technology and managerial innovations such as sourcing out, privatization or the establishment of more or less autonomous business units or profit centres. These new developments make many complex organisations less hierarchical, but they also create new forms of the problem of many hands. Consumers, citizens, and controlling bodies are faced with conglomerates of fluctuating, overlapping, and often temporary subunits or subcontractors of the corporate actor they thought they were dealing with.

The quangocratization and marketization of public services. In the public sector, the rise of 'quangos' and other forms of semi-independent agencies has created major gaps in the system of parliamentary accountability (O'Toole and Chapman 1995). Also, this quangocratization raises fundamental questions about the relations between politicians and civil servants and about their respective responsibilities. The rather simple, in fact Wilsonian, dichotomy between politics and administration that seems to be the philosophy behind the creation of many new agencies paradoxically gives rise to rather Weberian worries about *Beamtenherrschaft*. When these (semi) public bodies engage in commercial, marketdriven activities new issues of integrity and administrative responsibility come to the fore (LeGrand and Bartlett 1993; Walsh 1995; Nolan 1995; Bovens 1996).

These shifting relations within and between organisations require one to remain continuously on the alert, to gauge one's notions of responsibility again and again and to adjust them to those new relations. I hope the questions of responsibility that I have discussed in these pages will be useful in studying and assessing future fiascos and that they will help to make possible the formulation of new notions of employee responsibility for these new situations. For the quest for responsibility never ends.

References

Abbot, A. 1983. 'Professional Ethics', *American Journal of Sociology* 88: 855–85

1988. *The System of Professions: An Essay on the Division of Expert Labor.* Chicago

Ackerman, Bruce A. and Hassler, William T. 1981. *Clean Coal / Dirty Air: Or How the Clean Air Act Became a Multibillion Dollar Bail-Out for High-Sulfur Coal Producers and what Should Be Done about it.* New Haven

Adelberg, Sheldon and Batson, C. Daniel 1978. 'Accountability and Helping: When Needs Exceed Resources', *Journal of Personality and Social Psychology* 36: 343–50

Adkins, W. H. 1960. *Merit and Responsibility: A Study in Greek Values.* Oxford

Adorno, Th. W. 1971. *Kritiek: Kleine Schriften zur Gesellschaft.* Frankfurt-on-Main

Albrow, Martin 1970. *Bureaucracy.* London

Allison, G. T. 1971. *Essence of Decision: Explaining the Cuban Missile Crisis.* Boston

Ames, E. 1965. *Soviet Economic Processes.* Homewood

Andeweg, R. B. 1985. 'Overheid of overhead? De bestuurbaarheid van het overheidsapparaat', in M. A. P. Bovens and W. J. Witteveen (eds.) 1985, 207–24

Antunes, J. E. 1994. *Liability of Corporate Groups: Autonomy and Control in Parent-Subsidiary Relationships in US, German and EU Law: An International and Comparative Perspective.* Deventer

Arendt, Hannah 1958. *The Human Condition.* Chicago

1964. 'Personal Responsibility under Dictatorship', *The Listener* 6: 185–7, 205

1965. *Eichmann in Jerusalem: A Report on the Banality of Evil.* Revised and enlarged edn, New York

1968. *Between Past and Future: Eight Exercises in Political Thought.* New York

1972. *Crises of the Republic.* New York

Argyris, Chris 1964. *Integrating the Individual and the Organization.* New York

1982. *Reasoning, Learning and Action: Individual and Organisational.* San Francisco

Argyris, Chris and Schön, Donald A. 1978. *Organisational Learning: A Theory of Action Perspective.* Reading MA

1986. 'Reciprocal Integrity'. Paper presented at the Symposium on Functioning of Executive Integrity, Wheaterhead School of Management, Case Western Reserve University, 15–18 October

Aristotle 1980. *The Nicomachean Ethics.* Trans. with intro. David Ross; revised by J. L. Ackrill and J. O. Urmson, Oxford

Aron, M. W. 1992. 'Whistleblowers, Insubordination, and Employee Rights of Free Speech', *Labor Law Journal* 43: 211–20

Arrow, K. 1974. 'On the Agenda of Organizations', in R. Marris (ed.), *The Corporate Society.* New York

Austin, J. L. 1957. *A Plea for Excuses, Proceedings of the Aristotelian Society.* New Series Vol. LVII, Papers Read Before the Society 1956–57, London

Baelemans, C. and Zuilekom, A. van 1987. *De opkomst van corporatieve actoren in Nederland.* Paper Vakgroep politieke wetenschappen, Leiden

Baier, Kurt 1972. 'Guilt and Responsibility', in P. A. French (ed.), pp. 37–61

Barber, Benjamin R. 1984. *Strong Democracy: Participatory Politics for a New Age.* Berkeley

Barnard, Chester I. 1938. *The Functions of the Executive.* Cambridge MA

1950. 'Bureaucracy in a Democracy', review of Charles S. Hyneman, *Bureaucracy in a Democracy*, New York, 1950, *APSR* 44: 990–1004

Barnett, T. 1992a. 'A Preliminary Investigation of the Relationship Between Selected Organizational Characteristics and External Whistleblowing by Employees', *Journal of Business Ethics* 11: 949–59

1992b. 'Overview of State Whistleblower Protection Statutes', *Labor Law Journal* 43: 440–8

Barnett, T., Cochran, D. S. and Taylor, G. S. 1993. 'The Internal Disclosure Policies of Private Sector Employers: An Initial Look at Their Relationship to Employee Whistleblowing', *Journal of Business Ethics* 12: 127–36

Beauchamp, Tom L. and Bowie, Norman E. (eds.) 1983. *Ethical Theory and Business.* 2nd edn, Englewood Cliffs, NJ

Beck, Ulrich 1992. *Risk Society: Towards a New Modernity.* London

Beer, Stafford 1972. *Brain of the Firm.* London

1975. *Platform for Change.* London

Beiner, Ronald 1983. *Political Judgement.* London

Bendix, Reinhard 1952. 'Bureaucracy and the Problem of Power', in Merton, Gray, Hockey and Selvin (eds.), 114–34

1963. *Work and Authority in Industry: Ideologies of Management in the Course of Industrialization*. New York

Benjamin, M. 1976. 'Can Moral Responsibility Be Collective and Nondistributive?', *Social Theory and Practice* 4: 93–106

Benn, S. I. 1975. 'Freedom, Autonomy and the Concept of a Person', *Proceedings of the Aristotelian Society* 76: 109–30

Besselink, L. F. M. 1987. 'Aftredende bewindslieden dragen volle verantwoordelijkheid tegenover de kamer', *Namens* 2, 4: 214–20

Black, Max (ed.) 1962. *The Importance of Language*. Ithaca

Bloemen, E., Kok, J. and Van Zanden, J. L. 1993. *De top 100 van industriële bedrijven in Nederland 1913–1990*. Achtergrondstudie AWT. Den Haag

Blom, J. C. H. 1983. 'In de ban van goed en fout? Wetenschappelijke geschiedschrijving over de bezettingstijd in Nederland.' Inaugural address Amsterdam University, Amsterdam

Blumberg, P. I. 1993. 'The American Law of Corporate Groups' in J. McCahery, S. Picciotto, and C. Scott (eds.) 1993, 305–42

Boeke, Warren 1992. 'Power and Managerial Dismissal: Scapegoating at the Top', *Administrative Science Quarterly* 37: 400–21

Bok, Sissela 1980. 'Whistleblowing and Professional Responsibility', *New York University Education Quarterly* 2, nr 4: 2–7. Also in T. L. Beauchamp and N. E. Bowie (eds.), *Ethical Theory and Business*, 2nd edn, Englewood Cliffs, 1983, 261–9

1981. 'Blowing the Whistle' in Fleishman, Liebman and Moore (eds.) 1988, 204–20

1982. *Secrets: On the Ethics of Concealment and Revelation*. New York

Bonhoeffer, D. 1971. *Ethics*. London

Bosch, T. W. van den 1976. *Beschouwingen over het militair dienstbevel*. Zutphen

1981. *Huidig en toekomstig militair straf- en tuchtrecht*. Zwolle

Bovens, Mark 1996. 'The Integrity of the Managerial State', *Journal of Contingencies and Crisis Management* 4, 3: 125–32

Bovens, Mark, Geveke, H. G. and Vries, J. de 1995. 'Open Public Administration in the Netherlands: The Politics of Leaking', *International Review of Administrative Sciences* 61: 17–40

Bovens, Mark and 't Hart, Paul 1996. *Understanding Policy Fiascoes*. New Brunswick

Bovens, Mark, Schuyt, C. J. M. and Witteveen, W. J. (eds.) 1989. *Verantwoordelijkheid: retoriek en realiteit*. Zwolle

Bovens Mark and Witteveen W. J. (eds.) 1985. *Het schip van staat; beschouwingen over recht, staat en sturing*. Zwolle

1986. *Sturing van de samenleving*. Zwolle

Bozeman, Barry 1987. *All Organizations Are Public: Bridging Public and Private Organizational Theories.* San Francisco

Braithwaite, John 1985. 'Taking Responsibility Seriously: Corporate Compliance Systems', in B. Fisse and P. A. French (eds.) 1985, 39–61

Braithwaite, John and Geiss, Gilbert 1982. 'On Theory and Action for Corporate Crime Control', *Crime and Delinquency* 28: 292–306

Braithwaite, John and Makkai, Toni 1991. 'Testing an Expected Utility Model of Corporate Deterrence', *Law and Society Review* 25: 7–39

Brants, Chrisje 1988. 'Slavenburg en de grenzen van het strafrecht', *Recht en Kritiek* 14: 26–58

Bruinsma, F. 1988. *Cassatierechtspraak in civiele zaken: een rechtssociologisch verslag.* Rijksuniversiteit Utrecht, 2nd edn, Zwolle

Burke, John P. 1986. *Bureaucratic Responsibility.* Baltimore

Burnham, James 1947. *Machtsvorming der bewindvoerders.* The Hague

Burns, T. and Stalker, G. M. 1961. *The Management of Innovation.* London

Bussey, Ellen M. (ed.) 1984. *Federal Civil Service Law and Procedures.* Washington

Chandler, A. D. 1962. *Strategy and Structure: Chapters in the History of the Industrial Enterprise.* Cambridge MA

Chandler, A. D. and Salisbury, S. 1971. *Pierre S. Dupont and the Making of the Modern Corporation.* New York

Chandler, R. C. (ed.) 1987. *A Centennial History of the American Administrative State.* New York

Clinard, Marshall B. and Yeager, Peter C. 1980. *Corporate Crime.* New York

Coffee, John C. 1977. 'Beyond the Shut-Eyed Sentry: Toward a Theoretical View of Corporate Misconduct and an Effective Legal Response', *Virginia Law Review* 63: 1099–278
    1981. '"No Soul to Damn: No Body to Kick": An Unscandalized Inquiry into the Problem of Corporate Punishment', *Michigan Law Review* 79: 386–459

Coleman, James S. 1974. *Power and the Structure of Society.* New York
    1982. *The Asymmetric Society.* Syracuse
    1990. *Foundation of Social Theory.* Cambridge Mass

Cook, Scott D. N. and Yanow, Dvora 1993. 'Culture and Organizational Learning', *Journal of Management Inquiry* 2: 373–90

Cooper, D. E. 1968. 'Collective Responsibility', *Philosophy* 43: 258–68

Cooper, Terry L. 1987. 'Hierarchy, Virtue and the Practice of Public Administration: A Perspective for Normative Ethics', *Public Administration Review* 47: 320–8
    1991. *An Ethic of Citizenship for Public Administration.* Englewood Cliffs NJ

Crandall, R. W. and Lave L. B. (eds.) 1981. *The Scientific Basis of Health and Safety Regulation.* Washington

Crick, Bernard 1973. *Basic Forms of Government: A Sketch and a Model.*
London
Crook, S., Pakulski, J. and Waters, M. 1992. *Postmodernization: Change in
Advanced Society.* London
Dahl, Robert A. 1970. *After the Revolution.* New York
Davenport, Thomas H. 1993. *Process Innovation: Reengineering Work through
Information Technology.* Boston
Day, P. and Klein, R. 1987. *Accountabilities: Five Public Services.* London
DeGeorge, Richard T. 1983, 'Can Corporations Have Moral Responsibility?', in
T. L. Beauchamp and N. E. Bowie (eds.) 1983, 57–67
DeGeorge, Richard T. and Pichler, Joseph A. (eds.) 1978. *Ethics, Free
Enterprise and Public Policy: Original Essays on Moral Issues in Business.*
New York
Derksen, W. and Sande, M. L. van der (eds.) 1984. *De burgemeester, van
magistraat tot modern bestuurder.* Deventer
Doelder, H. de 1986. Requisitoir van het Openbaar Ministerie in de zaak
6918–83, Arrondissementsparket Rotterdam, 1 April 1986
Donaldson, Thomas 1982. *Corporations and Morality.* Englewood Cliffs NJ
Downie, R. S. 1969. 'Collective Responsibility', *Philosophy* 44: 66–9
Downs, Anthony 1967. *Inside Bureaucracy.* Boston
Dozier, Janelle B. 1988. 'Is Whistle-Blowing Helping Behaviour?: A Laboratory
Study of Team Member Reporting of an Unethical Team Leader', paper
presented at the 1988 Annual Meeting of the International Society of
Political Psychology, Secaucus NJ
Dozier, J. B. and Miceli, M. P. 1985. 'Potential Predictors of Whistle-Blowing: A
Prosocial Behavior Perspective', *Academy of Management Review* 10:
823–36
Dworkin, Ronald 1986. *Law's Empire.* Cambridge MA
Dworkin, T. M. and Callahan, E. S. 1991. 'Internal Whistlebowing: Protecting
the Interests of the Employee, the Organization, and Society', *American
Business Law Journal* 29: 267–308
Eastwood, Mary O. 1984. 'Prohibited Personnel Practices and Whistleblowing',
in E. M. Bussey (ed.), pp. 95–110
Eldersveld, Samuel J., Kooiman, Jan and Tak, Theo van der 1981. *Elite Images
of Dutch Politics: Accommodation and Conflict.* Ann Arbor/The Hague
Ellsberg, Daniel 1972. *Papers on the War.* New York
Elster, Jon 1983a. *Sour Grapes: Studies in the Subversion of Rationality.*
Cambridge
  1983b. *Explaining Technical Change: A Case Study in the Philosophy of
Science.* Cambridge
Elzinga, D. J. 1989. 'Politieke verantwoordelijkheid: Over verval en
vooruitgang in de politieke democratie', in M. A. P. Bovens, C. J. M.
Schuyt and W. I. Witteveen (eds.) 1989, pp. 63–80

Ermann, M. David and Lundman, Richard J. 1982a. *Corporate Deviance*. New York

Ermann, M. David and Lundman, Richard J. (eds.) 1982b, *Corporate and Governmental Deviance: Problems of Organizational Behavior in Contemporary Society*. 2nd edn, New York/Oxford

Etzioni, Amitai 1969. *A Sociological Reader on Complex Organizations*. 2nd edn, New York

1975. *A Comparative Analysis of Complex Organizations*. Revised and enlarged edn, New York

Ewing, David W. 1977. *Freedom inside the Organization: Bringing Civil Liberties to the Workplace*. New York

1983. *'Do it My Way or You're Fired!': Employee Rights and the Changing Role of Management Prerogatives*. New York

Falk Moore, Sally 1978. *Law as Process: An Anthropological Approach*. London

Fayol, H. 1916. *Administration Industrielle et Generale*. Paris

Feinberg, Joel 1970. *Doing and Deserving: Essays in the Theory of Responsibility*. Princeton

Finer, H. 1936. 'Better Government Personnel: America's Next Frontier', *Political Science Quarterly* 51: 569–99

1941. 'Administrative Responsibility in Democratic Government', *Public Administration Review* 1: 335–50

Finney, Henry C. and Lesieur, Henry R. 1982. 'A Contingency Theory of Organizational Crime', *Research in the Sociology of Organizations* 1: 255–99

Fishkin, James S. 1982. *The Limits of Obligation*. New Haven

Fisse, Brent 1985. 'Sanctions against Corporations: The Limitations of Fines and the Enterprise of Creating Alternatives', in B. Fisse and P. A. French (eds.) 1985, 137–57

Fisse, Brent and Braithwaite, John 1993. *Corporations, Crime and Accountability*. Cambridge

Fisse, Brent and French, Peter A. (eds.) 1985. *Corrigible Corporations and Unruly Law*. San Antonio

Fleishman, Joel L., Liebman, Lance and Moore, Mark H. (eds.) 1981. *Public Duties: The Moral Obligations of Government Officials*. Cambridge MA

Flores, A. and Johnson, D. G. 1983. 'Collective Responsibility and Professional Roles', *Ethics* 93: 537–45

Frankel, M. S. 1989. 'Professional Codes: Why, How, and What Impact?', *Journal of Business Ethics* 8: 109–15

Frederickson, H. G. and Chandler, R. C. (eds.) 1983. 'Citizenship and Public Administration, Proceedings of the National Conference on Citizenship and Public Administration, 14–16 April, 1983', *Public Administration Review* 44: special issue

French, Peter A. (ed.) 1972. *Individual and Collective Responsibility: The Massacre at My Lai*. Cambridge MA

French, Peter A. 1979. 'The Corporation as a Moral Person', *American Philosophical Quarterly* 16: 207–15
1984. *Collective and Corporate Responsibility.* New York
Friedrich, Carl J. 1935. *Constitutional Government and Politics.* New York
1940. 'Public Policy and the Nature of Administrative Responsibility', *Public Policy:* 15–24
Fuller, Lon L. 1967. *Legal Fictions.* Stanford
Galanter, Marc 1974. 'Why the "Haves" Come Out Ahead: Speculations on the Limits of Legal Change', *Law and Society Review* 9: 95–160
Galbraith, John Kenneth 1967. *The New Industrial State.* New York
1973. *Economics and the Public Purpose.* Boston
Gallie, W. B. 1962, 'Essentially Contested Concepts', in M. Black (ed.), pp. 121–46
Geach, Peter 1977. *The Virtues, Stanton Lectures 1973–1974.* Cambridge
George, Alexander L. 1980. *Presidential Decisionmaking in Foreign Policy: The Effective Use of Information and Advice.* Boulder CO
Gerding, G. 1986. 'Individuele autonomie, bestuurbaarheid en managers' in M. A. P. Bovens and W. J. Witteveen (eds.), *Sturing van de samenleving.* Zwolle pp. 143–53
Gersuny, Carl 1994. 'Industrial Rights: A Neglected Facet of Citizenship Theory', *Economic and Industrial Democracy* 15: 211–26
Gerth, H. H. and Wright Mills, C. 1946. *From Max Weber: Essays in Sociology.* New York
Glazer, Myron Peretz 1983. 'Ten Whistleblowers and How They Fared', *The Hastings Centre Report,* December: 33–41
Glazer, Myron Peretz and Glazer, Penina Migdal 1986. 'Whistleblowing', *Psychology Today,* 19: 36–43
1989. *The Whistleblowers: Exposing Corruption in Government and Industry.* New York
Glover, Jonathan 1970. *Responsibility.* London
Goodin, Robert E. 1982. *Political Theory and Public Policy.* Chicago
1985. *Protecting the Vulnerable: An Reanalysis of Our Social Responsibilities.* Chicago
Goodin, R. E. & Klingemann, H. D. (ed.) 1996. *A New Handbook of Political Science.* Oxford
Goodnow, Frank J. 1900. *Politics and Administration: A Study in Government.* New York
Goodsell, Charles T., et al. 1986. *Public Administration and the Governance Process: Refocusing the American Dialogue.* Mimeo Blacksburg VA.
Gosewehr, D. N. R. and Maas, W. P. M. 1984. *Booy Clean: Onderzoek naar bestuurlijke en juridische milieuhygiënische verwikkelingen rond het Rotterdamse cleaningsbedrijf.* Amsterdam
Gunsteren, H. R. van 1974. *Denken over politieke verantwoordelijkheid.* Rijksuniversiteit Leiden, Alphen aan den Rijn

1976. *The Quest for Control: A Critique of the Rational-Central-Rule Approach in Public Affairs.* London

1985. 'The Ethical Context of Bureaucracy and Performance Analysis', in F. X. Kaufman, G. Majone and V. Ostrom (eds.) 1985, 266–78

Haan, H. den 1987. 'De zaak Slavenburg'. Paper Vakgroep Politieke Wetenschappen, Rijksuniversiteit Leiden

Habermas, Jürgen 1981. *Theorie des Kommunikativen Handelns.* Volume 2, Frankfurt-on-Main

1989. *The Structural Transformation of the Public Sphere: An Inquiry into a Category of Bourgeois Society,* translated by Thomas Burger with the assistance of Frederick Lawrence. Boston

Hadden, Tom 1993. 'Regulating Corporate Groups', in J. McCahery, S. Picciotto, and C. Scott (eds.) 1993, 343–69

Haersolte, R. A. V. van 1971. *Personificatie van sociale systemen.* Deventer

Hampshire, S. (ed.) 1978. *Public and Private Morality.* Cambridge

Harmon, Michael M. 1971. 'Normative Theory and Public Administration: Some Suggestions for a Redefinition of Administrative Responsibility', in F. Marini (ed.) 1971, 172–85

1981. *Action Theory for Public Administration.* New York

1990. 'The Responsible Actor as Tortured Soul: The Case of Horatio Hornblower', in Kass and Catron (eds.), 151–80

1995. *Responsibility as Paradox: A Critique of Rational Discourse on Government.* Thousand Oaks, California

Hart, A. C. 't and Vries-Leemans M. J. H. J. de (1986). 'Enige opmerkingen betreffende het feitelijk leiding geven', in *Honderd jaar Wetboek van Strafrecht,* Arnhem, 289–301

Hart, H. L. A. 1968. *Punishment and Responsibility: Essays in the Philosophy of Law.* New York

Hart, H. L. A. and Honoré, Tony 1985. *Causation in the Law.* London

Hart, P. 't 1994. *Groupthink in Government: A Study of Small Groups and Policy Failure.* Baltimore

Haydon, Graham 1978. 'On Being Responsible', *The Philosophical Quarterly* 28: 46–57

Heady, Ferrel 1984. *Public Administration: A Comparative Perspective.* 3rd edn revised, New York

Heijden, P. F. van der 1988. *Grondrechten in de onderneming.* Rijksuniversiteit Groningen, Deventer

Held, Virginia 1970. 'Can a Random Collection of Individuals be Morally Responsible?', *Journal of Philosophy* 67: 471–81

Hellinga Commission, 1983. *Rapport van de onderzoekscommissie naar de bestuurlijke aspecten van de uitvoering van de milieu- en andere relevante wetgeving bij Drisolco B. V., E. M. K., Uniser e. a.,* ingesteld bij beschikking van de staatssecretaris van Volksgezondheid en Milieuhygiëne van 1 november 1982, 's-Gravenhage 14 September 1983

Heringa, A. W., Winter, R. E. de and Witteveen, W. J. (eds.), *Staatkundig Jaarboek 1987*. Nijmegen

Herzberg, A. J. 1962. *Eichmann in Jerusalem*. Den Haag

Hill, Michael J. 1972. *The Sociology of Public Administration*. New York

Hirschman, Alfred O. 1970. *Exit, Voice and Loyalty: Responses to Decline in Firms, Organizations and States*. Cambridge MA

Hollis, Martin 1987. *The Cunning of Reason*. Cambridge

Hood, Christopher C. 1983. *The Tools of Government*. London

    1991. 'A Public Management for All Seasons?', *Public Administration* 69, 3–19

Hosson, G. J. de 1995. 'Vertrouwenspersoon en bestuurlijke integriteit: Over de opvang van 'quasimodo's' in ambtelijke organisaties', *Bestuurswetenschappen* 49: 447–56

Hunt, John W. 1982a. 'Developing Middle Managers in Shrinking Organizations', *Journal of Management Development* 1: 10–22

    1982b. 'The Costs of Corporate Dependence: Managers Caught in the Middle', *London Business School Journal*. 7: 60–6

Jackall, Robert 1988. *Moral Mazes: The World of Corporate Managers*. New York/Oxford

Janis, Irving L. 1982. *Groupthink*. 2nd revised edn, Boston

Johnson, R. A. and Kraft, M. E. 1990. 'Bureaucratic Whistleblowing and Policy Change', *The Western Political Quarterly* 43: 849–74

Jonas, Hans 1979. *Das Prinzip Verantwortung: Versuch einer Ethik für die technologische Zivilisation*. Frankfurt-on-Main

Jörg, N. 1988. *De strafbaarheid van de leiding van corporaties in het Amerikaanse en Nederlandse recht*. Preadvies uitgebracht voor de Nederlandse Vereniging voor Rechtsvergelijking no. 39, Deventer

Jouvenel, B. de 1945. *Du Pouvoir*. Geneva

Kagan, Robert A. 1978. *Regulatory Justice: Implementing a Wage-Price Freeze*. New York

Kass, H. D. and Catron, B. L. (eds.) 1990. *Images and identities in public administration*. Newbury Park

Kastelein, J. 1985. *Modulair organiseren doorgelicht*. Groningen

Kaufman, Herbert 1973a. *Administrative Feedback: Monitoring Subordinates' Behavior*. Washington DC

    1973b, *Are Government Organizations Immortal?*. Washington DC

Kaufman, F. X., Majone G. and Ostrom V. (eds.) 1985. *Guidance Control and Performance Evaluation in the Public Sector*. Berlin

Kelman, H. C. and Hamilton, V. L. 1989. *Crimes of Obedience: Towards a Social Psychology of Authority and Responsibility*. New Haven

Kenny, Anthony 1978. *Freewill and Responsibility*. London

Koestler, Arthur 1979. *Janus: A Summing Up*. London

Lachs, J. 1978. '"I Only Work Here": Mediation and Irresponsibility', in DeGeorge and Pichler (eds.) 1978: 201–13.

Ladd, John 1970. 'Morality and the Ideal of Rationality in Formal Organisations', *The Monist* 54: 488–516

Laframboise, H. L. 1991. 'Vile Wretches and Public Heroes: The Ethics of Whistleblowing in Government', *Canadian Public Administration/Administration Publique du Canada* 34: 73–7

Lampert, Nicholas 1985. *Whistleblowing in the Soviet Union: Complaints and Abuses under State Socialism.* London

Lawrence, P. and Lorsch, J. W. 1967. *Organization and Environment: Managing Differentiation and Integration.* Boston

Leech, Tim J. 1991. 'Whistleblowing in Business: The Challenge and the Response', *Canadian Public Administration* 34: 78–83

Le Grand, J. and Bartlett, W. (ed.) 1993. *Quasi-Markets and Social Policy.* Basingstoke

Levinson, S. 1973. 'Responsibility for Crimes of War', *Philosophy and Public Affairs* 2: 244–73

Likert, Rensis 1961. *New Patterns of Management.* New York
     1967. *The Human Organization: Its Management and Value.* New York

Lucas, J. R. 1993. *Responsibility.* Oxford

McCahery, J., Picciotto, S., and Scott C. (eds.) 1993. *Corporate Control and Accountability: Changing Structures and the Dynamics of Regulation.* Oxford

McGregor, Douglas 1960. *The Human Side of Enterprise.* New York

Magruder, Jeb Stuart 1974. *An American Life: One Man's Road to Watergate.* New York

MacIntyre, Alasdair 1981. *After Virtue: A Study in Moral Theory.* Notre Dame
     1988. *Whose Justice? Which Rationality?* London

McLaughlin, Judith B. and Riesman, David 1986. 'The Shady Side of Sunshine', *Teachers College Record* 87: 471–94

Malchus, C. A. von 1823. *Politik der inneren Staatsverwaltung.* Erster Theil, Heidelberg

March, J. G. and Olsen, J. P. 1995. *Democratic Governance.* New York

Marini, F. (ed.) 1971. *Toward a New Public Administration: The Minnowbrook Perspective.* Scranton

Markesinis, B. S. and Deakin, S. F. 1994. *Tort Law.* 3rd edn, Oxford

Marx, Karl 1844. 'Zur Judenfrage' in *Deutsch-Französische Jahrbücher.* 1e u. 2e Lieferung, Paris

Mayo, Elton 1945. *The Social Problems of an Industrial Civilization.* Cambridge MA

Meeus, W. H. J. and Raaijmakers, Q. A. W. 1984. *Gewoon gehoorzaam: Een sociaal-psychologisch onderzoek naar gehoorzaamheid.* Rijksuniversiteit Utrecht

Merton, R., Gray, A., Hockey, B. and Selvin, H. C. (eds.) 1952. *Reader in Bureaucracy.* New York

Miceli, M. P. and Near, J. P. 1985. 'Characteristics of Organizational Climate and Perceived Wrongdoing Associated with Whistle-Blowing Decisions', *Personnel Psychology* 38: 525–44

Michels, Robert 1962 (1915). *Political Parties: A Sociological Study of the Oligarchical Tendencies of Modern Democracy*. Trans. by Eden and Cedar Paul, intro. Seymour Martin Lipset, New York

Milgram, Stanley 1974. *Obedience to Authority: An Experimental View*. New York

Mintzberg, Henry 1979. *The Structuring of Organizations: A Synthesis of the Research*. Englewood Cliffs NJ

MSPB 1984. *Blowing the Whistle in Federal Government: A Comparative Analysis of 1980 and 1983 Survey Findings*. A Report to the President and the Congress of the United States by the US Merit Systems Protection Board. Washington DC

    1986. *Getting Involved: Improving Federal Management with Employee Participation*. A Report to the President and the Congress of the United States by the US Merit Systems Protection Board. Washington DC

    1993. *Whistleblowing in the Federal Government: An Update*. A Report to the President and the Congress of the United States by the U. S. Merit Systems Protection Board. Washington D. C

Mulisch, Harry 1962. *De zaak 40/61: een reportage*. Amsterdam

Multatuli 1973 (1860). *Volledige Werken*. Deel I, Amsterdam

Nader, R., Petkas, P. and Blackwell, K. 1972. *Whistleblowing: The Report of the Conference on Professional Responsibility*. New York

Nagel, Stuart S. 1975. *Improving the Legal Process: Effects of Alternatives*. Lexington

Nagel, Thomas 1978. 'Ruthlessness in Public Life', in Hampshire (ed.) 1978, 75–91

Naisbitt, J. and Patricia Aburdene 1985. *Re-inventing the Corporation*. New York

Near, Janet P. and Miceli, Marcia P. 1985. 'Organizational Dissidence: The Case of Whistle-Blowing', *Journal of Business Ethics* 4: 1–16

    1995. 'Effective Whistleblowing', *Academy of Management Review* 20: 679–708

Niebuhr, H. R. 1963. *The Responsible Self: An Essay in Christian Moral Philosophy*. New York

Nielsen, Richard P. 1984. 'Arendt's Action Philosophy and the Manager as Eichmann, Richard III, Faust, or Institution Citizen', *California Management Review* 26: 191–201

Nolan. 1995. *Standards in Public Life: First report of the Committee on Standards in Public life*. Chairman Lord Nolan. Volume 1: Report. London

Norton-Taylor, Richard 1985. *The Ponting Affair*. London

OECD 1995, *Labour Force Statistics 1973–1993*. Paris

Olafson, F. A. 1967. *Principles and Persons: An Ethical Interpretation of Existentialism.* Baltimore

Olbers, M. M. 1984. 'Opdracht in strijd met de wet', *Sociaal Maandblad Arbeid* 39: 150–66

Osborne, D. and Gaebler, T. 1993. *Reinventing Government: How the Entrepreneurial Spirit Is Transforming the Public Sector.* New York

Ostrom, E. 1990. *Governing the Commons: The Evolution of Institutions for Collective Action.* Cambridge

Ostrom, E., Walker, J. and Gardner, R. 1992. 'Covenants with and Without a Sword: Self-Governance is Possible', *American Political Science Review* 86, 404–17

O'Toole, B. J. and Chapman, R. A. 1995. 'Parliamentary Accountability', in O'Toole and Jordan (eds.) 1995, 118–41

O'Toole, B. J. and Jordan, G. (eds.) 1995. *Next Steps: Improving Management in Government?* Aldershot

Oversloot, H. and Gunsteren, H. R. van 1987. 'Over corruptie, dubbele moraal en halve exit', in Heringa, Winter and Witteveen (eds.) 63–74

Paine, Lynn S. 1994. 'Managing for Organizational Integrity', *Harvard Business Review* 72: 107–17

Parfit, D. 1984. *Reasons and Persons.* Oxford

Parmerlee, Marcia A., Near, Janet P. and Jensen, Tamila C. 1982. 'Correlates of Whistleblowers' Perceptions of Organizational Retaliation', *Administrative Science Quarterly* 27: 17–34

Pennock, J. Roland 1952. 'Responsiveness, Responsibility, and Majority Rule', *APSR* 46: 790–807

Perrow, C. 1967. 'A Framework for the Comparative Analysis of Organizations', *American Sociological Review* 32: 194–208
   1979. *Complex Organizations: A Critical Essay.* 2nd edn, New York
   1984. *Normal Accidents: Living with High-Risk Technologies.* New York

Perry, J. L. 1992. The consequences of speaking out: Processes of hostility and issue resolution involving federal whistleblowers. *Academy of Management Best Paper Proceedings*; 52.

Peters, B. G. and Wright, V. 1996. 'Public Policy and Administration, Old and New', in Goodin, R. E. and Klingemann, H. D. (eds.) 1996. *A New Handbook of Political Science.* Oxford.

Peters, Charles and Branch, Taylor 1972. *Blowing the Whistle: Dissent in the Public Interest.* New York

Philips, J. C. 1972. 'Responsibility in Business Management', *American Behavioral Scientist* 15: 445–63

Pitkin, Hannah Fenichel 1972. *Wittgenstein and Justice: On the Significance of Ludwig Wittgenstein for Social and Political Thought.* Berkeley

Pollock, F. and Maitland, F. W. 1968. *The History of English Law before the Time of Edward I.* 2 vols. 2nd edn, Cambridge

Posner, Richard A. 1972. *Economic Analysis of Law.* Boston

Public Concern at Work 1995. *The Role for Whistleblowers in Tackling Financial Malparactice and Protecting the European Union Budget.* Report submitted to the European Parliament, London

Punch, Maurice 1981. *Management and Control of Organizations: Occupational Deviance, Responsibility and Accountability.* Nijenrode, Leiden

   1996. *Dirty Business: Exploring Corporate Misconduct/Analysis and Cases.* London

Putnam, R. D. 1993. *Making Democracy Work: Civic Traditions in Modern Italy.* Princeton

Rawls, J. 1971. *A Theory of Justice.* Cambridge MA

Robbins, S. P. 1980. *The Administrative Process.* 2d edn, Englewood Cliffs NJ

Romzek, Barbara S. and Dubnick, Melvin J. 1987. 'Accountability in the Public Sector: Lessons from the Challenger Tragedy', *Public Administration Review* 47: 227–38

RSV-enquête: Opkomst en ondergang van Rijn-Schelde-Verolme 1965–1971; 1971–1977, verslag van de Enquêtecommissie RSV (1983–1984), TK 1984–1985, 17817, no. 16

Sandel, Michael J. 1982. *Liberalism and the Limits of Justice.* Cambridge

Sartre, J. -P. 1946. *L'Existentialisme est un humanisme.* Paris

Scheltema, M. and Lubberdink, H. G. 1980. 'Ministeriële verantwoordelijkheid en parlementaire controle', in *Parlementaire controle en democratie in de verzorgingsstaat.* Utrecht

Schrag, Peter 1974. *Test of Loyalty: Daniel Ellsberg and the Rituals of Secret Government.* New York

Schumpeter, Joseph A. 1950. *Capitalism, Socialism and Democracy.* 3rd edn, New York

Schuyt, C. J. M. 1972. *Recht, orde en burgerlijke ongehoorzaamheid.* Rijksuniversiteit Leiden, Rotterdam

   1983. *Tussen macht en moraal: Over de plaats van het recht in verzorgingsstaat en democratie.* Alphen aan den Rijn

   1985. 'Sturing en het recht', in M. A. P. Bovens and W. J. Witteveen (eds.) 1985, 113–24

Schuyt, Kees, Groenendijk, Kees and Sloot, Ben 1976. *De weg naar het recht.* Deventer

Self, Peter 1977. *Administrative Theories and Politics: An Enquiry into the Structure and Processes of Modern Government.* 2nd edn, London

Seymour, Sally 1988. 'The Case of the Willful Whistle-Blower', *Harvard Business Review* 66: 103–9

Smart, J. J. C. T. and Williams B. (eds.) 1973. *Utilitarianism: For and Against.* Cambridge

Smigel, E. O. and Ross, H. L. 1970. *Crimes against Bureacracy.* New York

Snider, Laureen 1991. 'The Regulatory Dance: Understanding Reform Processes in Corporate Crime', *International Journal of the Sociology of Law* 19: 209–36

Sobel, R. 1984. *The Age of Giant Corporations: A Micro-Economic History of American Business 1914–1984*. 2nd edn, Westport CN

Spengler, Lukas van 1988. 'Veel ambtenaren zijn eerst aan zich zelf loyaal en dan pas aan hun baas, wie in conflict komt moet de betrekkelijkheid van z'n positie inzien', *Binnenlands Bestuur* 9: 24–5

Spicer, M. W., and Lundstedt, S. B. 1976. 'Understanding Tax Evasion', *Public Finance*, 31, 2: 295–305

Spiro, Herbert J. 1969. *Responsibility in Government: Theory and Practice*. New York

Stewart, Lea P. 1980. '"Whistle Blowing": Implications for Organizational Communication', *Journal of Communication* 30, 4: 90–101

Stivers, C. 1989. 'Organizational Citizenship: A Problematic Metaphor', *Administration and Society* 21: 228–33

    1990. 'The Public Agency as Polis: Active Citizenship in the Administrative State', *Administration and Society* 22: 86–105

Stone, Christopher D. 1975. *Where the Law Ends: The Social Control of Corporate Behavior* New York

    1985. 'Corporate Regulation: The Place of Social Responsibility', in B. Fisse and P. A. French (eds.), 1988, 13–38

Swaan, A. de 1982. 'Uitgaansbeperking en uitgaansangst; over de verschuiving van bevelshuishouding naar onderhandelingshuishouding', in De Swaan (ed.), *De mens is de mens een zorg: Essays 1971–1981*, Amsterdam

Taylor, F. W. 1911. *Principles and Methods of Scientific Management*. New York

Tetlock, Philip E. 1983. 'Accountability and Complexity of Thought', *Journal of Personality and Social Psychology* 45: 74–83

Teubner G. C. M., 1993. 'The Many-Headed-Hydra', in McCahery, Picciotto, and Scott (eds.) 1993, pp. 41–60

Thompson, Dennis F. 1980. 'Moral Responsibility of Public Officials: The Problem of Many Hands', *APSR* 74: 905–16

    1983. 'Ascribing Responsibility to Advisers in Government', *Ethics* 93: 546–60

    1987. *Political Ethics and Public Office*. Cambridge MA

    1995. *Ethics in Congress: From Individual to Institutional Corruption*. Washington, DC

Thomson, James C. Jr. 1968. 'How Could Vietnam Happen? An Autopsy', *Atlantic Monthly* 47–53

Toffler, A. 1985. *The Adaptive Corporation*. London

Torringa, R. A. 1984. *Strafbaarheid van rechtspersonen*. Groningen

    1988. *De rechtspersoon als dader: strafbaar leiding geven aan rechtspersonen*. 2e druk Arnhem

Tromp, B. A. G. M. 1985. 'Solidariteit als politieke pasmunt', in *Solidariteit: over wat mensen verbindt.* . . . Utrecht, pp. 72–85

Tullock, Gordon 1965. *The Politics of Bureaucracy.* Washington

Turpin, C. 1994. *British Government and the Constitution: Text, Cases and Materials.* 2nd edn, London

Tuurenhout, M. 1992. *Parlementaire controle en ambtelijke verantwoordelijkheid.* Arnhem

Vandivier, Kermit 1982. 'Why Should My Conscience Bother Me?', in M. D. Ermann and R. J. Lundman (eds.) 1982b, 102–22

Vaughan, Diane 1983. *Controlling Unlawful Organizational Behavior: Social Structure and Corporate Misconduct.* Chicago

1996. *The Challanger Launch Decision: Risky Technology, Culture, and Deviance at NASA.* Chicago/London

Vaughn, Robert G. 1977. 'Public Employees and the Right to Disobey', *Hastings Law Journal* 29: 261–95

1982. 'Statutory Protection of Whistleblowers in the Federal Executive Branch', *University of Illinois Law Review* 3: 615–67

Verkruisen, W. 1993. 'Dissatisfied patients: their experiences, interpretations, and actions,' PhD thesis, Groningen University

Vermeulen, B. P. 1989. *De vrijheid van geweten: een fundamenteel rechtsprobleem.* Erasmus Universiteit Rotterdam, Arnhem

Vinten, G. 1994. 'Asset Protection Through Whistleblowing', *The Journal of Asset protection and Financial Crime* 2: 121–31

Vogel, David 1986. *National Styles of Regulation: Environmental Policy in Great Britain and the United States.* Ithaca

Vos, J. G. 1985. 'De catacomben van de verzorgingsstaat', *Intermediair* 15 February 1985. 29–33

Waldo, Dwight 1948. *The Administrative State.* New York

Walsh, W. H. 1970. 'Pride, Shame and Responsibility', *The Philosophical Quarterly* 20: 1–13

1995. *Public Services and Market Mechanisms: Competition, Contracting, and the New Public Management.* London

Wamsley, Gary L., Charles T. Goodsell, John A. Rohr, Camilla M. Stivers, Orion F. White and James F. Wolf 1990. 'Public Administration and the Governance Process: Shifting the Political Dialogue', in Wamsley, Gary L., Robert N. Bacher, Charles T. Goodsell, Philip S. Kronenberg, John A. Rohr, Camilla M. Stivers, Orion F. White and James F. Wolf (eds.) *Refounding Public Administration.* Newbury Park

Weber, Max 1948. *From Max Weber: Essays in Sociology.* Trans., ed., and with intro. H. H. Gerth and C. Wright Mills. London

1938 (1919). *Gesammelte Politische Schriften.* 2e Auflage, Hrsg. Johannes Winckelman, Tübingen

1977 (1919). *Politik als Beruf.* 6e Auflage, Berlin

1980 (1920). *Wirtschaft und Gesellschaft: Grundriss der verstehende Soziologie.* 5e revidierte Auflage, besorgt von Johannes Winkelmann, Studiënausgabe, Tübingen

1981 (1920). *Die protestantische Ethik.* 6e durchgesehene Auflage, Hrsg. Johannes Winckelmann, Gütersloh

Weisband, Edward and Franck, Thomas M. 1975. *Resignation in Protest: Political and Ethical Choices between Loyalty to Conscience in American Public Life.* New York

Weldon, Elisabeth and Gargano, Gina M. 1988. 'Cognitive Loafing: The Effects of Accountability and Shared Responsibility on Cognitive Effort', *Personality and Social Psychology Bulletin* 14: 159–71

Wells, C. 1993, *Corporations and Criminal Responsibility.* Oxford

Westin, Alan F. (ed.) 1981. *Whistleblowing! Loyalty and Dissent in the Corporation.* New York

Westin, Alan F. and Salisbury, Stephan (eds.) 1980. *Individual Rights in the Corporation.* New York

Weston, J. F. (ed.) 1974. *Large Corporations in a Changing Society.* New York

Wildavsky, Aaron 1972. 'Why Planning Fails in Nepal', *Administrative Science Quarterly* 17: 508–28

1986. *Responsibilities are Allocated by Cultures.* Mimeo, Berkeley

1988. *Searching for Safety.* Berkeley

Wilensky, Harold L. 1967. *Organizational Intelligence. Knowledge and Policy in Government and Industry.* New York

Williams, Bernard 1973. 'A Critique of Utilitarianism', in J. J. C. T. Smart and B. Williams (eds.) 1973: 77–149

1981. *Moral Luck: Philosophical Papers 1973–1980.* Cambridge

Williamson, Oliver E. 1975. *Markets and Hierarchies: Analysis and Antitrust Implications.* New York

1985. *The Economic Institutions of Capitalism: Firms, Markets, Relational Contracting.* New York

Williamson, O. E. and Winter, S. G. (eds.) 1991. *The Nature of the Firm: Origins, Evolution, and Development.* New York/Oxford

Wilson, S. V. and Matz A. H. 1977. 'Obtaining Evidence for Federal Economic Crime Prosecutions: An Overview and Analysis of Investigative Methods', *American Criminal Law Review* 14: 651–716

Wilson, Woodrow 1925 (1887). 'The Study of Administration', reprinted in *College and State: Educational, Literary and Political Papers (1875–1913).* Vol. I, New York, 130–58

Wohlstetter, R. 1962. *Pearl Harbor: Warning and Decision.* Stanford

Wolin, Sheldon 1960. *Politics and Vision: Continuity and Innovation in Western Political Thought.* Boston

Young-Bruehl, Elisabeth 1982. *Hannah Arendt: For Love of the World.* New Haven

Subject index

Name index

Abbot, A, 162, 163
Ackerman, Bruce A., 64
Adelberg, Sheldon, 133
Adkins, W. H., 32
Adorno, Th. W., 10n.1
Albrow, Martin, 11
Allison, G. T., 78n.5
Ames, E., 75n.1, 76
Andeweg, R. B., 77
Antunes, J. E., 21n.8, 46, 229
Arendt, Hannah, 10n.1, 23n.1, 41, 52, 93, 95,
  101, 107, 116, 118, 126, 128n.14, 129, 155,
  160
Argyris, Chris, 157, 200, 215n.1, 224
Aristotle, 32
Aron M. W., 185, 187, 189, 194n.9, 195
Arrow, K., 70n.18
Austin, J. L., 112

Baelemans, C., 15
Baier, Kurt, 31n.11
Barnard, Chester I., 10, 23n.1, 36, 45, 58, 127,
  131, 132, 161
Barnett, T., 189, 194n.9, 207, 210, 211, 212, 221
Bartlett, W., 229
Batson, C. Daniel, 133
Beauchamp, Tom L., 56n.3, 146n.3
Beck, Ulrich, 18
Beer, Stafford, 154n.13
Dennei, Ronald, 99n.5
Bendix, Reinhard, 14, 55n.4, 149n.8
Benjamin, M., 95, 111
Besselink, L. F. M., 88n.15
Blackwell, K., 193, 194n.8, 196n.13

Bloemen, E., 17
Blom, J. C. H., 153
Blumberg, P. I., 229
Boeke, Warren, 79
Bok, Sissela, 194n.8, 196n.13, 198
Bonhoeffer, D., 33n.14
Bosch, T. W. van den, 122n.11
Bovens, Mark, 192n.6, 228, 229
Bowie, Norman E., 56n.5, 146n.5
Bozeman, Barry, 5
Braithwaite, John, 52, 57n.8, 58, 58n.9, 59n.11,
  62, 63, 65, 73n.21, 95, 107n.1, 108n.2,
  115n.5, 124, 218, 219, 219n.7, 221
Branch, Taylor, 194n.8
Brants, Chrisje, 80n.6, 81n.7, 82n.8, 83
Bruinsma, F., 16n.3
Burke, John P., 23n.1, 163, 164n.18, 166,
  166n.20, 179n.6
Burnham, James, 14
Burns, T., 154n.13

Callahan, E. S., 185, 194, 194n.9, 205n.31, 221
Calvin, J., 33
Chandler, A. D., 164n.18
Chandler, R. C., 16
Chapman, R. A., 86n.13, 91, 137, 137n.19, 229
Clinard, Marshall B., 19, 79, 80, 84n.11, 124,
  127, 130
Coffee, John C., 53n.1, 59n.11, 61n.12, 62n.13,
  69, 72, 73n.21, 92, 124, 196, 199
Coleman, James S., 3, 5, 9, 11, 12, 13, 14, 15,
  18n.5, 19, 20, 53, 59n.11, 67, 67n.17,
  73n.21, 107, 135, 215
Cook, Scott D. N., 71n.20

249

Printed in the United Kingdom
by Lightning Source UK Ltd.
114212UKS00001B/202